UNIT 15
OPERATING A CASH MANAGEMENT AND CREDIT CONTROL SYSTEM

AAT Technician NVQ/SVQ Level 4 in Accounting

British Library Cataloguing-in-Publication Data

A catalogue record for this book is available from the British Library.

Published by
Kaplan Publishing
Unit 2, The Business Centre
Molly Millars Lane
Wokingham
Berkshire
RG41 2QZ

ISBN 978-1-84710-328-4

Printed and bound in Great Britain.

We are grateful to the Association of Accounting Technicians for permission to reproduce past assessment materials. THe solutions have been prepared by Kaplan Publishinq.

CONTENTS

CONTENTS

PREFACE

STUDY TEXT

The study text is written in a practical and interactive style:

- key terms and concepts are clearly defined
- all topics are illustrated with practical examples with clearly worked solutions
- frequent practice activities throughout the chapters ensure that what you have learnt is regularly reinforced
- test your knowledge section at the end of each chapter helps you to check that you have really understood the topics covered.

WORKBOOK

The workbook comprises three main elements:

A question bank of key techniques to give additional practice and reinforce the work covered in each chapter. This comprises a series of short case studies which cover the major topics of the standards for this unit.

A practice simulation.

Two mock simulations which closely reflect the type of simulation students may expect.

STANDARDS OF COMPETENCE

Unit commentary

This unit is concerned with the management of cash and credit. The unit involves the management of cash balances as well as the granting of credit and the collection of outstanding debts.

Elements contained within this unit are:

Element: 15.1
Monitor and control cash receipts and payments

Element: 15.2
Manage cash balances

Element: 15.3
Grant credit

Element: 15.4
Monitor and control the collection of debts

Knowledge and Understanding

To perform this unit effectively you will need to know and understand:

		Chapter
The business environment		
1	The main types of cash receipts and payments: regular revenue receipts and payments; capital receipts and payments; drawings/dividends and disbursements; exceptional receipts and payments (Element 15.1)	1
2	The basic structure of the banking system and the money market in the UK and the relationships between financial institutions (Element 15.2)	3
3	Bank overdrafts and loans; terms and conditions; legal relationship between bank and customer (Element 15.2)	3, 4
4	Types of marketable security (bills of exchange, certificates of deposit, government securities, local authority short-term loans); terms and conditions; risks (Element 15.2)	5
5	Government monetary policies (Element 15.2)	3
6	Legal issues: basic contract; terms and conditions of contracts relating to the granting of credit; Data Protection legislation and credit control information (Element 15.3)	6
7	Sources of credit status information (Element 15.3)	6
8	External sources of information: banks, credit agencies and official publications (Element 15.3)	6
9	Legal issues: remedies for breach of contract (Element 15.4)	8
10	Legal and administrative procedures for the collection of debts (Element 15.4)	8
11	The effect of bankruptcy and insolvency on organisations (Element 15.4)	8
Accounting Techniques		
12	Form and structure of cash budgets (Element 15.1)	1
13	Lagged receipts and payments (Element 15.1)	1
14	Basic statistical techniques for estimating future trends: moving averages, allowance for inflation (Element 15.1)	2
15	Computer models to assess the sensitivity of elements in the cash budget to change (eg price, wage rate changes) (Element 15.1)	2
16	Managing risk and exposure (Element 15.2)	5
17	Discounts for prompt payment (Element 15.3)	6
18	Interpretation and use of credit control information (Elements 15.3 and 15.4)	7
19	Methods of collection (Element 15.4)	8
20	Factoring arrangements (Element 15.4)	8
21	Debt insurance (Element 15.4)	8
22	Methods of analysing information on debtors: age analysis of debtors; average periods of credit given and received; incidence of bad and doubtful debts (Element 15.4)	7
23	Evaluation of different collection methods (Element 15.4)	8

		Chapter
Accounting Principles and Theory		
24	Cash flow accounting and its relationship to accounting for income and expenditure (Element 15.1)	1
25	Liquidity management (Elements 15.2, 15.3 and 15.4)	4
The Organisation		
26	Understanding that the accounting systems of an organisation are affected by its organisational structure, its administrative systems and procedures and the nature of its business transactions (Elements 15.1, 15.2, 15.3 and 15.4	Throughout
27	Understanding that recording and accounting practices may vary in different parts of the organisation (Elements 15.1 and 15.4)	
28	An understanding that practice in this area will be determined by an organisation's specific financial regulations, guidelines and security procedures (Element 15.2)	
29	An understanding that in public sector organisations there are statutory and other regulations relating to the management of cash balances (Element 15.2)	
30	Understanding that practice in this area will be determined by an organisation's credit control policies and procedures (Element 15.3)	
31	An understanding of the organisation's relevant policies and procedures (Elements 15.1, 15.3 and 15.4)	

Element 15.1 Monitor and control cash receipts and payments

Performance criteria

In order to perform this element successfully you need to:

A	Monitor and control cash receipts and payments against budgeted cash flow.	1
B	Consult appropriate staff to determine the likely pattern of cash flows over the accounting period and to anticipate any exceptional receipts or payments.	2
C	Ensure forecasts of future cash payments and receipts are in accord with known income and expenditure trends.	2
D	Prepare cash budgets in the approved format and clearly indicate net cash requirements.	1
E	Identify significant deviations from the cash budget and take corrective action within defined organisational policies.	2

Range statement Chapter

Performance in this element relates to the following contexts:
Cash flows to be monitored:

- Regular revenue receipts and payments
- Capital receipts and payments
- Drawings or dividends and disbursements
- Exceptional receipts and payments

Element 15.2 Manage cash balances

Performance criteria

In order to perform this element successfully you need to:

A	Arrange overdraft and loan facilities in anticipation of requirements and on the most favourable terms available.	4
B	Invest surplus funds in marketable securities within defined financial authorisation limits.	5
C	Ensure the organisation's financial regulations and security procedures are observed.	4,5
D	Ensure account is taken of trends in the economic and financial environment in managing cash balances.	4
E	Maintain an adequate level of liquidity in line with cash forecasts.	4

Range statement

Performance in this element relates to the following contexts:
Maintain liquidity through the management of:

- Cash
- Overdrafts
- Loans

Element 15.3 Grant credit

Performance criteria

In order to perform this element successfully you need to:

A	Agree credit terms with customers in accordance with the organisation's policies.	6
B	Identify and use internal and external sources of information to evaluate the current credit status of customers and potential customers.	6
C	Open new accounts for those customers with an established credit status.	6
D	Ensure the reasons for refusing credit are discussed with customers in a tactful manner.	6

Range statement Chapter

Performance in this element relates to the following contexts:
Internal information derived from:

- Analysis of the accounts
- Colleagues in regular contact with current or potential customers or clients

External information derived from:

- Credit rating agencies
- Supplier references
- Bank references

Element 15.4 Monitor and control the collection of debts

Performance criteria

In order to perform this element successfully you need to:

A	Monitor information relating to the current state of debtors' accounts regularly and take appropriate action.	7
B	Send information regarding significant outstanding accounts and potential bad debts promptly to relevant individuals within the organisation.	7
C	Ensure discussions and negotiations with debtors are conducted courteously and achieve the desired outcome.	7,8
D	Use debt recovery methods appropriate to the circumstances of individual cases and in accordance with the organisation's procedures.	8
E	Base recommendations to write off bad and doubtful debts on a realistic analysis of all known factors.	7,8

Range statement

Performance in this element relates to the following contexts:
Information on debtors:

- Age analysis of debtors
- Average periods of credit given and received
- Incidence of bad and doubtful debts

Appropriate action:

- Information and recommendations for action passed to appropriate individual within own organisation
- Debtor contacted and arrangements made for the recovery of the debt

1

CASH BUDGETS

INTRODUCTION

In this initial chapter we will firstly consider the importance of cash flow to a business and the typical types of cash flows that a business will have. From this, the chapter moves on to the methods of preparing a cash budget or cash flow forecast for a business.

KNOWLEDGE & UNDERSTANDING

- The main types of cash receipts and payments: regular revenue receipts and payments; capital receipts and payments; drawings/dividends and disbursements; exceptional receipts and payments (Element 15.1)
- Form and structure of cash budgets (Element 15.1)
- Lagged receipts and payments (Element 15.1)
- Cash flow accounting and its relationship to accounting for income and expenditure (Element 15.1)

CONTENTS

PERFORMANCE CRITERIA

- Monitor and control cash receipts and payments against budgeted cash flow (Element 15.1A)
- Prepare cash budgets in the approved format and clearly indicate net cash requirements (Element 15.1D)

1 Cash flow and profit

1.1 The importance of cash flow

Clearly any business will wish to make a profit. This means that over a period of time sales made are worth more than the cost of making those sales together with the expenses incurred by the business. However, even if the business is making a profit, it must also have the cash available to pay its suppliers, pay its employees and pay for its expenses.

It is entirely possible for a profitable business to run short of cash. For example, a business may be making a profit but it has to replace a large item of machinery and this will deplete its cash resources to the extent that it may not be able to pay its creditors when they fall due. In the worst case scenario this might even mean that the business is forced into liquidation.

1.2 The difference between cash flow and profit

There are a variety of reasons why the profit of a business will not necessarily equate directly to cash inflows:

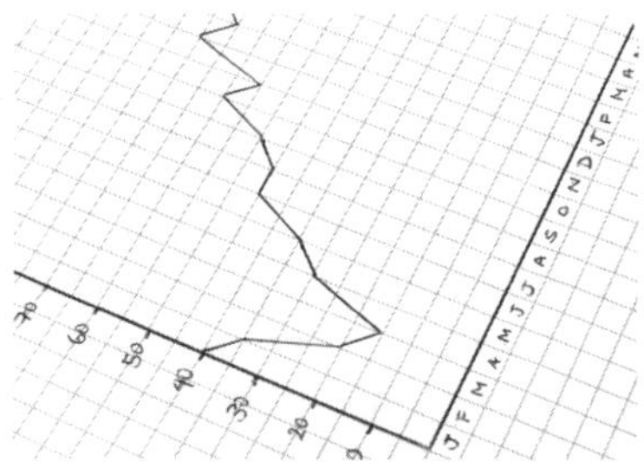

- Non-cash expenses – the profit and loss account of a business is charged with a number of non-cash expenses such as depreciation and provisions for doubtful debts. Although these are correctly charged as expenses in the profit and loss account, they are not cash flows and will not reduce the cash balance of the business.
- Purchase of fixed assets – these are often large cash outflows of a business but the only amount that is charged to the profit and loss account is the annual depreciation charge not the entire cost of the fixed asset.
- Sale of fixed assets – when a fixed asset is sold this will result in an inflow of cash to the business but the figure to appear in the profit and loss account is not the sales proceeds but any profit or loss on the sale.
- Financing transactions – some transactions, such as issuing additional share capital and taking out or repaying a loan, will result in large cash flows in or out of the business with no effect on the profit figure at all.

1.3 Accruals concept

One major reason for there being a difference between cash flow and profit is that the profit is calculated in the profit and loss account by applying the accruals concept.

DEFINITION

FRS 18 Accounting Policies defines the accruals concept as follows.

'The accruals basis of accounting requires the non-cash effects of transactions and other events to be reflected, as far as is possible, in the financial statements for the accounting period in which they occur and not, for example, in the period in which any cash involved is received or paid.'

The accruals basis of accounting covers the accounting for all income and expenditure but the differences that it causes between profit and cash flow are probably best illustrated for sales and purchases.

EXAMPLE

Jan set up in business selling computer accessories on 1 March 20X4 with cash in her bank account of £10,000. During the first month of trading she purchased £4,000 of goods on credit and sold them all on credit for £6,000. She is due to pay for the purchases on 15 April 20X4 and her customers are due to pay for the goods they have bought on 30 April.

What is her profit for the month of March and what is her cash flow?

Solution

Under the accruals concept the profit that would be reported would be the sales actually made during the month and the cost of making those sales.

	£
Sales	6,000
Cost of sales	(4,000)
Profit	2,000

However, as she has neither paid for the purchases nor received money for the sales, she has had no cash flow during the month.

The accruals concept therefore is one major reason for the difference between reported profit and cash flow. As well as applying to sales and purchases, the concept requires accruals and prepayments of expenses to be recognised at the end of a period. Also for non-cash expenses such as depreciation and provisions for doubtful debts to be recognised in the profit and loss account.

1.4 Closing stock

The accruals concept also applies to the accounting treatment of any stocks remaining at the end of a period when calculating the profit for the period. The sales for the period are compared to the cost of selling those goods so any unsold goods, the closing stock, are carried forward to the following period by being deducted from the purchases figure.

EXAMPLE

Ken set up in business selling flat pack furniture on 1 June 20X4 when he had £20,000 in his bank account. During the month of June he purchased furniture for cash of £7,000 and sold most of this on credit for £10,000. The debtors are not due to pay until 16 July. At the end of June the cost of the furniture that he had left was £1,500.

What is Ken's profit for the month of June and what is his cash flow?

Solution

Under the accruals concept not only will the sales appear in the profit calculation even though no cash has been received for them during the month but the purchases figures will be reduced by the cost of the goods not yet sold so that the sales figure is matched with the cost of the actual goods sold.

	£	£
Sales		10,000
Purchases	7,000	
Less: Closing stock	(1,500)	
Cost of sales		5,500
Profit		4,500

The cash flow of the business, however, is simply the cash spent on the purchases so although the profit appears as £4,500, the cash outflow is £7,000 leaving him with just £13,000 in his bank account at the end of the month.

2 Types of cash flows

2.1 Introduction

We must now start to focus on the different types of cash flow that a business is likely to have. Some will be regular receipts and payments such as sales, purchases and expenses. Some will be receipts and payments of a long-term nature, known as capital receipts and payments such as the raising of share capital or the purchase of fixed assets. Some payments will be made to the owners of a business either in the form of drawings for a sole trader or partnership or dividends for a company. There will also be necessary disbursements such as the payment of taxes to the government. Finally, there may be unusual or exceptional receipts or payments, for example for cash received from the sale of a fixed asset.

Every business will have different types of receipts and payments and different patterns of those receipts and payments but we will consider the typical types of cash flows that you may come across.

2.2 Cash inflows

- Revenue receipts for a business will be cash sales and cash from debtors who have purchased goods on credit.
- Capital receipts will include cash raised by issuing shares or raising a loan. Other types of capital cash inflow are the proceeds from the sale of fixed assets or the receipt of government grants. These are not likely to be regular cash inflows.

2.3 Cash outflows

- Revenue payments will include payments for cash purchases, cash paid to creditors, wages payments, payment of bills, cash payment of expenses.
- Capital payments could include the repayment of loans or the purchase of fixed assets. When new fixed assets are purchased this may be for a large sum on just one date or it may take the form of regular payments if, for example, the asset is acquired under a lease or hire purchase agreement.
- Businesses will also be likely to make payments or disbursements in the form of corporation tax, VAT and PAYE. These may be regular such as the monthly PAYE payments or one-off payments each year such as the annual payment of corporation tax.
- Payments will also be made to providers of finance such as dividends to shareholders and interest payments to banks and other providers of finance. The regularity of these payments will vary but, for example, companies usually pay any dividend twice a year, a small interim dividend during the year and a larger final dividend after the year end.
- Finally, in a sole trader's business or a partnership there may be either regular or irregular payments made to the owner or partners in the form of drawings.

2.4 Exceptional cash flows

The cash flows described above are the normal, everyday types of cash flows that most businesses will have. However in some cases there will also be exceptional cash flows which are not part of normal business operations. Exceptional cash outflows might include payment of legal damages or redundancy costs. Exceptional cash inflows might include items such as receipts from an insurance company for damaged stock.

▷ ACTIVITY 1

Cash flows can be classified between regular revenue receipts and payments and infrequent or irregular receipts and disbursements.
Give an example of each of the following:

(a) a regular revenue receipt
(b) an exceptional payment
(c) a capital payment
(d) an annual disbursement.

[Answer on p. 29]

3 Monitoring cash flow

3.1 The importance of monitoring cash flow

As we have seen earlier in this chapter, it is not enough for a business simply to be profitable; it must also have enough cash to meet its daily commitments. Therefore it is an important part of the management and accounting function to monitor the cash position of the business.

3.2 Actual and budgeted cash flow

One way of monitoring the cash position of the business is a careful and regular scrutiny of the bank statement when it is received. This will show the actual cash paid in and out of the business bank account. However, although the checking and analysis of actual cash flows from the bank statement is an important element of financial control, it does not provide information which management can use for planning.

Therefore a more useful approach is to prepare budgets of expected cash flows which can be used to forecast the cash position at the end of each day, week or month.

3.3 Cash budget

A cash budget or cash flow forecast is an estimate of all of the cash inflows and all of the cash outflows for the period. When these are applied to the opening cash figure, the closing estimated cash balance at the end of each period can be determined and management can plan to take any necessary action: for example agreement with the bank for an overdraft facility if the budgeted cash balance is negative or the arrangement for short-term investment if the cash balance is budgeted to be healthy.

EXAMPLE

At 1 March 20X4 Apple Ltd expects to have a bank balance of £2,000. It is estimated that cash from sales in March, April and May will be £24,000 each month. Cash payments for expenses each month are estimated to be £21,000 but in May some new equipment must be purchased at a cost of £12,000 paid for on 1 May by cheque.

Prepare the cash budget for the next three months and determine the net cash position at the end of each of the three months.

Solution

Cash budget

	March	April	May
	£	£	£
Cash inflows	24,000	24,000	24,000
Cash outflows:			
Expenses	(21,000)	(21,000)	(21,000)
Capital expenditure			(12,000)
Net cash inflow/(outflow)	3,000	3,000	(9,000)
Opening cash balance	2,000	5,000	8,000
Closing cash balance	5,000	8,000	(1,000)

Note that the closing cash balance at the end of each month is derived by adding or deducting the net cash flow for the month to or from the cash balance at the start of the month. The closing cash balance of one month therefore becomes the opening cash balance the following month.

This indicates to management that although there will be cash in the bank at the end of March and April, there is expected to be a shortage at the end of May. Management can then use this information to plan for this eventuality by, for example, arranging for a bank overdraft or bank loan or selling some surplus assets.

4 Preparation of cash budgets

4.1 Introduction

We will now look at the detailed preparation of cash budgets by looking at the main elements individually and then bringing it all together in a full-scale worked example.

Cash budgets are not difficult to produce but in an assessment you will often find that a lot of information has to be absorbed and used, which can be daunting. A logical approach is what is required.

4.2 Proforma receipts and payments cash budget

Cash budget for the six months to December 20X4

	July	Aug	Sept	Oct	Nov	Dec
	£	£	£	£	£	£
Receipts						
Cash sales						
Cash from debtors						
Capital introduced						
Payments						
Fixed costs						
Payments to creditors						
Purchases of fixed assets						
Balance b/f						
Net cash flow						
Balance c/f						

Each cash budget has to be amended to reflect the particular circumstances of the business.

For example, businesses with only cash sales will not need the line for cash from debtors. Also, other sources of income may arise, such as proceeds from the sale of fixed assets. There are many sorts of cash payments; possibly cash purchases as well as credit purchases, wages and salaries to employees or the drawings of a proprietor, and each must be detailed line by line under the payments heading.

The crucial point to remember is that all cash inflows and all cash outflows over the budget period must be considered. As you work through the following examples and questions, you will see examples of different receipts and payments but note how the basic proforma above is used to find the net cash balance.

In a simulation you will be given a proforma cash budget which will help you to make sure that you have included all relevant figures.

4.3 Lagged receipts and payments

Sales are often made on credit and customers do not pay until subsequent periods. The credit terms offered to customers will be decided by the managers and a general pattern of receipts from these customers can therefore be established. The cash budget needs to show the actual cash expected to be received from debtors in the period rather than the actual sales made to debtors in the period.

The same principle applies to payments to creditors which will be considered later in the chapter.

O EXAMPLE

A business makes sales on credit and finds that it receives 50% of the money due in the month of sale and 50% in the following month. We need to state cash receipts for the first three months of the year.

Solution

	Dec	Jan	Feb	March
	£	£	£	£
Sales	10,000	12,000	14,000	16,000
The cash receipts will be:				
50% in month of sale	5,000	6,000	7,000	8,000
50% in subsequent month	–	5,000	6,000	7,000
Giving:				
Total cash receipts	5,000	11,000	13,000	15,000

The above example shows how payments from debtors for a particular month are not the same as sales to debtors for that month, so in a simulation do not fall into the trap of simply using the credit sales figures.

4.4 Sales on credit and discounts

In some businesses a cash or settlement discount is offered to customers for payment within a certain time period. This means that although the cash is received sooner, a lower amount is received than was invoiced. This must be taken into account when preparing the cash budget.

EXAMPLE

A business offers a 3% discount for payment received from credit customers in the month of sale. The business has found that 40% of customers take advantage of this by paying in the month of sale, 50% of customers pay in the month after the sale and 10% of customers pay two months after the month of sale.

Credit sales for the business are as follows:

	Actual		Budgeted		
	February	March	April	May	June
	£	£	£	£	£
Credit sales	20,000	22,000	24,000	18,000	21,000

What are the cash receipts from debtors for the three months ending 30 June?

Solution

		Cash inflow April	May	June
		£	£	£
February sales	– 20,000×10%	2,000		
March sales	– 22,000×50%	11,000		
	22,000×10%		2,200	
April sales	– 24,000×40%×97%	9,312		
	24,000×50%		12,000	
	24,000×10%			2,400
May sales	– 18,000×40%×97%		6,984	
	18,000×50%			9,000
June sales	– 21,000×40%×97%			8,148
Cash inflow		22,312	21,184	19,548

Note that the cash received in the month of sale is 97% of the amount invoiced as these customers have taken advantage of the settlement discount.

4.5 Bad debts

It is also entirely possible that some debts will become bad debts. This means that the cash will never be received from these debtors. Therefore the amounts due from these debtors must not be included in the cash budget as it is likely that the cash will never be received.

4.6 Sales quantities and prices

In the examples so far you have been given the monetary amount of the sales in each month in order to calculate the receipts from debtors. However, you may be given information about the sales quantity in units each month and the selling price per unit. From this, the total monetary amount of the sales for the month can be calculated.

▷ ACTIVITY 2

Kelly Limited sold 3,000 units of its only product in June 20X3 at a selling price of £45 each. Owing to an increase in production costs, this price increases to £48 with effect from 1 July 20X3 and this is expected to reduce demand for July to 2,900 units. Thereafter, however, demand is expected to increase by 10% per month.

Cash sales account for 500 units per month and are expected to remain at this level. Credit sales account for the balance and debtors pay as follows:
(a) 60% by value in the month of sale, receiving a 2% discount
(b) 40% by value in the following month.

What is the budgeted cash received in August 20X3?

[Answer is on p. 29]

4.7 Payments to creditors

The determination of the cash payments that are to be made to creditors each month can be a little more complicated than the calculation of the receipts from debtors as the information can be expressed in a variety of different ways. The simplest form in which you might come across payments to creditors information is similar to that for receipts from debtors – you will be told the amount of credit purchases and the payment pattern to creditors.

EXAMPLE

A business estimates that its credit purchases for February and March will be £14,000 but will increase by 10% each month thereafter. Its payment pattern to creditors is that 60% are paid in the month following the purchases and the remaining 40% two months after the purchase.

What are the payments to creditors for the three months of April, May and June?

Solution

	February	March	April	May	June
	£	£	£	£	£
Purchases (increasing by 10% each month)	14,000	14,000	15,400	16,940	18,634
Payments to creditors					
– February purchases					
14,000×40%			5,600		
– March purchases					
14,000×60%			8,400		
14,000×40%				5,600	
– April purchases					
15,400×60%				9,240	
15,400×40%					6,160
– May purchases					
16,940×60%					10,164
Cash payments			14,000	14,840	16,324

4.8 Purchases expressed in terms of sales value

In some cases the information supplied about purchases will be expressed in terms of the sales value which has been budgeted for i.e. sales figures will be provided together with the anticipated gross profit margin. The purchases each month will then be calculated using the gross profit percentage given to find the cost of purchases. Once the purchases are known then the cash payments to the suppliers can be calculated.

EXAMPLE

A business has the following budgeted sales:

	February	March	April	May	June	July
	£	£	£	£	£	£
Budgeted sales	38,000	40,000	44,000	46,000	45,000	50,000

The business operates at a gross margin of 40% and its policy is to make purchases on credit each month which are enough to cover the following month's sales. Creditors are paid two months after the month of purchase.

What are the payments to creditors for each of the three months of April, May and June?

Solution

The first step is to calculate the cost of purchases incurred in each month.

	February	March	April	May	June	July
	£	£	£	£	£	£
Budgeted sales	38,000	40,000	44,000	46,000	45,000	50,000
Purchases (60% of following month's sales)						
February 40,000 ×60%	24,000					
March 44,000 ×60%		26,400				
April 46,000 ×60%			27,600			
May 45,000 ×60%				27,000		
June 50,000 ×60%					30,000	
Payments (two months after purchase)			24,000	26,400	27,600	

4.9 Increase or decrease in stock levels

Another method of expressing information about purchase quantities is to include plans for any increases or decreases in stock levels during the period. If stock levels are to be increased then purchases must be larger but if stock levels are budgeted to decrease then the amount of purchases will also decrease.

O EXAMPLE

A business generally has purchases of £80,000 each month on credit. These are paid for in the month following the purchase. However, it is budgeted to increase stock levels at the end of May by £20,000 and that stock levels will then remain at that value. There is no anticipated increase in sales.

What are the cash payments to creditors for each of the three months of April, May and June?

Solution

Again the first step is to calculate the amount of purchases each month. This will generally be £80,000 but in May must be £100,000 in order to increase the stock levels. As there is no anticipated increase in sales levels then purchases in June can revert to £80,000.

	March	April	May	June
	£	£	£	£
Purchases	80,000	80,000	100,000	80,000

As payments are made in the month following the purchase then the cash payments will be as follows:

	April	May	June
	£	£	£
Payments	80,000	80,000	100,000

4.10 Cash budgets and manufacturing organisations

If you are preparing a cash budget within a manufacturing organisation then in order to determine the payments to creditors you may have to calculate the production budget and materials purchases budget first.

The production budget is the amount of finished goods to be made in a period. This is calculated as follows:

		Units
Sales		X
Add:	Closing stock	X
Less:	Opening stock	(X)
Production		X

If finished goods stock levels remain constant then the quantity of production will be the same as that of sales, but if the stock levels are budgeted to change this will affect the amount of production.

Once the number of units that are to be produced each month has been determined then the amount of raw materials required to be purchased for that production can be determined. The amount to be purchased will depend upon any changes in raw materials stock levels and the purchases can be calculated as:

		Units
Production		X
Add:	Closing stock	X
Less:	Opening stock	(X)
Purchases		X

Take care not to confuse opening and closing stocks of finished goods and opening and closing stocks of raw materials. The finished goods stock levels are used to determine the production budget and the raw materials stock levels are used in the determination of the purchases budget.
Finally the cost of these purchases and the payment pattern for these materials can be calculated.

EXAMPLE

A business has planned sales of its product of 4,000 units in March which will be expected to increase by 200 units each month. Finished goods stock at the start and end of March is anticipated to be 500 units and these are budgeted to be increased to 600 units at the end of April, 700 units at the end of May and 750 units at the end of June.

Each unit of the finished product requires 2 kg of raw materials which are purchased on credit in the month of production and cost £20 per kg payable one month after the date of purchase. At the beginning of March there will be 1,000 kg of raw materials in stock but these stock levels are to be decreased by 100 kg at the end of March and by 100 kg at the end of each month thereafter.

What are the payments to creditors in each of the months of April, May and June?

Solution

Production budget

	March Units	April Units	May Units	June Units
Sales	4,000	4,200	4,400	4,600
Add: Closing stock (finished goods)	500	600	700	750
Less: Opening stock (finished goods)	(500)	(500)	(600)	(700)
Production quantity	4,000	4,300	4,500	4,650

Note that the closing finished goods stock at the end of each month is the opening stock at the start of the following month.

Once the amount of production is known then the raw materials purchases can be determined in quantities first of all. Start with the materials needed for the actual production but then take into consideration the fact that there is 1,000 kgs of material at the start of March, but this stock level is to decrease by 100 kgs per month thereafter.

Materials purchases budget – kgs

	March kgs	April kgs	May kgs	June kgs
Production × 2 kg	8,000	8,600	9,000	9,300
Add: Closing stock (raw materials)	900	800	700	600
Less: Opening stock (raw materials)	(1,000)	(900)	(800)	(700)
Purchases in kgs	7,900	8,500	8,900	9,200

The materials purchases in each month are therefore the number of kgs required at the price of £20 per kg.

Materials purchases budget – £

	March £	April £	May £	June £
Purchases in kg × £20	158,000	170,000	178,000	184,000

Finally, the cash payments pattern is determined. In this case each month's purchases are paid for in the following month:

	April £	May £	June £	July £
Payments to creditors	158,000	170,000	178,000	184,000

▷ ACTIVITY 3

Srnicek's purchases in May were £100,000 and these are expected to increase by £10,000 per month for the next three months. 30% of purchases are for cash, the balance being credit purchases. Creditors are paid as follows:

(a) 50% in the month of purchase (this qualifies for a 5% discount)

(b) 30% in the month after sale

(c) 20% in the following month.

What is the cash outflow during July?

[Answer on p. 29]

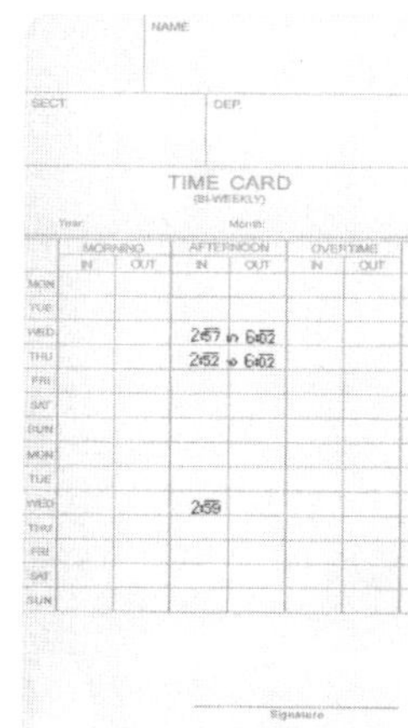

4.11 Wages and salaries

Wages and salaries are normally paid in the month in which they are incurred and the only usual complication is that they may have to be calculated on a per unit basis based upon the production budget or there may be increases in the wage rate during the budget period.

O EXAMPLE

The production budget for a company shows the following monthly production:

	April	May	June
	Units	Units	Units
Production	6,200	6,800	7,000

Each unit of production requires two labour hours and the wage rate is £7.00 per hour for April and May increasing to £7.40 per hour in June. Wages are paid in the month in which they are incurred.

What figures should appear for wages costs in the cash budget for April, May and June?

Solution

	April	May	June
	£	£	£
6,200 units × 2 × £7.00	86,800		
6,800 units × 2 × £7.00		95,200	
7,000 units × 2 × £7.40			103,600

4.12 Fixed overheads

Care should be taken with fixed overheads or expenses that are to appear in the cash budget. You will often be told that the monthly figure includes a cetain amount which relates to depreciation. Depreciation is not a cash flow and therefore this amount should be excluded from the cash budget.

5 Worked example

5.1 Introduction

From the following information which relates to The Magic Lantern Company Limited, we are going to prepare a month by month cash budget for the second half of 20X5:

(a) A magic lantern sells for £40 and has a variable cost of £26 made up as follows:
Materials £20 Labour £4 Overhead £2

(b) Fixed costs amount to £6,000 per month and are paid on the 25th of each month.

(c) Credit sales, in units:

May	June	July	Aug	Sept	Oct	Nov	Dec	Jan
1,000	1,200	1,400	1,600	1,800	2,000	2,200	2,600	2,400

(d) Production quantities
The company produces goods one month before they are sold. The demand for the product fluctuates and the company therefore decides to adjust its stocks to cater for this as follows:

Month	Aug	Sept	Oct	Nov	Dec
Increase/(decrease) in stocks (units)	200	400	400	(200)	(200)

(e) Cash sales, at a discount of 5%, are expected to average 100 units a month.

(f) Customers are expected to settle their accounts in the second month following sale.

(g) Suppliers of materials are paid two months after the materials are used in production.

(h) Wages are paid in the same month as the magic lanterns are produced.

(i) 70% of the variable overhead is paid in the month of production and the remainder in the following month.

(j) Corporation tax of £18,000 is to be paid in October.

(k) A new delivery vehicle costing £8,000 was bought in June and is to be paid for in August. The old vehicle was sold for £600, the buyer undertaking to pay in July.

(l) The company is expected to be £3,000 overdrawn at the bank at 30 June 20X5.

5.2 Approach to cash budget questions

The approach to a question like this is vital, especially under timed conditions. The key point to remember is that, unless you write a point down, the assessor will think that you do not know it. This means that the work should be done in the following order:

1. Read the question and be aware of what is in it.
2. Set out a proforma cash budget (this will be done for you in simulations).
3. Deal with the easy items first.
4. Only then attempt the more difficult items.

This approach will ensure that you do not omit points that you are able to deal with simply because you have run out of time.

5.3 Easy items

Having read the question and set out a proforma, return to the question and look for the easy items. Points (b), (j), (k) and (l) give information which can be copied straight from the question paper onto the answer. Even in a simulation there will be information like this and copying it out will score marks!

Point (e) is also relatively easy to deal with, so we should also calculate the cash sales.

At this point, the answer is as follows

The Magic Lantern Company Limited
Cash budget for the six months to December 20X5

	July	Aug	Sept	Oct	Nov	Dec
	£	£	£	£	£	£
Receipts						
Cash sales (W1)	3,800	3,800	3,800	3,800	3,800	3,800
Proceeds from sale of vehicle	600					
	July	Aug	Sept	Oct	Nov	Dec
	£	£	£	£	£	£
Payments						
Fixed costs	6,000	6,000	6,000	6,000	6,000	6,000
Purchase of new vehicle		8,000				
Corporation tax				18,000		
Balance b/f	(3,000)					
Net cash flow						

Working 1

100 × £40 × 95% = £3,800

Note that the figures in the cash budget are cross-referenced to the appropriate workings.

This is not yet the finished article, but it is beginning to look like a cash budget and that provides encouragement to attempt the remainder of the question.

5.4 The final stage

Each question should be taken on its merits but, typically, production and hence associated cash flows will depend upon sales. So the next stage is usually to work out the credit sales figure and calculate when the cash is received.

(a) Calculate cash receipts from debtors

The cash received from credit sales is calculated as follows:

	May	June	July	Aug	Sept	Oct	Nov	Dec
Credit sales (units)	1,000	1,200	1,400	1,600	1,800	2,000	2,200	2,600
	£	£	£	£	£	£	£	£
Credit sales (£)	40,000	48,000	56,000	64,000	72,000	80,000	88,000	104,000
Cash received			40,000	48,000	56,000	64,000	72,000	80,000

Having calculated the cash received, write the information on the cash budget.

(b) Calculate the production budget

Now that sales are known (not forgetting the cash sales), we can work out our production.

	April	May	June	July	Aug	Sept	Oct	Nov	Dec	Jan
Credit sales (units)	–	1,000	1,200	1,400	1,600	1,800	2,000	2,200	2,600	2,400
Cash sales (units)	–	100	100	100	100	100	100	100	100	100
Total sales (units)	–	1,100	1,300	1,500	1,700	1,900	2,100	2,300	2,700	2,500
Production for sales (one month before) (units)	1,100	1,300	1,500	1,700	1,900	2,100	2,300	2,700	2,500	–
Stock increase/ (decrease) (units)	–	–	–	–	200	400	400	(200)	(200)	–
Total production (units)	1,100	1,300	1,500	1,700	2,100	2,500	2,700	2,500	2,300	–

(c) Calculate the materials purchases budget

Now that production is known, we can work out the material cost and when that cost is paid.

	April	May	June	July	Aug	Sept	Oct	Nov	Dec
Production (units)	1,100	1,300	1,500	1,700	2,100	2,500	2,700	2,500	2,300
	£	£	£	£	£	£	£	£	£
Material cost of production (£20 per unit)	22,000	26,000	30,000	34,000	42,000	50,000	54,000	50,000	46,000
Payments to suppliers									
Two-month delay	–	–	22,000	26,000	30,000	34,000	42,000	50,000	54,000

This information should now be written onto the cash budget.

(d) Calculate the wages and variable overhead

Knowledge of production facilitates calculation of the cash paid in respect of these items as well.

	June	July	Aug	Sept	Oct	Nov	Dec
Units produced	1,500	1,700	2,100	2,500	2,700	2,500	2,300
	£	£	£	£	£	£	£
Wages paid (£4 per unit)	6,000	6,800	8,400	10,000	10,800	10,000	9,200
Variable overhead (£2 per unit)	3,000	3,400	4,200	5,000	5,400	5,000	4,600
Cash paid							
70% in month	2,100	2,380	2,940	3,500	3,780	3,500	3,220
30% next month	–	900	1,020	1,260	1,500	1,620	1,500
Total variable overhead paid		3,280	3,960	4,760	5,280	5,120	4,720

5.5 Complete solution

The Magic Lantern Company Limited
Cash budget for the six months to December 20X5

	July	Aug	Sept	Oct	Nov	Dec
	£	£	£	£	£	£
Receipts						
Cash from debtors	40,000	48,000	56,000	64,000	72,000	80,000
Cash sales (W1)	3,800	3,800	3,800	3,800	3,800	3,800
Proceeds from sale of vehicle	600					
	44,400	51,800	59,800	67,800	75,800	83,800

	July	Aug	Sept	Oct	Nov	Dec
	£	£	£	£	£	£
Payments						
Fixed costs	6,000	6,000	6,000	6,000	6,000	6,000
Payments to creditors	26,000	30,000	34,000	42,000	50,000	54,000
Wages	6,800	8,400	10,000	10,800	10,000	9,200
Variable overhead	3,280	3,960	4,760	5,280	5,120	4,720
Corporation tax				18,000		
Purchase of new vehicle		8,000				
	42,080	56,360	54,760	82,080	71,120	73,920
Summary						
Balance b/f	(3,000)	(680)	(5,240)	(200)	(14,480)	(9,800)
Net cash flow	2,320	(4,560)	5,040	(14,280)	4,680	9,880
Balance c/f	(680)	(5,240)	(200)	(14,480)	(9,800)	80

This shows that until December the company will have an overdraft, which will rise as high as £14,480 in October.

5.6 Overdraft interest

One of the purposes of a cash budget is to identify the cash balance at the end of each month and to determine whether an overdraft facility is required. If an overdraft is agreed with the bank and the facility is used then the bank will charge interest on the amount of the overdraft.

In practice the amount of the overdraft interest will be calculated on a daily basis. However, for cash budgeting purposes the amount of overdraft interest will normally be calculated on the basis of the amount of the overdraft outstanding at the end of the previous month. This figure for interest will then be included in the following month's cash payments.

EXAMPLE

A business anticipates having an overdraft of £2,000 at the end of March. The budgeted cash receipts and payments (excluding overdraft interest) for the following three months are expected to be as follows:

	April	May	June
	£	£	£
Cash receipts	16,500	18,000	17,200
Cash payments	17,400	17,500	17,000

Overdraft interest is charged at 0.5% per month on the basis of the overdraft balance at the start of each month.

Prepare the completed cash budget including the amount of overdraft interest.

Solution

		April	May	June
		£	£	£
Cash receipts		16,500	18,000	17,200
Cash payments		(17,400)	(17,500)	(17,000)
Overdraft interest	(2,000× 0.5%)	(10)		
	(2,910× 0.5%)		(15)	
	(2,425× 0.5%)			(12)
Net cash flow		(910)	485	188
Opening balance		(2,000)	(2,910)	(2,425)
Closing balance		(2,910)	(2,425)	(2,237)

▷ ACTIVITY 4

Data

Kirkton Jeans Limited started in business on 1 November 20X4 with share capital of £200,000. It received £100,000 in enterprise grants from a Regional Enterprise Company and has negotiated a £325,000 overdraft facility from a local bank.

The company is a fashion manufacturer specialising in the manufacture of denim jeans for the domestic market. At the commencement of business, the company bought cutting and sewing machinery costing £130,000 and fixtures and fittings of £11,000.

Kirkton Jeans will sell a small range of denim jeans, each with a similar cost structure and sold at a similar price:

	£	£
Selling price		15.00
Costs		
Direct labour	6.50	
Direct material	3.25	
Variable overheads	1.50	
		11.25
Contribution		3.75

Fixed overheads are property expenses of £240,000 per annum, paid monthly in advance, and energy costs of £115,200 per annum, paid quarterly in arrears in February, May, August and November. Other fixed costs are estimated at £15,000 per month, to be paid monthly.

Forecast sales in units are as follows:

Nov	Dec	Jan	Feb	Mar	Apr	May
Nil	20,000	24,000	24,000	22,000	20,000	26,000

The planned production profile is as follows:

Nov	Dec	Jan	Feb	Mar	Apr	May
24,000	24,000	22,000	20,000	26,000	26,000	28,000

50% of sales are for cash. The remainder are credit sales. Industry experience and market research suggests that all credit sales will be paid in the month following sale (i.e. 'net monthly').

Material purchases are paid for in the month incurred. Labour costs and variable overheads are also paid for in the month in which they are incurred.

The bank charges interest on overdrafts at the rate of 1% per month, calculated on the closing balance at the end of the month. Interest is then paid on the first banking day of the following month.

Task

Using the proforma cash flow budget supplied, prepare a month-by-month budgeted cash flow forecast.

Kirkton Jeans Limited

	Nov	Dec	Jan	Feb	Mar	Apr	May
Receipts							
Cash sales							
Credit collections							
Share capital							
Enterprise grants							
Cash income							
Payments							
Direct labour							
Material purchases							
Variable overheads							
Property costs							
Energy costs							
Other fixed costs							
Capital costs							
Interest							
Cash outflows							
Net cash flow							
Balance b/f							
Balance c/f							
Sales (units)							
Production (units)							

[Answer on p. 30]

▷ ACTIVITY 5

Data

Wilson Limited produces bicycle saddles. By increasing exports, it plans to increase production and sales during the first half of next year. The actual figures for November and December were as follows.

Month (20X6)	Production (units)	Sales (units)
November	7,000	7,000
December	8,000	8,000

The plans for the next six months are shown below.

Month (20X7)	Production (units)	Sales (units)
January	10,000	8,000
February	12,000	10,000
March	12,000	12,000
April	14,000	13,000
May	15,000	14,000
June	15,000	16,000

- The selling price is £20.50 per unit, with an anticipated price increase to £21.50 per unit from 1 June.
- Raw material costs £4 per unit.
- Wages and other variable costs are £8 per unit.
- Other fixed costs are £1,800 per month rising to £2,200 from 1 May onwards.
- 20% of sales are for cash, the remainder being credit sales which are paid for two months after the sale.
- Material purchases are paid one month after delivery and are held in stock for one month before entering production.
- Wages and variable and fixed costs are paid in the month of production.
- A new machine costing £450,000 is to be purchased in February to cope with the planned expansion of demand. 20% of payment is to be made on 1 February and the remainder retained until the machine is operational (expected 1 July 20X7).
- An advertising campaign is also to be launched, involving payments of £20,000 in each of February and May.
- Corporation tax of £56,000 is due to be paid on 30 June 20X7.
- The company is financed by share capital of 1 million £1 shares and a debenture of £0.5 million paying semi-annual interest of 3.5% on 30 June and 31 December.
- The directors plan to pay a dividend of £0.10 per share in May.
- An overdraft of £0.5 million has been agreed with Wilson Limited's bankers.
- The current overdraft interest rate is 7.2% per annum on the prior month closing balance.
- Interest is received on cash balances at 6.0% per annum on the prior month closing balance.
- On 1 January the firm expects to have £185,000 in the bank.

Task

Complete the cash budget provided below

Wilson Limited – Cash budget 20X7

	Jan	Feb	Mar	Apr	May	June
Inflows						
Receipts from cash sales						
Receipts from debtors						
Interest received						
Total inflows						

	Jan	Feb	Mar	Apr	May	June
Outflows						
Payments to creditors for purchases						
Variable costs						
Fixed costs						
Advertising						
Capital expenditure						
Corporation tax						
Dividends						
Interest on overdraft						
Interest on long-term loan						
Total outflows						
Net cash flow						
Opening cash balance						
Closing cash balance						

[Answer on p. 31]

6 Test your knowledge

1 Give four reasons why the net profit of a business may differ from the net cash inflows.

2 What is the accruals concept?

3 Give an example of an annual disbursement.

4 What is meant by the term lagged receipts?

5 Credit sales of a product are 2,000 units in May and 2,500 units in June, each at a selling price of £10. 40% of credit customers pay in the month following the sale, taking a 2% cash discount. The remainder pay two months after the sale. What is the cash inflow for in July?

6 Purchases in May are expected to be £40,000 and are to increase by 5% per month. 20% of purchases are for cash and the remainder are on credit. 60% of the credit purchases are paid one month after the purchase and the remainder two months after the purchase. What was the cash outflow in July?

[Answers on p.32]

7 Summary

In this chapter we have considered the importance of cash to a business and therefore the importance of monitoring cash flows. The most effective method of monitoring the cash position is to prepare a cash budget for the forthcoming periods. When the estimated cash receipts and payments are brought together in a cash budget then the estimated net cash position at the end of each month can be determined and management can take action to deal with this net cash position in the most appropriate manner (for detail see later in this text).

The preparation of a cash budget requires a logical approach to determining the more difficult cash flows such as cash from credit sales or cash paid to creditors. Make sure that you do put in all of the easy figures as well as spending your time on the more complicated calculations.

Answers to chapter activities & 'test your knowledge' questions

ACTIVITY 1

(a) **A regular revenue receipt**
Examples might include cash sales, investment income (bank interest or dividends).

(b) **An exceptional payment**
Examples might include redundancy costs or closure costs.

(c) **A capital payment**
Examples might include purchase of fixed assets or the purchase of a new business.

(d) **An annual disbursement**
Examples might include payments to the HM Revenue and Customs, a final dividend to shareholders, a bonus to the directors.

ACTIVITY 2

August cash receipts

	June	July	August
Credit sales	£	£	£
(3,000 – 500 =) 2,500 × £45	112,500		
(2,900 – 500 =) 2,400 × £48		115,200	
((2,900 × 1.1) – 500 =) 2,690 × £48			129,120

	£
Cash receipts from credit sales	
60% × 129,120 × 0.98	75,923
40% × 115,200	46,080
Cash sales 500 × £48	24,000
	146,003

ACTIVITY 3

July cash outflow

	£
May credit purchases (100,000 x 70%) x 20%	14,000
June credit purchases (110,000 x 70%) x 30%	23,100
July – Cash purchases 120,000 x 30%	36,000
– Credit purchases 120,000 x 70% x 50% x 95%	39,900
	113,000

▷ ACTIVITY 4

	Nov	Dec	Jan	Feb	Mar	Apr	May
	£	£	£	£	£	£	£
Receipts							
Cash sales		150,000	180,000	180,000	165,000	150,000	195,000
Credit collections			150,000	180,000	180,000	165,000	150,000
Share capital	200,000						
Enterprise grants	100,000						
Cash income	300,000	150,000	330,000	360,000	345,000	315,000	345,000
Payments							
Direct labour	156,000	156,000	143,000	130,000	169,000	169,000	182,000
Material purchases	78,000	78,000	71,500	65,000	84,500	84,500	91,000
Variable overheads	36,000	36,000	33,000	30,000	39,000	39,000	42,000
Property expenses	20,000	20,000	20,000	20,000	20,000	20,000	20,000
Energy costs				28,800			28,800
Other fixed costs	15,000	15,000	15,000	15,000	15,000	15,000	15,000
Capital costs	141,000						
Interest		1,460	3,025	2,580	1,894	1,738	1,880
Cash outflows	446,000	306,460	285,525	291,380	329,394	329,238	380,680
Net cash flow	–146,000	–156,460	44,475	68,620	15,606	–14,238	–35,680
Balance b/f	0	–146,000	–302,460	–257,985	–189,365	–173,759	–187,997
Balance c/f	–146,000	–302,460	–257,985	–189,365	–173,759	–187,997	–223,677
Sales (units)		20,000	24,000	24,000	22,000	20,000	26,000
Production (units)	24,000	24,000	22,000	20,000	26,000	26,000	28,000

▷ ACTIVITY 5

Wilson Limited: cash budget 20X7

Month ending (£)	January	February	March	April	May	June
Inflows						
Receipts from cash sales	32,800	41,000	49,200	53,300	57,400	68,800
Receipts from debtors	114,800	131,200	131,200	164,000	196,800	213,200
Interest received	925	1,059	646	822	1,064	829
Total inflows	148,525	173,259	181,046	218,122	255,264	282,829
Outflows						
Payments to creditors for purchases	40,000	48,000	48,000	56,000	60,000	60,000
Variable costs	80,000	96,000	96,000	112,000	120,000	120,000
Fixed costs	1,800	1,800	1,800	1,800	2,200	2,200
Advertising		20,000			20,000	
Capital expenditure		90,000				
Corporation tax						56,000
Dividends					100,000	
Interest on overdraft						
Interest on long-term loan						17,500
Total outflows	121,800	255,800	145,800	169,800	302,200	255,700
Net cash flow	26,725	(82,541)	35,246	48,322	(46,936)	27,129
Opening cash balance	185,000	211,725	129,184	164,430	212,752	165,816
Closing cash balance	211,725	129,184	164,430	212,752	165,816	192,945

Test your knowledge

1
- Non-cash expenses such as depreciation
- Purchase of fixed assets
- Sale of fixed assets
- Financing transactions

2 Transactions are accounted for in the period in which they occur rather than in the period in which the cash was received or paid.

3 Dividends, Corporation Tax, Drawings.

4 Sales are made to customers on credit and the cash is received in a later period than that in which the sale was made.

5

	£
May sales (2,000× £10×60%)	12,000
June sales (2,500×£10×40%×98%)	9,800
July cash receipts	21,800

6

	£
May purchases (£40,000×40%×80%)	12,800
June purchases (£40,000×1.05×60%×80%)	20,160
July purchases (£40,000×1.05×1.05×20%)	8,820
	41,780

2

FORECASTING AND MONITORING CASH FLOWS

INTRODUCTION

This chapter begins with consideration of methods that can be used to forecast cash payments and cash receipts. One of the most common of these methods is time series analysis which can be used to try to forecast as accurately as possible sales in future periods. Cash flow forecasts might also be affected by changes in quantities of sales or production and by inflation of costs and prices.

Once a cash flow forecast has been prepared then it has a variety of uses to management. By changing individual assumptions within the forecast it is possible to see what effect this might have on the eventual cash balance. This process of sensitivity analysis can be performed more easily by a computer package and therefore this chapter considers the basic techniques for preparing a cash flow forecast on a computer spreadsheet. Finally this chapter considers how cash flows will be monitored and how the cash flow forecast will be compared to the actual cash flows and the importance of this area for management.

KNOWLEDGE AND UNDERSTANDING

- Basic statistical techniques for estimating future trends: moving averages, allowance for inflation
- Computer models to assess the sensitivity of elements in the cash budget to change (e.g. price, wage rate changes)

CONTENTS

PERFORMANCE CRITERIA

Consult appropriate staff to determine the likely pattern of cash

- flows over the accounting period and to anticipate any exceptional receipts or payments — B 15.1
- Ensure forecasts of future cash payments and receipts are in accord with known income and expenditure trends — C 15.1
- Identify significant deviations from the cash budget and take corrective action within defined organisational policies — E 15.1

1 Information for cash budgets

1.1 Introduction

In the previous chapter we have seen how much information is required in order to produce a cash budget. In an assessment this information will all be provided for you; however in practice you will need to know where the information comes from.

1.2 Sales information

The starting point for information for the cash budget will normally be sales quantities and prices as this will be the basis for the production budget and expenses figures. The sales information will normally be provided by the sales or marketing director or manager. Both the quantity of sales and the price that will be charged is vital for the cash budget and we will look at methods of estimating future sales later in the chapter.

1.3 Production information

Details such as the amount of production, the levels of closing stocks and the labour hours to be worked should all be available from the production manager or director. The production manager may also have information about variable and fixed expenses of the factory but equally that information may come from the accountant.

The production manager or director may also be able to provide information about any planned capital expenditure or any planned sales of fixed assets.

1.4 Accounting information

Some further information required may come from the accounts department in the form of materials prices, labour hour rates, variable and fixed costs, details of sales of fixed assets. The accounts department should also have the information required to determine the payment pattern of debtors and creditors.

1.5 Forecast information

All of this information required for the cash budget has to be forecast. This will start with forecasts of sales quantities which could be done using time series analysis. The sales price must also be forecast and this may be done by considering inflation rates.

Once the sales figures have been forecast the production expenses must be estimated which will include forecasts of materials prices, wage rates and expense items.

2 Time series

2.1 Introduction

The sales director may know that sales are changing but may not be able to quantify the changes without undertaking some basic analysis. A method of finding the underlying trend is to use time series analysis which enables a general linear trend to be isolated from a fluctuating pattern of changing values.

☐ DEFINITION

A time series is a set of values for some variable (e.g. monthly sales) which varies with time. The set of observations will be taken at specific times, usually at regular intervals.

Examples of figures which can be plotted as a time series are:
(a) monthly rainfall in London
(b) daily closing price of a share on the Stock Exchange
(c) weekly sales in a department store.

2.2 Time series graph

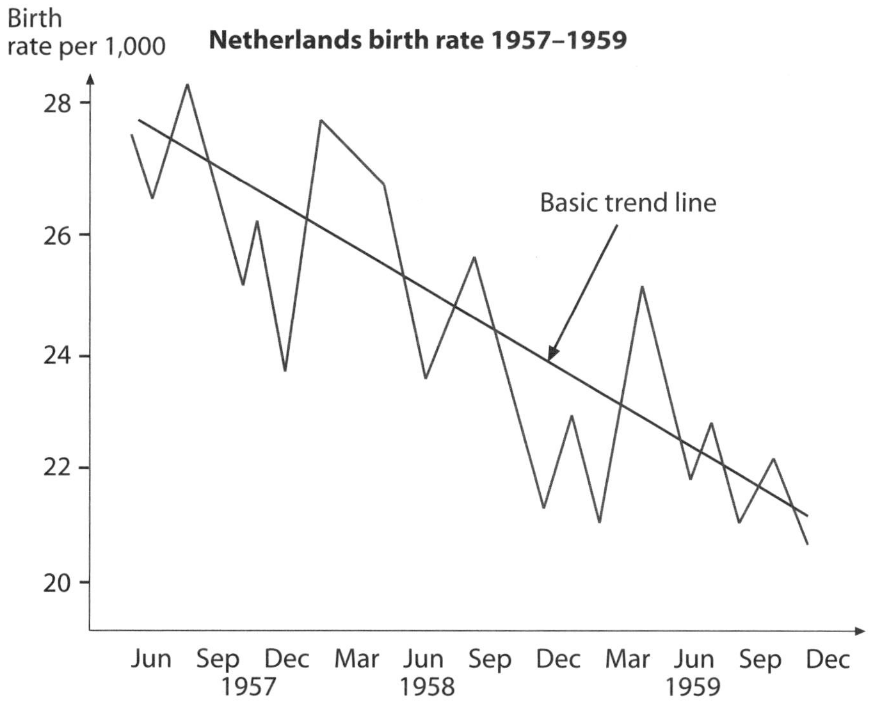

The graph below shows the birth rate in the Netherlands from 1957–1959.

In such a graph, each point is joined by a straight line – hence the typically 'jagged' appearance.

2.3 Characteristic movements

Analysis of time series has revealed certain characteristic movements or variations. These movements are the components of the time series. Analysis of these components is essential for forecasting purposes.

The four main types of components are:
- long-term movements or basic trends
- cyclical movements
- seasonal movements
- irregular or random movements.

2.4 Basic trend

The basic trend refers to the general direction in which the graph of a time series goes over a long interval of time. This movement can be represented on the graph by a trend curve or line.

For example, the government often refers to unemployment in terms of the 'underlying trend'; it is this that is considered important.

2.5 Cyclical variations

Cyclical variations refer to long-term oscillations or swings about the trend line or curve. These cycles may or may not be periodic; i.e. they do not necessarily follow exactly similar patterns after equal intervals of time. In business and economic situations, movements are said to be cyclical if they recur after time intervals of more than one year. A good example is the trade cycle, representing intervals of prosperity, recession, depression and recovery.

For cyclical variations to be apparent, data must be available over very long periods of time since the periods of oscillation are so long. This is impractical for simulation tasks and, for that reason, the calculation of cyclical variations is ignored in this chapter although you must, of course, realise that they exist.

2.6 Seasonal variations

Seasonal fluctuations are the identical, or almost identical, patterns which a time series follows during corresponding intervals of successive periods. Such movements are due to recurring events, such as the sudden increase in department store sales before Christmas. Although, in general, seasonal movements refer to a period of one year, this is not always the case and periods of hours, days, weeks, months, etc may also be considered, depending on the type of data available.

2.7 Random variations

Random variations are the sporadic motions of time series due to chance events such as floods, strikes, elections etc.

By their very nature they are unpredictable and therefore cannot play a large part in any forecasting, but it is possible to isolate the random variations by calculating all other types of variation and removing them from the time series data. It is important to extract any significant random variations from the data before using them for forecasting.

3 Time series analysis

3.1 Analysis of a time series

The analysis of a time series consists of:

Step 1 Breaking the series down into trend and seasonal variations.

Step 2 Projecting the trend into the future.

Step 3 Adding together the projected trend and appropriate seasonal variation to arrive at one forecast figure.

The analysis which follows concentrates on solely on isolating only the basic trend which is all that is required for Unit 15.

3.2 Isolating the trend

There are many methods of analysing time series; some sophisticated, others simple. The method covered in this chapter is the best known and most commonly used, though not necessarily the most sophisticated.

You may have noticed earlier that a trend curve was drawn in on the time series graph. Indeed one way of isolating the trend, admittedly not very scientific, is simply to draw it in freehand on the graph.

This is not usually good enough for most purposes and we will use the method of moving averages in order to isolate the trend figures.

3.3 Moving averages

By using moving averages, the variations in a time series can be eliminated leaving a 'smoothed' set of figures which is taken as the trend. It is important that the correct cycle is chosen for the moving average, otherwise the result will not be as good as it should be. For instance, if there are seasonal variations present in a time series and the pattern is repeated every fourth period, then moving averages with a cycle of 4 should be used for the best results.

Types of variation	Cycle	
Seasonal	4	Calculate the average for each successive 4 periods.
Daily	5	Calculate the average for each successive 5 days.

This should be apparent from the wording of the question. The technique is best illustrated by way of an example.

O EXAMPLE

The following data will be used to demonstrate the various techniques in the subsequent paragraphs. The figures shown are the quarterly sales figures.

	Quarter			
Year	1	2	3	4
	£000	£000	£000	£000
1	74	100	94	127
2	84	106	120	141
3	94	112	130	147
4	112	118	148	169
5	138	140		

Solution

The underlying trend is estimated using moving averages. Generally speaking, the idea is that each successive 12-month period is considered (rolling on one quarter at a time) to see whether the annual total is increasing or decreasing (i.e. if the 'trend' is up or down).

Year	(a) Quarter	(b) Value	(c) 4-quarter moving total	(d) 8-quarter moving total	(e) Trend(T) (d)/8
1	1	74			
	2	100			
			395 (W1)		
	3	94		800 (W3)	100
			405 (W2)		
	4	127		816 (W4)	102
			411		
2	1	84		848	106
			437		
	2	106		888	111
			451		
	3	120		912	114
			461		
	4	141		928	116
			467		
3	1	94		944	118
			477		
	2	112		960	120
			483		
	3	130		984	123
			501		
	4	147		1,008	126
			507		
4	1	112		1,032	129
			525		
	2	118		1,072	134
			547		
	3	148		1,120	140
			573		
	4	169		1,168	146
			595		
5	1	138			
	2	140			
	3				
	4				

Positioning of figures in column (c) , (d) and (e) should be noted.

- Points on column (c)

  (W1) 395 is the total of the first four quarters (i.e. 74 + 100 + 94 +127). This figure is shown in between quarter 2 and quarter 3 as this is the mid-point of the four quarters being totalled.
  (W2) 405 is the total of quarters 2 to 5 (i.e. 100 + 94 + 127 + 84), or (395 + 84 - 74) may be easier.
  This figure is shown in between quarter 3 and quarter 4 as this is the mid-point of the four quarters being totalled.
  This line could be used to isolate the trend itself; however, for various reasons (not least of which is accuracy), an eight-quarter total is produced.

- Points on column (d)

  (W3) 800 is the total of quarters 395 + 405
  (W4) 816 is the total of 405 and 411.

- Point on column (e)

  The trend can now be found, by taking the eight-quarter moving total and dividing by 8 (e.g. 800 / 8 = 100). This average figure is the average of quarters 1, 2, 3 and 4, together with quarters 2, 3, 4 and 5 and is taken to represent quarter 3's trend figure, being the middle quarter of the five quarters under consideration:

  1 2 3 4 5

  Middle quarter ↑

Therefore this figure (100) is shown adjacent to the original figure for quarter 3.

The above gives rise to the fact that column (e) is known as the centred average.

The trend shown in column (e) can be used to calculate the average increase per quarter.

Total increase over range: 146 – 100 = 46.

Number of increases = 13 (i.e. 14 quarters but only 13 steps up!).

Average increment per quarter = 3.54.

Therefore the trend figure for the next quarter will be 146 + 3.54 = 149.54.

3.4 Disadvantages of moving averages

- Values at the beginning and end of the series are lost; therefore, the moving averages do not cover the complete period.
- The moving averages may generate cycles or other movements that were not present in the original data.
- The averages are strongly affected by extreme values. To overcome this, a weighted moving average is sometimes used, giving the largest weights to central items and small weights to extreme values.

▷ ACTIVITY 1

The following represents quarterly output of a product:

	March	June	September	December
Year 1	100	104	110	109
Year 2	102	108	112	108

What are the trend figures that would be obtained by a four-quarter centred moving average?

[Answer on p. 64]

The basic idea here will be to take a predicted trend figure and adjust it for an 'average' seasonal variation.

▷ ACTIVITY 2

Stenwater's cash flow is typically very seasonal with the maximum borrowing requirement in the summer months. From the figure below it can be seen that the maximum borrowing is expected to occur in June.

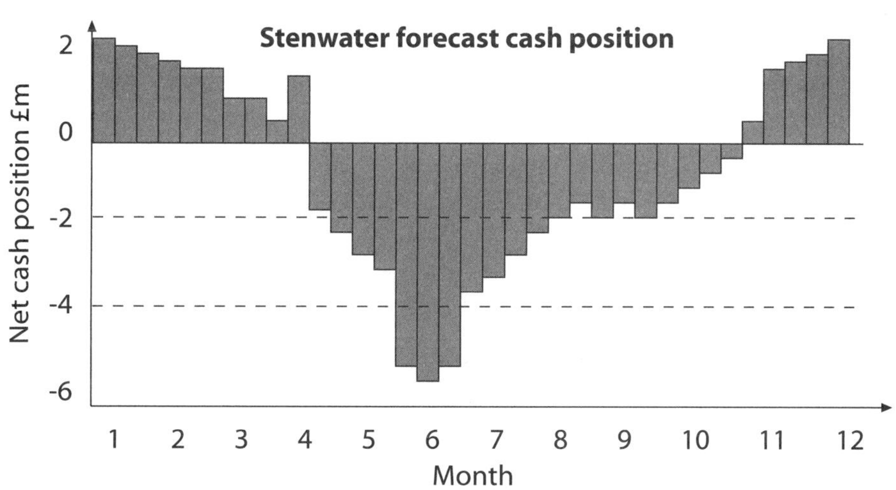

Task 1

The finance manager has suggested monitoring cash flow by a series of moving averages. Calculate the three-day moving average for the series of cash flows given below.

Date	Net cash position (£ million)	Three-day moving average (£ million)
6 June	(5.351)	–
7 June	(5.415)	
8 June	(5.451)	
9 June	(5.587)	
10 June	(5.654)	
13 June	(5.487)	
14 June	(5.478)	–

(a) When does the net cash position trend cross the three-day moving average?

(b) What does this indicate?

Further data

Some time has now passed and Stenwater Limited's cash management procedures have become more sophisticated. You now personally prepare weekly and monthly cash flow forecasts in 'receipts and payments' style format.

As these forecasts are short run with most items occurring in the near future, many managers believe that financial transactions over this period could be forecast very accurately.

Task 2

What four categories of transactions might create the sources of uncertainty which make short-term cash flow difficult to forecast? Give an example of each.

[Answer on p. 64]

▷ ACTIVITY 3

Seasonal variations or fluctuations may affect many companies' cash flows.

(a) Explain the meaning of the term 'seasonal variation'.

(b) Give two examples of seasonal variations in a company's cash flow.

(c) The table below provides details of Masham plc's monthly cash flow. Calculate the three-month moving average of Masham's cash flow (to the nearest thousand) in the spaces provided below.

Month	Sales £000	Three-month moving average
June	770	–
July	750	
August	910	
September	905	
October	925	
November	870	
December*	990	–

*Forecast

(d) What do you deduce from the moving averages calculated for Masham's monthly cash flows?

(e) What features, other than seasonal variations and long-term trends, could be identified from time series data? Identify **two** such features.

[Answer on p. 65]

4 Quantity increases and inflation

4.1 Introduction

In arriving at expected sales, purchases and other cost figures, department heads need some method of calculating the numbers and here statistical methods may provide a useful tool.

4.2 Percentage increases

In some situations, it may be quite easy to predict future sales. From past experience and knowledge of the market, a sales director may predict sales quantities to rise by 1% each month.

So, for example, if sales are 100,000 units at £1 each (i.e. £100,000 in January), he could predict:

February	$(100{,}000 \times 1.01)$	=	101,000 units
March	$(100{,}000 \times 1.01^2)$ (i.e. $100 \times 1.01 \times 1.01$)	=	102,010 units
April	$(100{,}000 \times 1.01^3)$	=	103,030 units
etc			

4.3 Inflation increases

Alternatively, the only rise in sales may be due to inflation, say of 3% per month, which means the price rises. So, if January sales are £100,000, then:

February sales will be	(£100,000 × 1.03)	=	£103,000
March sales will be	(£103,000 × 1.03)	=	£106,090 etc

4.4 Quantity and inflation increases

Sales may be both rising by 1% in volume terms and increasing in value by 3% due to inflation each month. In which case, when January sales are 100,000 units×£1 = £100,000:

February sales will be	(100,000 × 1.01) units (£1 × 1.03)		
	i.e. £100,000 × 1.01 × 1.03	=	£104,030
March sales will be	100,000×1.01 × 1.01 × 1.03 × 1.03		
	or $100{,}000 \times 1.01^2 \times 1.03^2$	=	£108,222 etc

5 Sensitivity of the cash budget elements

5.1 Introduction

In many cases managers may need to consider how the bank position will alter if there is a change in any of the receipt or expenditure items. What may seem a healthy positive cash position could change with a 1% increase in wages or a 2% fall in sales. It is therefore advisable to assess the sensitivity of the balance to such changes.

O EXAMPLE

Consider the following cash flow.

	January	February	March
	£	£	£
Receipts			
Sales	10,000	20,000	15,000
Payments			
Creditors	10,000	10,000	20,000
Wages	2,000	3,000	2,000
Sundry	500	500	500
	12,500	13,500	22,500
Balance b/f	4,000	1,500	8,000
Net cash flow	(2,500)	6,500	(7,500)
Balance c/f	1,500	8,000	500

What would be the net cash position each month if:

(i) wages increased by 5%?

(ii) wages increased by 8%?

(iii) What is the maximum increase in wages over the period before the bank balance becomes an overdraft?

Solution

(i) If wages increase by 5% you can see that the wage expense will become:

	£	£	£
Wages	2,100	3,150	2,100

and the bank balance changes to:

Balance b/f	4,000	1,400	7,750
Net cash flow	(2,600)	6,350	(7,600)
Balance c/f	1,400	7,750	150

Thus, although wages have increased, the bank balance is still positive and corrective measures are not required.

(ii) If, however, an 8% wage increase were agreed, then wages would become:

	£	£	£
Wages	2,160	3,240	2,160

causing:

Balance b/f	4,000	1,340	7,600
Net cash flow	(2,660)	6,260	(7,660)
Balance c/f	1,340	7,600	(60)

i.e. the bank balance would become overdrawn.

(iii) The credit manager can calculate exactly what the maximum rise in wages can be without causing the company to become overdrawn at the bank.

Taking the original figures, it is possible to have a £500 wages increase over the current total wages of £7,000 over the period without having a negative cash figure at the end of March, i.e.:

500 / 7,000= 0.0714

i.e. a 7.14% pay rise is possible.

Therefore, when negotiating staff salaries, the credit manager can state that pay rises up to 7.14% will not be detrimental to the company's cash position, but figures above this will cause the company to become overdrawn at the bank.

5.2 Changes in payment patterns

The cash flows that appear in the cash budget are heavily dependent upon the payment patterns of debtors or the timescale on which the business pays its creditors. In some cases managers may need information about the effect that a change in those payment patterns would have on the net cash position.

O EXAMPLE

A business is producing its cash budget for the next three months. Credit sales in February and March were £50,000 and £58,000. Credit sales are forecast as £60,000, £70,000 and £50,000 respectively for each of the months of April, May and June. Credit customers are currently offered one month's credit and they all pay in the month after the sale.

Cash outflows in each month are estimated to be:

April	May	June
£48,000	£57,000	£60,000

At the end of March there is an overdraft of £10,000.

What would be the effect on the net cash position at the end of each month if credit customers took two months' credit?

Solution

Current policy cash budget (one month credit)

	April	May	June
	£	£	£
Receipts from debtors			
(previous months sales)	58,000	60,000	70,000
Cash outflows	(48,000)	(57,000)	(60,000)
Net cash flow	10,000	3,000	10,000
Cash balance b/f	(10,000)	–	3,000
Cash balance c/f	–	3,000	13,000

New policy cash budget (two months credit)	April	May	June
	£	£	£
Receipts from debtors			
(sales from two months ago)	50,000	58,000	60,000
Cash outflows	(48,000)	(57,000)	(60,000)
Net cash flow	2,000	1,000	–
Cash balance b/f	(10,000)	(8,000)	(7,000)
Cash balance c/f	(8,000)	(7,000)	(7,000)

The effect of debtors paying two months after the sale rather than one month has been to reduce a positive cash balance to an overdraft balance at the end of each month.

This is a favourite element of simulations – once you have produced the original cash budget you are then required to assess the affect that a change in payment policy would have on the net cash position.

5.3 Discount to credit customers

A further way in which the payment pattern of debtors can be altered is by the offering of a cash or settlement discount for earlier payment of outstanding debts.

This will mean that less cash will be received from debtors but that this cash will be received earlier which may alleviate any anticipated cash flow problems.

EXAMPLE

A business has the following budgeted credit sales and budgeted cash payments:

	January	February	March	April	May	June
	£	£	£	£	£	£
Budgeted sales	100,000	120,000	110,000	140,000	150,000	160,000
Budgeted cash payments	80,000	94,000	108,000	120,000	130,000	145,000

The current credit terms are payment within 60 days and the current payment pattern is that 20% of customers pay during the month following sale, 70% pay two months after the sale and 10% three months after the date of sale.

The company is considering introducing a settlement discount of 2% for payment during the month after sale. This is anticipated to result in 60% of customers paying in the month after sale, 30% two months after the date of sale and 10% three months after the date of sale.

The company anticipates a bank overdraft of £20,000 at the start of April.

(i) Determine the net cash balance at the end of each of the months of April, May and June under the existing credit terms.

(ii) Calculate the effect on the net cash balance at the end of each of the three months if the new policy of offering a settlement discount were introduced from March sales onwards.

(iii) Comment on how the new policy affects the net cash balance for each of the three months.

Solution

Under existing policy

		April	May	June
		£	£	£
January sales	(10%×100,000)	10,000		
February sales	(70%×120,000)	84,000		
	(10%×120,000)		12,000	
March sales	(20%×110,000)	22,000		
	(70%×110,000)		77,000	
	(10%×110,000)			11,000
April sales	(20%×140,000)		28,000	
	(70%×140,000)			98,000
May sales	(20%×150,000)			30,000
		116,000	117,000	139,000
Cash payments		(120,000)	(130,000)	(145,000)
Net cash flow		(4,000)	(13,000)	(6,000)
Opening balance		(20,000)	(24,000)	(37,000)
Closing balance		(24,000)	(37,000)	(43,000)

Under new policy

		April	May	June
		£	£	£
January sales	(10%×100,000)	10,000		
February sales	(70%×120,000)	84,000		
	(10%×120,000)		12,000	
March sales	(60%×110,000×98%)	64,680		
	(30%×110,000)		33,000	
	(10%×110,000)			11,000
April sales	(60%×140,000×98%)		82,320	
	(30%×140,000)			42,000
May sales	(60%×150,000×98%)			88,200
		158,680	127,320	141,200
Cash payments		(120,000)	(130,000)	(145,000)
Net cash flow		38,680	(2,680)	(3,800)
Opening balance		(20,000)	18,680	16,000
Closing balance		18,680	16,000	12,200

Under the new policy of offering the settlement discount, the overdraft is eliminated immediately and the business continues to have a healthy, although diminishing, cash balance throughout the period. This compares to the old policy which would see the overdraft of £20,000 at the start of April increasing to one of £43,000 at the end of June.

5.4 Assessing a proposed discount policy

In the last example we saw how the significant change in debtor payments patterns under the new cash discount policy immediately eliminated the overdraft, therefore dramatically improving the cash position. However, this will tend to be a short term improvement in cash flow as sales receipts will be lower in later months.

Therefore, in a simulation you might be asked to assess a discount policy and to recommend whether the company should pursue such a policy. This will require an assessment of not only the improvement in monthly cash flow but also a comparison of the discount itself to that cash flow improvement in order to determine the monthly cost of the discount.

O EXAMPLE

At the end of March a business has debtors of £28,400, all of which it is anticipated will be received by the end of April. Invoiced sales are anticipated to be £20,000 in April, £30,000 in May and £40,000 in June. Current credit terms are payment within 60 days but the anticipated cash flows from these invoiced sales will be:

- 40% in the month the invoice is issued
- 50% in the month after the invoice is issued
- 10% in two months after the invoice is issued.

The finance director is considering introducing a settlement discount of 3% for payments received in the month that the sales invoice is raised. This policy is expected to result in 80% of customers paying within the month of the invoice and the remainder paying in the following month.

Recommend whether the company should pursue this discount policy.

Solution

Cash inflows without discount

		April	May	June
		£	£	£
From opening debtors		28,400		
April invoices	(20,000×40%)	8,000		
	(20,000×50%)		10,000	
	(20,000×10%)			2,000
May invoices	(30,000×40%)		12,000	
	(30,000×50%)			15,000
June invoices	(40,000×40%)			16,000
Budgeted cash receipts		36,400	22,000	33,000

Cash inflows with discount

		April	May	June
		£	£	£
From opening debtors		28,400		
April invoices	(20,000×80%×97%)	15,520		
	(20,000×20%)		4,000	
May invoices	(30,000×80%×97%)		23,280	
	(30,000×20%)			6,000
June invoices	(40,000×80%×97%)			31,040
Budgeted cash receipts		43,920	27,280	37,040

The proposed discount policy has a significant effect of accelerating receipts from customers which results in £7,520 additional cash being received in April. However, the sales receipts in later months will be lower due to the discount.

If the cost of the discount is related to the improvement in cash flow then a percentage cost of the discount can be calculated:

Discount = 3%×20,000
= £600

Improvement in cash flow = £7,520

Percentage cost = $\frac{600}{7{,}520} \times 100$
= 8.0%

This represents a monthly interest rate of 8%, but with annual interest rates considerably lower than this it would be advisable for the company to borrow from its bank if it requires additional short term funds rather than offering the discount as the bank borrowing would undoubtedly be cheaper.

5.5 Cost of a discount

The analysis carried out in the previous example of the cost/benefit of the proposed discount was one that was required for a Unit 15 AAT simulation. However, it is also possible to approximate the annual cost of offering a discount to debtors by the following formula:

$$\frac{d}{100 - d} \times \frac{365}{N - D}$$

where d = discount percentage given
N = normal payment term
D = discount payment term

EXAMPLE

Using the example above we can calculate the approximate annual cost of the proposed discount.

The discount was 3% for payment within 30 days whereas the normal credit terms were 60 days.

$$\text{Annual cost} = \frac{d}{100 - d} \times \frac{365}{N - D}$$

$$= 38\%$$

As it would cost 38% per annum to offer this discount, it would most certainly be cheaper to borrow from the bank to raise any funds required.

ACTIVITY 4

	April	May	June
	£	£	£
Sales	2,600	3,100	1,600
Creditors	1,300	1,550	700
Wages	1,000	1,000	1,000
Power	200	200	200
	2,500	2,750	1,900
Balance b/f	100	200	550
Net cash flow	100	350	(300)
Balance c/f	200	550	250

(a) In the above cash flow, how sensitive is the bank balance at the end of June to a 1% increase and a 2% decrease in sales?

(b) Ignoring part (a), what is the maximum wage rise that can be agreed without causing the bank balance to become overdrawn?

(c) For each of the two variations to sales in part (a) and ignoring part (b), how much can the payments to creditors increase without causing the bank balance to become negative?

[Answer on p. 66]

6 Computer spreadsheets

6.1 Introduction

We have already seen that once a cash budget has been produced the managers may be interested in the effects on the net cash position of changes in the assumptions upon which the cash budget was based, such as wage rates and credit periods. If computer packages such as spreadsheets are used then the effect of any number of changes and any combination of changes can be calculated quickly and easily.

6.2 Areas of sensitivity

The cash budget might be sensitive to a variety of different changes in assumptions regarding the cash flows:

- change in sales volume
- change in sales price
- change in material costs
- change in wages costs
- change in overhead costs
- change in debtor payment periods
- change in creditor payment periods.

If sensitivity analysis is carried out manually, it is both time consuming and difficult to combine more than one change in variable. However, a computer spreadsheet can carry out such calculations effortlessly.

6.3 Uses of computer spreadsheets

Spreadsheets can be used for a variety of purposes when assessing the sensitivity of cash budget figures:

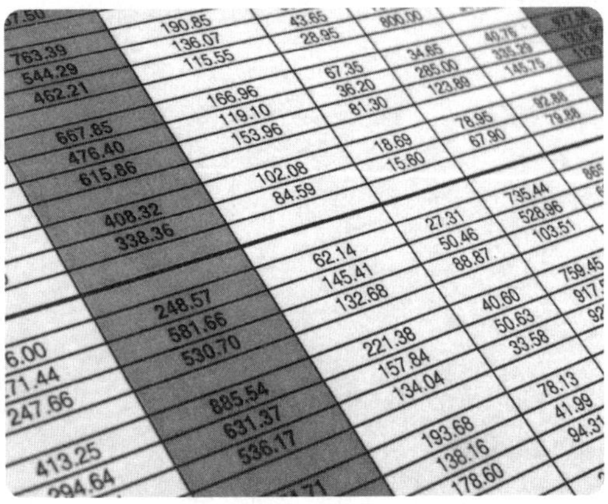

- determining the effect of changes in quantity and timing of amounts
- preparing cash forecasts for a range of different outcomes, from the worst to the best
- preparing cash forecasts for different scenarios of growth, expansion, inflation, etc
- using probability analysis to assign different probabilities to different possible outcomes.

6.4 Preparing a cash flow forecast on a spreadsheet

Many of you will be familiar with spreadsheets from your earlier studies or from the workplace. In a simulation you might be asked to set up a spreadsheet for a cash budget by determining the formulae that would be used to calculate the figures for particular cells on the spreadsheet. This is not difficult, just a question of a logical approach as with cash budgets themselves.

O EXAMPLE

A company wishes to set up a computer spreadsheet to help with the preparation of its monthly cash budget starting from 1 January 20X4 when the balance on the bank account is an overdraft of £25,400. The following information is available:

- Sales in January 20X4 are expected to be £36,000 and are expected to rise by 1% each month.
- Sales are all on credit and the average payment pattern for debtors is that 30% pay in the month after the sale and 70% two months after the sale.
- Sales in November and December 20X3 were £30,000 in each month.
- Materials purchases in January are expected to be £24,000 and are expected to rise on average by 0.5% per month.
- All materials purchases are on credit and are paid for in the month of purchase.
- Overhead costs are £8,400 for January and are expected to increase by 2% per month.
- Overhead costs are paid for in the month that they are incurred.
- Corporation tax of £8,600 is due in October.
- Capital expenditure of £24,000 is budgeted for April 20X4 and a further £10,000 in August.
- Overdraft interest is charged at 2.5% per month based on the balance at the end of the previous month.

Set up a computer spreadsheet that can prepare the cash budget.

Solution

The first stage is to set up the basic proforma for the spreadsheet just as you would for a manual cash budget. Then enter the figures that are known:

- January sales, purchases, cash receipts, overheads and cash balance.
- February receipts from December sales.
- Enter the exceptional payments for corporation tax and capital expenditure (due to lack of space on the page we have only shown the first four months of the cash budget but in practice it may go many months into the future).

	A	B	C	D	E
1		Jan	Feb	Mar	Apr
2		£	£	£	£
3	Sales	36,000			
4	Cash receipts				
5	One month	9,000			
6	Two months	21,000	21,000		
7	Total receipts				
8					
9	Cash payments				
10	Materials	24,000			
11	Overheads	8,400			
12	Tax				
13	Capital expenditure				24,000
14	Interest				
15	Total payments				
16					
17	Cash receipts less payments				
18	Cash balance b/f	–25,400			
19	Cash balance c/f				

The next stage is to insert other figures that we know such as growth rates and the interest rate into further cells in the spread sheet. For example:

	A	B	C	D	E
20	Sales growth	1.01			
21	Debts paid in one month	0.3			
22	Debts paid in two months	0.7			
23	Purchases growth	1.005			
24	Overheads growth	1.02			
25	Interest	0.025			

Now we can produce formulae for each further cell in the spreadsheet based upon the initial information that we were given. (Not all of the formulae have been completed, just enough for you to see how it works.)

	A	B	C	D	E
1		Jan	Feb	Mar	Apr
2		£	£	£	£
3	Sales	36,000	B3 x B20	C3 x B20	D3 x B20
4	Cash receipts				
5	One month	9,000	B3 x B21	C3 x B21	D3 x B21
6	Two months	21,000	21,000	B3xB22	C3 x B22
7	Total receipts	B5 + B6	C5 + C6		
8					
9	Cash payments				
10	Materials	24,000	B10 x B23	C10 x B23	
11	Overheads	8,400	B11 x B24	C11 x B24	
12	Tax				
13	Capital expenditure				24,000
14	Interest	B18 x B25	C18xB25		
15	Total payments	B10 + B11 + B12 + B13 + B14			
16					
17	Cash receipts less payments	B7 – B15			
18	Cash balance b/f	–25,400	B19	C19	D19
19	Cash balance c/f	B17 + B18			

Not only can the computer now quickly calculate all of the figures in the cash flow statement but any of the assumptions can also be changed and the figures will be automatically updated. So, for example, if in March it was realised that sales growth was only 0.75% per month then cell B20 can be changed and the computer will put through all of the changes that stem from this.

7 Monitoring cash flow

7.1 Introduction

Once a cash flow budget has been drawn up, the management of the business are in a position to plan their working capital requirements. Knowing the business's projected cash position, it is possible to estimate:

(a) the need for cash and the ability to finance this

(b) the possible sources from which any shortfall can be financed, and

(c) what to do with any surplus cash.

7.2 Investing a surplus

From production of the cash budget and surpluses/deficits of cash can be anticipated and so expected. A known surplus needs to be planned for. It should be invested sensibly to earn interest or income for the business. The type of investment depends on various factors:

- the size of funds available for investment
- the length of time the money can be tied up
- the acceptable risk.

This will all be covered in more detail in a later chapter of this text book.

7.3 Funding a deficit

If a deficit of cash is projected, then the business will need to plan to find the extra funds to cover the shortfall.

The choices of funding method will be considered in detail in later chapters of this text book.

However, the directors need to be sure that the need for extra funds is not arising because of overtrading.

7.4 Overtrading

Overtrading usually occurs when a company tries to expand too quickly and over-stretches its working capital due to inadequate financing for its growth rate. If sales increase too rapidly, then working capital requirements may increase as more money is tied up in stocks of raw materials to support the increased sales levels; debtors will also rise. This can lead to a situation in which the company is operating at a profit but suffers a liquidity crisis as it has insufficient cash to pay its bills and expenses.

This problem happens over a period of time, with the working capital gradually being stretched and without the managers of the company realising what is happening as the company continues to be profitable. The balance sheet eventually reveals the problem.

7.5 Identifying signs of overtrading

Signs of overtrading can be identified as follows:

- sharply and rapidly increasing sales volumes
- falling profit margins despite increased sales as higher discounts are given to attract more customers and production costs increase due to overtime costs, etc
- greater reliance on short-term funding such as overdrafts
- longer debtor/creditor collection ratios.

7.6 Controlling overtrading

Planned overtrading is not dangerous; it is the unmanaged and undetected overtrading that causes company downfalls.

If, however, the symptoms of unmanaged overtrading are detected, then the problem may be averted by:

- issuing new share capital or loan stock
- taking out long-term loans rather than overdrafts
- reducing the operating cycle by controlling debtors and creditors
- slowing down the company's expansion.

7.7 Over-capitalisation

The opposite of overtrading is over-capitalisation. There is too much cash. Consequently profit is suppressed in relation to the capital investment in the company and earnings per £ of capital are low. Unless this surplus can be invested by the company to earn a good return, it could be distributed to shareholders through a higher dividend or a buyback of shares.

ACTIVITY 5

Data

Sparkle Toothbrushes Inc have established a small UK subsidiary, Sparkle Toothbrushes (UK) Limited, which has been trading for two years. Their future plans are as follows:

(a) New equipment costing £160,000 will be bought and paid for on 1 January 20X6.
(b) Wages will be £20,000 per month.
(c) Selling and administration costs are expected to be £12,000 per month.
(d) Premises are rented at £72,000 per annum payable quarterly in advance starting on 1 January.
(e) Terms of trade are for customers to pay in the month following receipt of goods and suppliers to be paid two months after the month of purchase.
(f) For planning purposes the bank overdraft is expected to be £100,000 at the end of December 20X5.

Planned sales and purchases are as follows:

	Sales	Purchases
	£000	£000
November	115	100
December	120	110
January	120	130
February	160	160
March	200	160

Task

(a) You are asked to put together a quarterly cash flow forecast (starting 1 January 20X6) based on the information above. Your forecast should clearly show the cash position at the start and end of each month. Complete the forecast on the form below.

Sparkle Toothbrushes (UK) Limited – Cash flow for quarter ending March 20X6

Month	January	February	March	Total
	£	£	£	£
Receipts				
Sales				
Total receipts				
Payments				
Purchases				
Wages				
Selling and admin				
Rent				
Equipment				
Total payments				
Net cash flow				
Cash balances				
At start of month				
At end of month				

(b) What steps could be taken to get the cash in more quickly? Identify TWO ways to achieve this.

(c) What will be the overall effect on cash flow if, on average, 50% of customers pay one month late? Show your workings below:

Month	January	February	March	Total
	£	£	£	£
Net cash flow (from (a) above)				
Adjustment				
New net cash flow				

[Answer on p. 67]

8 Reconciliation of actual cash flow to budgeted cash flow

8.1 Introduction

As well as using the cash budget to identify any anticipated surplus or deficit in future periods, it is also important to monitor the actual performance of the business compared to the budgeted performance. This is part of the management process of control whereby the actual cash flows are compared to the budgeted cash flows and any significant variances between the two are highlighted and investigated.

8.2 Comparison of actual to budgeted cash flows

For each line of the cash budget the actual cash flow for each month and for the period in total can be compared to the corresponding budgeted figure. Any major differences should be investigated to determine why the variance happened and to consider how this can be dealt with in terms of future operations or future budgeting.

EXAMPLE

Given below are the actual and budgeted cash flows for the month of April:

	Actual	Budget
	£	£
Cash sales	6,400	9,000
Receipts from debtors	27,800	34,000
Payments to creditors	(20,500)	(16,700)
Production wages	(3,600)	(3,600)
Administration costs	(2,100)	(2,000)
Capital expenditure	(14,000)	–
Net cash flow	(6,000)	20,700
Opening cash balance	3,200	3,200
Closing cash balance	(2,800)	23,900

What are the significant differences between the actual cash flows for the month and the budgeted cash flows and how might the company have tried to avoid the overdraft balance that actually occurred at the end of the month?

Solution

Cash sales are £2,600 less than budgeted.

Receipts from debtors are £6,200 less than budgeted.

Payments to creditors are £3,800 more than budgeted.

There is capital expenditure of £14,000 which was not budgeted for.

Taking these factors all together, this means that the company has an overdraft of £2,800 at the end of the month rather than the healthy budgeted cash balance of almost £24,000.

The company could have tried to avoid the overdraft situation in the following ways:

- Better credit control and collection procedures leading to higher receipts from debtors.
- Delaying payments to creditors or negotiating longer credit terms with the suppliers.
- Postponing the capital expenditure.
- Purchasing the capital items on lease or hire purchase terms rather than outright.
- Finding specific finance for the capital expenditure such as a bank loan.

8.3 Reconciliation of budgeted cash balance to actual cash balance

After determining the variances between the actual cash flows and the budgeted cash for the period then it should be possible to use these differences to reconcile the budgeted cash balance at the end of the period to the actual cash balance. This provides a useful summary to the management of the business for the causes of the unexpected actual position.

EXAMPLE

Given below are the actual and budgeted cash flows for April from the previous example:

	Actual	Budget
	£	£
Cash sales	6,400	9,000
Receipts from debtors	27,800	34,000
Payments to creditors	(20,500)	(16,700)
Production wages	(3,600)	(3,600)
Administration costs	(2,100)	(2,000)
Capital expenditure	(14,000)	–
Net cash flow	(6,000)	20,700
Opening cash balance	3,200	3,200
Closing cash balance	(2,800)	23,900

Prepare a reconciliation of the budgeted cash balance of £23,900 to the actual overdraft figure of £2,800 at the end of the month.

Solution

Reconciliation of budgeted cash balance to actual cash balance

	£
Budgeted cash balance at 30 April	23,900
Shortfall in cash sales	(2,600)
Shortfall in receipts from debtors	(6,200)
Additional payments to suppliers	(3,800)
Additional administration costs	(100)
Unbudgeted capital expenditure	(14,000)
Actual overdraft at 30 April	(2,800)

▷ ACTIVITY 6

Given below are the actual and budgeted cash flows for the month of October for a business:

	Actual £	Budget £
Receipts from debtors	106,000	132,400
Payments to suppliers	(79,000)	(70,000)
Production wages	(17,500)	(17,000)
Production expenses	(1,500)	(1,000)
Selling expenses	(3,400)	(4,000)
Administration expenses	(4,100)	(4,100)
Dividend	(20,000)	
Net cash flow	(19,500)	36,300
Opening cash balance	10,000	10,000
Closing cash balance	(9,500)	46,300

(a) Reconcile the actual cash balance at the end of October to the budgeted cash balance at that date.

(b) Identify three significant deviations from the cash budget and suggest what action could have been taken to avoid each of these variances.

[Answer on p. 68]

9 Test your knowledge

1 What are the four main types of components in a time series?

2 What does the basic trend of a time series denote?

3 What are seasonal variations in a time series?

4 Given below are six months of sales figures:

	£
Jan	10,000
Feb	11,300
Mar	10,800
Apr	11,000
May	10,400
June	11,500

Calculate the three-month moving average for these figures.

5 March sales were £160,000 and estimated to increase in volume by 2% in April and in price by 5%. What are the estimated April sales in value?

6 What is meant by overtrading?

7 What is meant by over-capitalisation?

8 What will be the overall effect of the introduction of a settlement discount for debtors?

[Answers on p.69]

10 Summary

When preparing cash budgets a lot of forecast information is required, particularly regarding sales forecasts. One method of forecasting the sales figure is to use time series analysis where the trend is determined and this information is then used to forecast future sales. A further method of forecasting sales is to use anticipated growth of sales and inflation rates to update the current sales figures and produce a forecast.

The figures in the cash budget are all estimates based upon projected sales figures and assumptions regarding factors such as the payment pattern of debtors and the speed of payment to creditors. Management may be interested in how the net cash position would change if these estimates or assumptions change. This can be determined by various forms of sensitivity analysis. Computer spreadsheets can be used not only to speed up the preparation of cash budgets but also to easily carry out a variety of forms of sensitivity analysis.

As well as using cash budgets in order to plan for anticipated deficits or surpluses, management will also need to compare the actual cash flows for a period to the budgeted cash flows as part of the process of control. Useful information for management will be a reconciliation between the budgeted cash balance at the end of the period and the actual cash balance in order to highlight areas that can be improved in terms of operations or budgeting.

Answers to chapter activities & 'test your knowledge' questions

▷ ACTIVITY 1

Four-quarter moving totals:

(100 + 104 + 110 + 109)	=	423
(423 - 100 + 102)	=	425
(425 - 104 + 108)	=	429
(429 - 110 + 112)	=	431
(431 - 109 + 108)	=	430
Trend	=	moving totals (order 2) of above / 8
	=	(423+425) / 8 , (425+429) / 8
		(429+431) / 8, (431+430) / 8
	=	106, 106.75, 107.5, 107.625

▷ ACTIVITY 2

Task 1

Date	Net cash position (£ million)	3-day moving average (£ million)
6 June	(5.351)	–
7 June	(5.415)	(5.406)
8 June	(5.451)	(5.484)
9 June	(5.587)	(5.564)
10 June	(5.654)	(5.576)
13 June	(5.487)	(5.540)
14 June	(5.478)	–

(a) 13 June

(b) That the trend of decreasing cash position has been reversed

Task 2

- **Sales uncertainty** – the risk relating to an organisation's future sales. Examples could include changes in revenue due to economic (e.g. inflation) or competitive factors, changes in the sales mix, price or volume variances.
- **Collection rate uncertainty** – uncertainty regarding the organisation's future collection patterns of amounts due from debtors. Examples might refer to the uncertainty caused by changing economic and competitive conditions which will affect historic collection patterns.
- **Production cost uncertainty** – the risk of labour and material costs that go into a product or service. Examples may include unexpected changes in labour productivity, materials prices and volumes of material used.
- **Capital outflow uncertainty** – the uncertainty relating to the timing of an organisation's cash disbursements for major capital expenditure and construction programmes. Examples might include the risks attached to a large construction project and the delays that might occur.

▷ ACTIVITY 3

(a) Short-term fluctuations in recorded values, due to different circumstances which affect results at different times of the year, or different days of the week.

(b) Jewellery sales: two-thirds of annual sales made in the last third of the year.
Ice cream sales: high in the summer months, low in winter.

(c)

Month	Sales (£000)	Three-month moving average
Jun	770	–
Jul	750	810
Aug	910	855
Sept	905	913
Oct	925	900
Nov	870	928
Dec	990	–

(d) There is a clear upward movement in Masham's monthly cash flows.

(e) Cyclical variations (cycles) or random variations (non-recurring).

▷ ACTIVITY 4

(a) **1% increase in sales**

	April	May	June
	£	£	£
Sales (x 1.01)	2,626	3,131	1,616
Resulting in:			
Balance b/f	100	226	607
Net cash flow	126	381	(284)
Balance c/f	226	607	323

i.e. a 1% increase in sales results in the bank balance increasing from £250 to £323. This is an increase of £73 (i.e. 29%).

2% decrease in sales

	April	May	June
	£	£	£
Sales (x 0.98)	2,548	3,038	1,568
Resulting in:			
Balance b/f	100	148	436
Net cash flow	48	288	(332)
Balance c/f	148	436	104

A 2% decrease in sales has not caused the bank balance to become overdrawn but cash has fallen to £104. This is a £146 (i.e. 58%) fall.

(b) There is a £250 cash balance at the end of the quarter. If this were allocated to wages a 250/3,000 (i.e. an 8.33 % pay rise could be given without the company becoming overdrawn this quarter).

(c) Increase in sales by 1%
This resulted in a surplus of £323 at the end of the quarter, i.e.:
(323/3,550)= 9.1%

So a 9.1% increase in payments to creditors could be sustained without the company becoming overdrawn in the quarter.

Decrease in sales by 2%

This resulted in a cash balance of £104.

Here, (104 / 3,550) = 2.9% is the maximum increase in payments which can be made to creditors.

▷ ACTIVITY 5

(a) **Sparkle Toothbrushes (UK) Limited – Cash flow for quarter ending March 20X6**

Month	January	February	March	Total
	£	£	£	£
Receipts				
Sales	120,000	120,000	160,000	400,000
Total receipts	120,000	120,000	160,000	400,000
Payments				
Purchases	100,000	110,000	130,000	340,000
Wages	20,000	20,000	20,000	60,000
Selling and admin	12,000	12,000	12,000	36,000
Rent	18,000			18,000
Equipment	160,000			160,000
Total payments	310,000	142,000	162,000	614,000
Net cash flow	(190,000)	(22,000)	(2,000)	(214,000)
Cash balances				
At start of month	(100,000)	(290,000)	(312,000)	(100,000)
At end of month	(290,000)	(312,000)	(314,000)	(314,000)

(b) Two from:

- Offer trade discounts for prompt payment
- Reduce credit sales
- Negotiate to pay rent in arrears, rather than in advance.

(c) Month	January	February	March	Total
	£	£	£	£
Net cash flow	(190,000)	(22,000)	(2,000)	(214,000)
Adjustment (working)	(2,500)	–	(20,000)	(22,500)
New net cash flow	(192,500)	(22,000)	(22,000)	(236,500)
Opening balance	(100,000)	(292,500)	(314,500)	(100,000)
Closing balance	(292,500)	(314,500)	(336,500)	(336,500)

Working

	Nov	Dec	Jan		Feb		March		April	May
	£000	£000	£000		£000		£000		£000	£000
Sales	115	120	120		160	200				
Cash for part (a)			120	(Dec)	120	(Jan)	160	(Feb)	200	
Cash for part (c)			57.5	(50%Nov)	60.0	(50%Dec)	60.0	(50% Jan)		
			60.0	(50% Dec)	60.0	(50% Jan)	80.0	(50% Feb)		
			117.5		120.0		140.0			
Adjustment			(2.5)		–		(20.0)			

ACTIVITY 6

(a) **Reconciliation of budgeted cash balance to actual cash balance**

	£
Budgeted cash balance	46,300
Shortfall in receipts from debtors	(26,400)
Additional payments to suppliers	(9,000)
Additional production wages	(500)
Additional production expenses	(500)
Shortfall in selling expenses	600
Unbudgeted dividend	(20,000)
Actual overdraft	(9,500)

(b) Receipts from debtors were £26,400 less than budgeted – this could have been addressed by tighter credit control and collection procedures to collect more money from invoiced sales during the month.

Payments to suppliers were £9,000 more than budgeted – this could have been dealt with by delaying payment to the suppliers or by negotiating longer credit terms.

Unbudgeted dividend of £20,000 – this could possibly have been delayed until the business had more cash or reduced in size.

Test your knowledge

1
- Basic trend
- Cyclical variations
- Seasonal variations
- Random variations

2 The general movement of the time series over time.

3 Similar variations in corresponding time periods.

4

		Moving average
	£	£
Jan	10,000	–
Feb	11,300	10,700
Mar	10,800	11,033
Apr	11,000	10,733
May	10,400	10,967
June	11,500	–

5 Estimated sales = £160,000×1.02×1.05 = £171,360

6 Overtrading is when a company expands too quickly and over-stretches its working capital due to inadequate funding.

7 Over-capitalisation is where a business has too much cash which is not being invested to earn a suitable return for the owners of the business.

8 The introduction of a settlement discount for debtors should initially increase immediate cash flows but reduce cash inflows over the longer term as less cash is received from debtors.

Cheque No.
Sort Code

3

BANKS AND FINANCIAL MARKETS

INTRODUCTION

This chapter provides the background information required regarding the UK banking system and money market. This information will then be used in the following two chapters when considering the issues of raising finance and investing surplus funds.

KNOWLEDGE AND UNDERSTANDING

- The basic structure of the banking system and the money market in the UK and the relationships between financial institutions
- Government monetary policies
- Bank overdrafts and loans; terms and conditions; legal relationship between bank and customer

CONTENTS

1 Cash management

1.1 Introduction

In the previous two chapters we have seen how to prepare a cash budget and the importance of having enough cash in the business at all times. The cash budget highlights the net cash position at the end of each period that is budgeted for. In some organisations this will be every month whereas in other, probably larger, organisations the net cash position at the end of each day is determined from the budget.

1.2 Net cash position

The importance of highlighting the net cash position is that the personnel responsible for cash management within the organisation can then plan ahead as to how to manage this net cash position.

1.3 Deficit of funds

If the net cash position at a point in the future is budgeted as a deficit then plans must be laid for how to finance this deficit. This may be by an overdraft or loan from the bank or longer term financing such as a share or debenture issue.

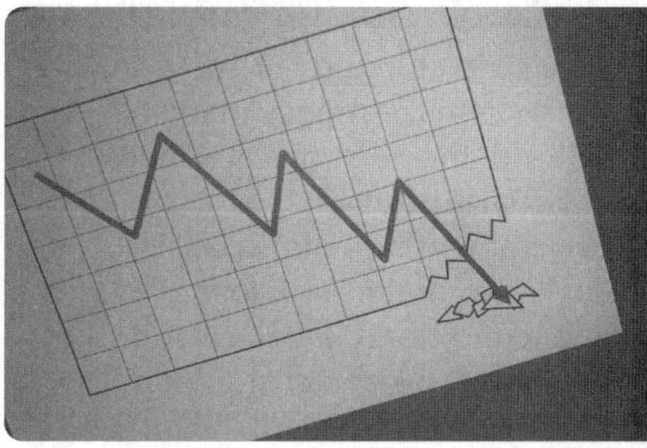

1.4 Surplus of funds

A budgeted surplus of funds means that the business will be solvent and will be able to pay its creditors and others. However, it also means that a valuable asset, cash, is not being used profitably within the business. The interest that the cash will earn in the business cheque account is likely to be negligible, if any is earned at all. To make the cash surplus work for the business it should be invested.

Raising of finance and investment of funds will be considered in detail in the next two chapters. However, in order for the right decisions to be taken regarding either raising additional finance or investing surplus funds, you need to understand how the financial markets and the banking system work. Therefore in the rest of this chapter we will be covering the detailed workings of the financial markets.

2 The UK banking system

2.1 Introduction

There will always be individuals, partnerships, companies and governments with surplus funds. They will want to invest their excess funds to earn a return.

Similarly, there will always be entities without enough funds. For example, an individual might want to buy a car or a house, a company might want to undertake an ambitious expansion project, or a government might want to buy an expensive weapons system.

The financial system brings both groups together; its intermediaries act as links in the chains joining savers and borrowers. The system is seen at its simplest when individuals deposit their savings at the bank, which then lends the money on to others, but the path can get much more complicated.

2.2 Financial intermediation

Why are the intermediaries needed? Why don't the savers and borrowers get together directly and save the costs which the intermediaries involve? The reason is that financial intermediation brings benefits as follows.

- 'Maturity transformation' occurs, in which deposits by customers, usually short term, are lent out to borrowers for much longer periods of time.
- The risk profile of a saver is reduced. If financial intermediaries did not exist, a person or organisation with money to lend would have to seek out a potential borrower, who might eventually default. An intermediary is likely to aggregate the deposits of individual depositors for the purpose of granting fewer but more substantial advances, whilst reducing or eliminating the risk of default to savers.
- Intermediaries also provide considerable benefits to borrowers, who might otherwise have difficulty locating potential savers who are willing to lend appropriate amounts of funds at reasonable interest rates. Moreover, the use of a financial institution will provide greater flexibility for borrowers in that they almost certainly will be permitted to repay loans earlier than originally specified if circumstances permit, or reschedule debts if they have cash flow problems. It is unlikely that, with direct saving and lending, these provisions would be possible.

▷ ACTIVITY 1

List three advantages of financial intermediation.

[Answer on p.83]

2.3 Types of financial institutions

There are many different types of financial institutions that play some role in the operation of securities and other capital markets. Some act solely in the role of intermediary, collecting money from investors and passing it on to borrowers; others act as investors/borrowers in their own right. We shall now look at some of the most common types of institution:

- brokers – stock and money
- banks – clearing and merchant
- institutional investors – pension funds, insurance companies, investment and unit trusts
- venture capitalists.

2.4 Brokers

Brokers, in their purest form, act as agents for investors who wish to buy or sell shares or funds. They seek out a source or outlet for the required shares or funds and act as a go between in settling price and other terms of the deal. Their profits are generally made by commission and fees.

2.5 Banks

There are two main types of banks in the UK: primary and secondary banks. Primary banks are those which operate the money transmission service in the economy, the banks which operate cheque accounts and deal with cheque clearing. These are often known as the commercial banks, retail banks or clearing banks.

The secondary banks consist of a wide range of merchant banks, other British banks and foreign banks in the UK. They do not tend to take part in the cheque clearing system.

2.6 Types of deposit

Banks take deposits from customers.

The banks offer a variety of deposit facilities to their customers, one useful distinction being between retail deposits and wholesale deposits.

2.7 Retail deposits

Those banks which operate an extensive branch network obtain a substantial proportion of their sterling resources as retail deposits: current account deposits held by individuals or organisations in connection with their ordinary payments and receipts, and other interest-bearing deposits held as a supplementary store of liquidity. Retail banking is the traditional high street banking with relatively small deposits from and loans to customers.

2.8 Wholesale deposits

Wholesale deposits are large interest-bearing deposits – usually of at least £50,000 - on which the interest rate is negotiated. Deposits may be received directly from customers or indirectly through money brokers. The market is very competitive and the rate paid for funds is generally identical for institutions of the same standing. Sources of wholesale deposits include institutions at home and abroad, large companies, non-bank financial institutions and other banks with temporary surplus funds.

2.9 Certificate of deposit

The certificate of deposit (CD) is a particular type of wholesale deposit. The CD is a document issued by a bank certifying that a deposit has been made with that bank which is repayable to the bearer on surrender of the certificate at maturity. A CD is a negotiable instrument so that, while the bank has a deposit for a fixed term, the depositor has the option of obtaining cash before maturity by selling the certificate in the market.

2.10 Lending facilities

The banks offer a variety of lending facilities to their customers with terms varying according to the type of lending and customer involved.

(a) Companies are offered overdraft and term lending, syndicated loan finance and services such as instalment credit, leasing and factoring which are often provided through subsidiaries.
(b) Personal customers get overdraft and bridging finance, personal loans, revolving credit and budget accounts, instalment credit (often through subsidiaries) and credit card finance.

2.11 Relationship of the banker and customer

There are in fact four main contractual relationships between the banker and the customer.

The debtor/creditor relationship where the customer deposits his money with the bank and the bank becomes the debtor and the customer, the creditor. If the customer's account is overdrawn, however, the bank becomes the creditor and the customer the debtor.

There are a number of essential areas in this element of the contract:
- The bank must receive cheques for the customer's account.
- The bank borrows the customer's deposits and undertakes to repay them.
- The bank will only cease to do business with the customer with reasonable notice.
- The bank is not liable to pay until the customer demands payment.
- The customer exercises reasonable care when writing cheques.

The bailor/bailee relationship concerns the bank accepting the customer's property for storage in its safe deposit. The bank undertakes to take reasonable care to safeguard the property against loss or damage and then re-deliver it only to the customer or someone authorised by the customer.

The principal/agent relationship where, for example, the customer pays a crossed cheque into the bank, the bank acts as agent when presenting the cheque for payment and paying the proceeds into the customer's account.

The mortgagor/mortgagee relationship exists where the bank asks the customer to secure a loan with a charge over the customer's assets. If the customer does not repay the loan then the bank can sell the asset and use the proceeds to pay off the loan.

2.12 Fiduciary relationship

The bank and the customer also have a fiduciary relationship which means that the bank is expected to act with the utmost good faith in its relationship with the customer.

2.13 The duties of the bank

The bank has the following duties to its customers:

- It must honour customer's cheques as long as they are correctly made out, there is no legal reason for not honouring it and their customer has enough funds or overdraft limit to cover the amount of the cheque.
- The bank must credit cash/cheques paid in to the customer's account.
- If the customer makes a written request for repayment of funds in its account, for example by writing a cheque, the bank must repay the amounts on demand.
- The bank must comply with the customer's instructions by a direct debit mandate or standing order.
- The bank must provide a statement showing the transactions on the account and be prepared to provide details of the balance on the customer's account.
- The bank must respect the confidentiality of the customer's affairs unless the bank is required by law or public duty to disclose, or the interest of the bank requires disclosure or where the customer gives his consent for disclosure.
- The bank must tell the customer if there has been an attempt to forge the customer's signature on a cheque.
- The bank should use care and skill in its actions.
- The bank must provide reasonable notice if it is to close a customer's account.

2.14 Customer's duties

The customer has two main duties:

- to exercise care in drawing cheques such that fraud is not facilitated
- to tell the bank of any forgeries known of.

2.15 The rights of the bank

The rights of the bank are:

- to charge reasonable charges and commissions over and above interest
- to use the customer's money in any way provided that it is legal and morally acceptable
- to be repaid overdrawn balances on demand
- to be indemnified against possible losses when acting on a customer's behalf.

2.16 Services offered by merchant banks

Merchant banks may be subsidiaries of clearing banks, part of a large financial group of companies, or independent. Their main functions include:

- Provision of financial advice – mainly to larger commercial companies, on such aspects as the raising of finance, the investment of cash surpluses, and merger and acquisition activities. Such assistance can contribute significantly to a firm's financial management strategy.
- Provision of finance – merchant banks specialise in the provision of large, longer term lending through the money markets. They also have specialised 'issuing houses' that handle share and other security issues.

2.17 Institutional investors

Only about 20-25% of quoted company shares in the UK are currently held by private individuals.

The vast majority of equity finance for quoted companies comes from institutional investors, in particular the pension funds. The most important types of institutional investors are:

- Pension fund – buys securities with the pension contributions it receives. These produce income to pay current pensioners, and provide for the need to pay future pensioners.
- Insurance company – buys securities with the insurance premiums it receives. These produce income to pay for claims (for example, when life assurance policies mature) and provide for future claims.
- Investment trust – buys securities with the money raised by selling shares in the trust. The income and capital gains produced are distributed amongst the shareholders in the trust.
- Unit trust – buys securities with the money raised by selling units in the trust. These produce income and capital gains to give the unit holders a return on their investment.

2.18 Venture capitalists

Venture capital is a source of long-term (mainly equity) finance where the investor relies on growth rather than income and is prepared to accept much greater risk.

It is normally provided under the condition of 'hands-on', the venture capitalist having a continuing involvement in the business of the company.

It is not subject to repayment on demand at a specified time, and realisation occurs only on the sale of the company or on flotation.

Venture capital is therefore a potentially valuable source of capital for small companies which would not prove attractive to the average investor on the Stock Exchange.

3 The Bank of England

3.1 Introduction

The Bank of England is the UK's central or national bank charged with overall control of the banking system in the interest of the nation.

The Bank of England is in the control of the UK government. The Governor, Deputy Governor and 16 directors are appointed by the Sovereign on the recommendation of the Prime Minister. Consequently, the Treasury is able to implement government policies through:
(a) the use of monetary policy
(b) the Bank's overall control of the banking system, and
(c) the Bank's influence over the financial institutions.

The Bank of England acts as the government's bank in the widest possible sense, i.e. examining and anticipating banking problems.

3.2 The Bank of England's role as a banker

The Bank acts as banker:
(a) to the government
(b) to foreign central banks and international organisations.

All commercial banks have a bank account with the Bank which is used to settle debts between each other and to pay amounts due to the government.

3.3 The Bank of England's operations in the markets

- The Bank ensures implementation of government policy to control the economy by controlling the money market for short-term loans by the issue of Treasury bills.
- The Bank issues long-term government debt, referred to as gilt-edged securities or gilts.
- The Bank sets interest rates via a committee appointed by the government.
- The Bank manages the exchange rate to protect the pound. If sterling's value is too high the Bank sells sterling for foreign currencies, if its value is too low the Bank will buy sterling with its foreign currency reserves.
- The Bank meets the government's long-term borrowing requirements by open market operations on the Stock Exchange.
- The Bank is a lender of last resort and will provide funds for banks which are short of cash.

▷ ACTIVITY 2

What are the main functions of the Bank of England?

[Answer on p.83]

4 The money markets

4.1 Introduction

The term money markets covers a vast array of markets buying and selling different forms of money or marketable securities, which are short-term highly liquid investments that are readily convertible into cash. The money markets provide the financial institutions with a means of borrowing and investing to deal with short-term fluctuations.

The main traders in the money markets are banks, the government through the Bank of England, local authorities, brokers, jobbers and other intermediaries in the market.

4.2 Money market financial instruments

The main types of financial instrument that are traded in the money markets are:

- Bills – short-term financial assets that can be converted into cash by selling them in the discount market.
- Deposits – money in the bank accounts of banks and other financial intermediaries.
- Commercial paper – IOUs issued by large companies which can be either held to maturity or sold to third parties.
- Certificates of deposit (CDs) – a certificate for deposits of £50,000 or more for a fixed term which can be sold earlier than maturity in the CD market.

4.3 The primary market

This market consists of the banks and securities firms and the Bank of England. The primary market is used by the Bank to smooth out fluctuations in cash balances by buying bills and other short-term financial instruments from the financial institutions in order to provide more cash, and selling government bills to deal with any surplus cash.

4.4 The local authority market

In this market the local authorities borrow short-term funds by issuing local authority bills with a maturity of about one year.

4.5 The inter-bank market

This is a market for very short-term borrowing, often overnight, between the banks. It is used to smooth fluctuations in the banks' receipts and payments.

4.6 The foreign exchange market

Like the money market, the foreign exchange market operates through the general offices of its constituent banks. The aim of the foreign exchange dealers is to secure supplies of foreign currency as required to finance international trade.

The price of foreign currency is determined by demand and supply i.e. the demand for the country's goods and services by foreigners, and the supply of overseas goods and services which its own home nationals wish to buy.

4.7 The capital market

Many institutions apart from banks are used to provide capital, such as:

(a) Issuing houses who issue new shares or debentures for expanding firms.

(b) Building societies who collect funds for those wishing to purchase their own home.

(c) Finance houses who deal in the more risky but more profitable hire-purchase field for financing purchase of consumer goods (e.g. cars).

(d) Investment trusts and unit trusts which accumulate small amounts from many individuals and purchase a balanced portfolio of investments, thus providing a good source of fixed capital for industry.

(e) Insurance companies who have large sums to invest from premiums received from insuring the public.

(f) The Stock Exchange which raises long-term capital not only via the provision of a market for existing stocks and shares but also by issuing new shares.

4.8 The Stock Exchange

Stock exchanges are based in many of the world's financial centres – such as New York, Tokyo and Paris. The function of such exchanges is to provide a market place for the buying and selling of stocks and shares so that companies can raise long-term finance and investors can buy or sell shares.

The Stock Exchange also provides a market for government bonds or gilts.

ACTIVITY 3

(a) Describe briefly how the money markets operate.
(b) Briefly describe what is meant by the term marketable security.
(c) Give two examples of a marketable security that is used in liquidity management.

[Answer on p.83]

5 Government monetary policies

5.1 Introduction

Government monetary policies are the policies that are implemented by the Treasury and the Bank of England in order to deal with the supply of money, interest rates and the availability of credit.

5.2 Market operations

The government can influence the amount of money in the economy by restricting or encouraging bank lending. By selling attractively priced gilts the government takes money from financial institutions and individuals who pay for these gilts out of their bank accounts thereby reducing the banks' asset bases and the amount that they can lend.

The government also controls bank lending and influences the interest rate by the selling or buying of Treasury bills. By selling Treasury bills the government is taking money out of the system and by buying Treasury bills it can put money back into the system and through supply and demand can influence interest rates.

5.3 Interest rate policy

The Bank of England controls the interest rate through its operations in the primary money market. If interest rates rise then this reduces the demand for borrowing which in turn will have the effect of reducing consumer demand as less credit is available and the credit that is available is too costly.

5.4 Government spending and borrowing

If the government spends more than it raises in taxes then this will increase the money supply. This is known as the Public Sector Borrowing Requirement (PSBR). The government will wish to control the PSBR and to keep it within certain limits so as not to increase the money supply too much. If, however, the government spends less than it raises this will reduce the money supply, this is known as the Public Sector Debt Repayment (PSDR).

6 Test your knowledge

1 What are the three main reasons why financial intermediaries are required?

2 What are the primary banks?

3 What is a Certificate of Deposit?

4 What is meant by there being a fiduciary relationship between a bank and its customer?

5 What are the customer's duties to a bank?

6 What are the main rights of a bank?

7 What are the two main services offered by merchant banks?

8 State three ways in which the Bank of England operates in the money markets.

9 What are the main types of financial instrument traded in the money markets?

[Answers on p. 84]

7 Summary

In this chapter we have summarised the main operations of the banks, the money markets and the government. The primary or retail banks deal in the transmission of money as high street banks, whereas the secondary banks deal with the wholesale business. The Bank of England plays an important role in controlling the banking system and operating the government's monetary policy and regulation of interest rates. Interest rates are controlled by the Bank in the primary market and short-term finance is provided to banks, financial institutions and large commercial organisations through the secondary market which is made up of the local authority market, the inter-bank market, the CD market, the inter-company market and the commercial paper market. Finally, we considered government monetary policy which is concerned with the supply of money, interest rates and the amount of credit that is available.

Answers to chapter activities & 'test your knowledge' questions

▷ ACTIVITY 1

- Links lenders with savers
- Maturity transformation
- Reduction in risk to the lender

▷ ACTIVITY 2

- Supervision of the financial system
- Banker to the government
- Lender of last resort
- Holding operational deposits from the banks for settling their balances
- Implementing government monetary policy
- Sole note-issuing authority

▷ ACTIVITY 3

(a) The money markets even out short-term cash flow between banks, companies and governments; what is bought and sold is the use of money for a set time.

The price of money in this market is the interest rate charged. Interest rates are set by the supply of and demand for money but, for economic reasons, the government may try to influence the level of rates.

The linchpin of the money markets is the inter-bank deposit market where banks swap deposits with one another; other similar markets are allied to this.

Money is also traded as IOUs or securities. A certificate of deposit is an IOU for a bank deposit, a treasury bill is a short-term government IOU and a commercial bill is an IOU for international trade which has been guaranteed by a bank.

To supply money to the banking system, the Bank of England buys bills in the money market at rates it advertises. It uses this mechanism to influence the level of interest rates.

Interest rates go up when the economy is booming, inflation is high, overseas interest rates are rising or the pound is falling.

Rates fall when the economy is in recession, inflation is falling, international rates are coming down or sterling is strong.

(b) Short-term, highly liquid investments which are readily convertible to cash.

(c) Any two of:
- Bills of exchange
- Certificates of deposit
- Government securities
- Local authority short-term loans.

Test your knowledge

1
- Maturity transformation
- Reduction in risk profile of lender
- Links lenders and borrowers.

2 The primary banks are the commercial, retail or high street banks.

3 A document issued by a bank certifying that a deposit has been made with that bank which is repayable to the bearer on surrender of the certificate at maturity.

4 The bank is expected to act with the utmost good faith in its relationship with the customer.

5
- To exercise care in drawing cheques such that fraud is not facilitated
- To tell the bank of any forgeries known of.

6
- To charge reasonable charges and commission
- To use the customer's money in any way provided that it is legal and morally acceptable
- To be repaid overdrawn balances on demand
- To be indemnified against possible losses when acting on a customer's behalf.

7
- Provision of financial advice
- Provision of finance.

8 Any three of:
- Implementation of government policy to control the economy
- Issuing long-term government debt
- Setting interest rates
- Managing the exchange rate
- Meeting the government's long-term borrowing requirements
- Lender of last resort.

9
- Bills
- Deposits
- Commercial paper
- Certificates of deposit.

4

RAISING FINANCE

INTRODUCTION

In an earlier chapter we saw that one of the purposes of preparing a cash flow forecast was in order for the management of a company to be able to forecast whether there is likely to be any cash surplus or cash deficit in the future periods. If a cash deficit is forecast then management will need to make arrangements well in advance for how to deal with that deficit. In this chapter we consider the various forms of finance that can be raised to deal with any known shortage of cash at a future date, how that finance can be arranged and the most appropriate form of finance for specific situations.

KNOWLEDGE AND UNDERSTANDING

- Bank overdrafts and loans; terms and conditions; legal relationship between bank and customer
- Liquidity management

CONTENTS

PERFORMANCE CRITERIA

· Arrange overdraft and loan facilities in anticipation of requirements and on the most favourable terms available	A 15.2
· Ensure the organisation's financial regulations and security procedures are observed	C 15.2
· Ensure account is taken of trends in the economic and financial environment in managing cash balances	D 15.2
· Maintain an adequate level of liquidity in line with cash forecasts	E 15.2

1 The need to raise finance

1.1 Introduction

Any business will have an initial amount of capital which is either contributed by the owner or, in the case of a company, is issued share capital. However at various stages in the business life cycle the management may find that there is a need to raise additional finance.

1.2 Reasons for additional finance

There are many reasons why a business may need to raise additional finance but the most common are:

- to fund working capital
- to increase working capital
- to reduce creditors
- to purchase fixed assets
- to acquire another business.

The need to raise the finance may be highlighted by a deficit in the cash budget, by management decisions regarding investment in fixed assets or by the business strategy of growth by acquisition.

1.3 Funding working capital

☐ DEFINITION

Working capital is the short-term net assets of the business made up of stock, debtors, creditors and cash.

One of the most common reasons for additional finance which is normally highlighted by a deficit in the cash budget is in order to fund working capital. The working capital of a business will have an operating cycle which is effectively the period between the payment of money for goods and the receipt of money from debtors. If creditors are being paid more quickly than money is being received from debtors then at some time it is likely that the business will require funds to tide them over until the money from the debtors is received.

EXAMPLE

A business has a turnover of £1,200,000 per annum and cost of sales of £720,000. Debtors at the year end are £200,000, creditors total £60,000 and stocks of £120,000 are being held.

What is the operating cycle of the business?

Solution

The operating cycle can be calculated in days by determining the debtor and creditor payment periods and the stock turnover in days.

Debtors payment period	200,000/1,200,000×365	=61 days
Creditors payment period	60,000/ 720,000×365	=30 days
Stock turnover period	120,000/ 720,000×365	=61 days

The operating cycle is

	Days
Debtors payment period	61
Stock turnover period	61
	122
Creditors payment period	(30)
Operating cycle	92

This means that stock is being held on average for 61 days before it is sold and then there is a further 61 days before the money from the sale is received. However the creditors are being paid 30 days after the purchase, meaning that there is a 92-day lag between making the payment for the stock and receiving the money from the sale.

This time lag between money out and money in will need to be funded.

1.4 Increasing working capital

After a period of operating, a business may find that it needs an increase in its working capital. This may be due to increased sales turnover which in turn requires increases in stocks and debtors. The business may be able to gain additional credit from its trade creditors but in the absence of that may have to raise funds to finance this increase. Care should be taken in such circumstances to ensure that the business is not overtrading (see earlier chapter).

Alternatively the additional finance required might be due to an increase in debtors. This might be due to inefficiencies in the credit control of the business or it may be that increased credit has had to be offered to customers in order to keep their custom in a competitive market or to increase market share and sales turnover.

Often additional finance might be required due to an increase in stock levels which is not associated with a general increase in turnover. Such a stock increase will normally only be temporary and could be due to:

- taking advantage of an attractive price by placing a bulk order
- building up stocks in advance of a peak period in a seasonal business
- receipt of a large order from a customer.

1.5 Reduction of creditors

A business may need to reduce its trade creditors either in order to take advantage of settlement discounts or due to the fact that trade creditors may be pressing the business for quicker payment for their own reasons. This reduction in trade credit will need to be funded by some other source of finance. If creditors are to be paid earlier, then the cash to do this will have to be found.

Equally additional finance might be required for the short term to fund payments such as quarterly VAT payments or the annual Corporation Tax payment.

1.6 Purchase of fixed assets

Not only will a business require enough cash to pay its creditors and expenses, such as wages, when they fall due, but most businesses will also need to invest in additional or replacement fixed assets on a fairly regular basis. In many cases a business will not have enough cash to purchase the fixed assets required to maintain or expand operations out of cash and will therefore need to raise finance in order to fund the purchase.

1.7 Acquisition of another business

Many businesses have a policy of growth by acquisition of other businesses. Such a major amount of expenditure will almost always require funding by some form of external finance.

In general terms the types of finance available can be categorised as:

- short term – anything up to 3 years
- medium term – 2 to 10 years
- long term – over 10 years.

In the rest of this chapter we will consider all three of these types of finance but as a rule of thumb the time scale of the finance should match the time scale of the reason for the finance. Therefore if the finance is required for working capital reasons then the finance should be short term whereas if the finance is required for longer term investment in fixed assets or another business then the appropriate finance may be medium or long term.

▷ ACTIVITY 1

A business has turnover of £680,000 and cost of sales of £470,000. At the year end it has the following working capital:

	£
Stock	106,000
Trade debtors	136,000
Trade creditors	118,000

What is the operating cycle of the business in days?

[Answer on p.101]

2 Short-term debt finance

2.1 Introduction

Short-term debt finance is used for:

(a) temporary working capital

(b) bridging finance for assets being financed from the sale of existing assets, and

(c) purchase of short-lived assets.

The most common type of short-term finance is a bank overdraft.

2.2 Bank overdraft

Bank overdrafts are most often negotiated for a fixed period in terms of a maximum available facility. In other words, the bank undertakes to advance anything up to, say £50,000, and the business can take advantage of the facility as and when it needs to. The interest will generally be at a variable rate, calculated on a day-to-day basis with reference to the bank's base rate. The principal advantage of an overdraft is flexibility. The business only pays interest on the amount actually drawn, although there may be an additional flat charge of perhaps 0.25% on the maximum facility.

Overdrafts are (technically) repayable on demand and should never be regarded as substitutes for adequate medium term finance.

2.3 Short-term bank loan

A term loan with a bank is a loan for a fixed amount, for an agreed period on pre-arranged terms. The loan will be governed by formal documentation which will include:

- the term of the loan
- the interest rate
- the way in which the interest is charged
- the repayment date/dates
- any security required for the loan
- any covenants attached to the loan.

Term loans can be for virtually any period and the repayment terms can be negotiated with the bank:

- Interest rates may be fixed or variable.
- There are a variety of methods of repaying interest and capital (see later in the chapter).
- The loan can be drawn upon in stages, e.g. 50% now and 50% in three months' time.

2.4 Commercial paper

In recent years (partly in response to government attempts to curtail bank lending) there has been a trend towards the 'securitisation' of short-term loans. This means the sale by companies of promissory notes (promises to pay, often called commercial paper) in preference to the taking out of bank loans.

Commercial paper is unsecured borrowing and is usually issued for short-term borrowings - generally maturing within a three-month period. Commercial paper can be traded and it can be issued in any currency. In order to provide some credence to the market, a credit rating system has been developed so that some reliance can be placed on the commercial paper.

2.5 Debt factoring

A further method of raising short-term finance without resorting to an overdraft or a bank loan is a debt factoring service. Debt factoring is a continuing arrangement by which the factoring company purchases all the trade debts due to a business as they arise. The business will be paid up to 80% of the value of invoices as they are raised, with the balance coming on the date the invoice is settled. The factoring may be with recourse or without recourse.

DEFINITION

With recourse factoring means that the business is liable to the factoring company if a debtor defaults.

DEFINITION

Without recourse factoring means that the factor takes over all responsibility for bad debts as well as collected amounts.

In a factoring arrangement the factoring company will generally take over responsibility for debt collection and sales ledger accounting. The factoring company will obviously make a charge which is proportional to the services it provides and the risk which it assumes.

2.6 Invoice discounting

Invoice discounting is another service provided by factoring companies. It is similar to factoring, in that debts are assigned to the factoring company as they arise, but whereas a factoring arrangement applies to all debtors, discounting is generally negotiated piecemeal for particular selections of invoices. When a batch of debts is assigned, the factoring company will advance up to 75% of the gross invoice value. The payments from customers are forwarded to the factoring company as and when the business receives them (debt collection remains the responsibility of the supplier) and at the end of the month the balance of the purchase price (less charges) is received from the factoring company.

Invoice discounting is simple and flexible, it can be used as and when short-term funds are needed and enables the business to maintain a normal relationship with its customers (who need not know about the third party involvement).

2.7 Hire purchase

If a fixed asset is to be purchased by the business but there is not enough cash available for outright purchase, one simple method is to purchase the asset on a hire purchase scheme.

Hire purchase and instalment credit arrangements can be set up quickly and can generally offer fairly flexible repayment terms. The security for the 'advance' is clearly provided by the asset being purchased.

2.8 Trade credit

Trade credit in the form of extending the time taken to pay trade creditors can be used to provide finance which is apparently cheap and easy to obtain (as the creditors' permission is not sought). However, the company runs the risk of losing suppliers and ultimately prices will rise. If the company extends the payment period beyond 30 days without the supplier's prior agreement, then the supplier is entitled to charge interest.

Increasing the creditors payment period is often the first reaction to a cash deficit but it must be appreciated that it is not without its costs and it does have limits beyond which the credit period cannot be extended without loss of supplies.

▷ ACTIVITY 2

A business has produced its cash budget for the following six months. The cash budget shows that from month four onwards the current overdraft facility will be exceeded, largely due to the extension of additional credit to debtors in order to maintain market share in the face of stiff competition.

List the options the business has in dealing with this situation.

[Answer on p.101]

3 Medium-term debt finance

3.1 Introduction

On the whole medium-term debt finance should be used to fund the purchase of assets with a three- to ten-year life such as plant and machinery. However it can also be useful to fund a medium term deficit in working capital.

3.2 Bank loans

An obvious source of finance for say the purchase of major fixed assets is a medium term bank loan. The term of the loan should not exceed the life of the asset being purchased and will normally be approximately the same as the asset's useful life. The interest on the loan will either be fixed or variable. If the interest is variable then the interest charged will depend upon market rates of interest and will normally be a certain percentage above the bank's base rate or the London Inter-Bank Offered Rate (LIBOR).

3.3 Security

In some cases the bank may only be prepared to advance the money on the basis of some security given by the business. Security can be in the form of a fixed charge or a floating charge.

☐ DEFINITION

A fixed charge is where the security is a particular asset or group of assets.

The bank would have the right to sell this asset if the business defaults on the loan repayments.

☐ DEFINITION

A floating charge is a charge on a certain group of assets of the business such as debtors or stock which will be constantly changing.

If the business defaults on the loan then the bank has the right to however much of those assets the business has at the time.

3.4 Medium-term loan and working capital

In most cases a bank loan is most appropriate for the purchase of major assets which will hopefully provide income over the loan period out of which the loan interest and repayments can be made. However in some cases it may be necessary to raise a medium-term loan to finance a working capital deficit.

For example suppose that a company has consistently had an overdraft of between £20,000 and £30,000 for the last two years. This would appear to be part of the permanent working capital of the business and is known as the hardcore overdraft. Overdraft finance tends to be at a higher rate of interest than loan finance as it is harder to monitor from the bank's perspective and is more volatile. Therefore this company might convert the hardcore overdraft into say a £20,000 five-year loan which will be paid off over the period but which should reduce the amount of additional overdraft finance required.

3.5 Leasing

If a business is to buy a fixed asset such as plant and machinery or motor vehicles it may find that leasing the asset is a cheaper option than taking out a bank loan and purchasing the asset outright. Many financial intermediaries such as banks and insurance companies provide lease finance for a wide range of assets.

There are two types of lease, an operating lease and a finance lease.

3.6 Finance leases

DEFINITION

A finance lease is one where the lessee has all the significant risks and rewards associated with the asset.

Under a finance lease the lessee has the use of the asset for most, if not all, of its useful life. The lessee may even be able to sell the asset at the end of its life with only a proportion of the sale proceeds being returned to the lessor. However the lessee, although having use of the asset, never actually gains legal title to the asset.

The lessee will be responsible for the upkeep and maintenance of the asset and to all intents and purposes owns the asset. The finance lease charges will reflect the repayment of the value of the asset and the finance charge to the lessor.

This may often be a cheaper form of financing the purchase of an asset than taking out a loan to purchase the asset outright.

3.7 Operating leases

DEFINITION

An operating lease is any lease other than a finance lease. Typically, the lessor hires out the asset to the lessee for a short period which is normally substantially less than the asset's total life.

Once the lease period is over then the lessor will lease the same asset to another lessee. The lessor is responsible for servicing and maintaining the asset and the lessee simply gets the use of the asset for the lease period in return for the lease payments.

This type of lease might be useful for example if a particular specialised type of equipment is only required for a fairly short time period. However if an asset is required for substantially its entire useful life then a finance lease would be required.

In simulations if you are asked how a business should raise additional finance required do not concentrate solely on term loans and overdrafts. You may be required to suggest other methods such as leasing, debt factoring, invoice discounting, etc.

▷ ACTIVITY 3

A business has produced its cash budget for the following six months. The cash budget shows that from month four onwards the current overdraft facility will be exceeded, largely due to the necessity to replace the fleet of delivery vans in month four.

List the options the business has in dealing with this situation.

[Answer on p.101]

4 Long-term debt finance

4.1 Introduction

Long-term debt finance is typically used for the purchase of long life, major fixed assets and for acquisitions of other businesses.

4.2 Loan stock and debentures

Any loan raised by the issue of a series of negotiable units could be described as 'loan stock' (the term is not used with a precise meaning) and the word debenture itself merely describes the document which acknowledges the indebtedness. All company borrowing could be referred to as debentures or debenture stock. In practice, the term debenture is usually restricted to secured loans.

Loan stock commonly has a fixed rate of interest, although in recent years a number of companies have issued floating rate debentures. They are repaid at a specified date.

4.3 Advantages of debentures

Advantages of debenture finance are as follows:

(a) It is generally cheaper to raise than a new issue of equity.

(b) It may be cheaper to finance than equity since debenture-holders suffer less risk and may be satisfied by a lower return. However, this must be tempered by the fact that shareholders may perceive there to be a greater gearing risk if the company is already highly geared and may therefore require a higher return.

(c) The existing shareholders will retain the same degree of control.

(d) The interest paid will be allowable for corporation tax.

4.4 Disadvantages of debentures

Disadvantages of debenture finance include the following:

(a) The company may be committed to the fixed interest payments and will therefore have less flexibility than with equity.

(b) The manner in which future finance may be raised could be affected, as future lenders will consider the level of gearing already in existence.

(c) In the event of any default on the interest payments, the debenture-holders would have the power to appoint a receiver to run the company.

4.5 Mortgages

Mortgage loans are loans for specific assets and for which these specific assets (land or buildings) are the security. They are most commonly for 20 or 25 years, but can sometimes be for as long as 35 years. Interest rates on such loans can be fixed, but are more usually variable, at say 1.75% above base rate. The specialists in such loans for businesses are pension funds and insurance companies, who prefer a lower limit of at least £50,000, although smaller loans have been arranged with policy-holders.

4.6 Sale and leaseback

Sale and leaseback arrangements most commonly relate to property and (less likely) large items of capital equipment. The company sells such an asset to the financial institution (perhaps an insurance company) which then leases it back to the company for a term of, generally, between 20 and 25 years.

4.7 Convertible loan stock

DEFINITION

Convertible loan stock is a debenture loan of a company which can be converted by the holder at some point in the future into equity shares of the company.

Convertible loan stock carries as one of the terms of issue the option for the holder to convert his stock within a given time period into equity shares at a specified price. If the option is not exercised, the loan stock will continue its normal term to redemption. If a majority of stockholders decide to convert, the company may take powers to convert the remaining stock or to repay it at a pre-determined price.

4.8 Advantages of convertibles

The advantages of a convertible loan stock issue from the company's point of view are as follows:

(a) In many cases it will be possible to offer convertible loan stock at a lower interest rate than ordinary debentures. This can be particularly useful for a business which is just starting up or is developing a new product, because the conversion date can be planned to coincide with the growing availability of profits sufficient to pay acceptable dividends.

(b) The incentive of a future share in profits may encourage lenders who would not otherwise invest in the company.

(c) If the company is in need of permanent capital but the market price of shares is currently depressed, the issue of convertible loan stock can be used as a delaying tactic in the hope that the conversion period will coincide with higher share prices, thus giving the company a higher amount per share issued.

The big advantage from the point of view of the investor is that he can wait to see how the share price of the company moves before deciding whether to invest in the equity i.e. whether or not to convert his convertible debentures or to simply redeem them.

▷ ACTIVITY 4

Suggest why the interest rate charged on an overdraft might be higher than that charged on a term loan by a bank.

[Answer on p.101]

5 Choosing the form of finance

5.1 Introduction

As we have seen, there are a variety of forms of finance available to a business from the very short term to the long term. Each of these forms of finance have different characteristics and different costs and it is vital that the most appropriate and cheapest form of finance is chosen to meet the funding requirements of each situation.

In some situations a specific form of finance will be clearly the most appropriate. For example the acquisition of a fleet of salesmen's cars under a leasing arrangement. However, in many cases, the choice that must be made by the accounting function is the choice between financing by bank overdraft or by taking out a term loan.

5.2 Overdraft or bank loan

In general terms the financing method should be matched to the life of the asset for which the financing is required. Therefore, in most cases, an overdraft is most suitable for increased working capital requirements and a loan is more suitable for the purchase of fixed assets or another business. However, you do need to appreciate the advantages and disadvantages of each of these two main sources of finance.

5.3 Advantages of a bank overdraft

A bank overdraft as a source of short term funding has a number of advantages:

- Flexibility. An overdraft facility is the amount that the business could borrow from the bank in the form of an overdraft. However, the full facility does not need to be used and therefore the precise amount of funding required does not need to be estimated. For example, a business may have been granted an overdraft facility of £50,000 but currently only requires £30,000 of regular overdraft finance.
- Cost. Although the interest rate on an overdraft may be higher than that which could be negotiated on a loan, the important point about overdraft interest is that it is calculated daily on the amount of the actual overdraft each day rather than on a fixed amount as would be the interest on a loan.
- Short-term. Technically an overdraft is repayable on demand and therefore should only be used to fund short-term working capital requirements. The benefit of this is that when the short-term funding requirement is over the overdraft facility is simply not required. There is no necessity to negotiate paying off a loan early or incurring a penalty for early repayment.

5.4 Disadvantages of a bank overdraft

However, there are also some drawbacks to the use of overdraft finance:

- Repayable on demand. Technically the overdraft is repayable on demand and if the business is seen by the bank as not meeting its cash flow forecasts or business plan then the bank could cancel the overdraft facility and require any outstanding amount to be repaid possibly causing severe cash flow repercussions for the business.
- Increasing the facility. Once an overdraft facility has been agreed with the bank it may be difficult to persuade the bank to increase that facility if additional finance is required.
- Short term. As the overdraft is repayable on demand, it is only really suitable for the financing of short term assets such as investment in additional working capital rather than longer term situations such as the purchase of fixed assets or acquisition of another business.

5.5 Advantages of loan finance

The main advantages of loan finance is that it can be tailored to meet the requirements of the borrower. It can be taken out for a period which matches the assets which it is financing and the repayment terms can be negotiated to match with the cash flows from the asset or the other business cash flows.

5.6 Disadvantages of loan finance

- Interest rate. If the interest on the loan is fixed rate then this is often more expensive than an overdraft or a variable rate loan.
- Security. The bank will normally require some form of security for the loan, either a fixed or a floating charge.
- Restrictions. The bank may impose certain restrictions or covenants which will limit the freedom of action of the management of the business, for example restrictions on payment of dividends or on other forms of finance taken out by the business.
- Interest charged. On a loan the interest charge is based upon the full amount of the loan, whereas with a bank overdraft interest is only charged on the amount of the overdraft facility actually being used at the current time.

6 Test your knowledge

1 Sales of a business are £390,000 and debtors are £55,000. What is the debtors payment period?

2 Sales of a business are £600,000 and these are made at a gross profit margin of 40%. The stock at the year end was £80,000. What is the stock turnover in days?

3 The cost of sales of a business is £680,000 and the period end creditors are £251,000. What is the creditors payment period?

4 A business makes sales of £200,000 at a gross profit margin of 38%. Debtors at the period end are £11,500, creditors are £31,500 and stocks are £38,000. What is the operating cycle for the business?

5 Suggest three appropriate methods of finance for a shortfall in working capital.

6 Distinguish between a fixed charge and a floating charge for a bank loan.

7 What is the essential difference between a finance lease and an operating lease?

8 What is a sale and leaseback agreement?

[Answers on p.102]

7 Summary

There are many choices facing a business that needs to raise finance but it is important that the right choice of the form of finance is made. This will start with an initial consideration of the reason for the additional finance. If it is due to the need for increased working capital then a form of short-term or possibly medium-term finance would be most appropriate. If the finance is required for the purchase of fixed assets then medium- or long-term finance to match with the life of the asset is probably the best option.

Answers to chapter activities & 'test your knowledge' questions

▷ ACTIVITY 1

	Days
Stock turnover (106,000/470,000×365)	82
Debtors payment period (136,000/680,000×365)	73
	155
Creditors payment period (118,000/470,000×365)	(92)
Operating cycle	63

▷ ACTIVITY 2

- Negotiate an increased overdraft
- Delay payment to creditors
- Issue commercial paper
- Take out a short-term bank loan
- Debt factoring
- Invoice discounting

▷ ACTIVITY 3

- Negotiate an increased overdraft
- Delay payment to creditors
- Take out a medium-term bank loan
- Purchase the vans on a finance lease

▷ ACTIVITY 4

From the bank's point of view a term loan is safer and easier to monitor than an overdraft. A loan must be paid off over a fixed term according to the loan agreement. If the lender falls behind with payments the bank will be aware of this immediately. However with an overdraft the bank has less control over its use. The facility has to be kept open but it may not be used. Equally the bank has little idea of any problems behind the use of the overdraft therefore it could be viewed as more risky. To compensate for the additional risk to the bank of overdraft finance the rate of interest charged will tend to be higher than that on a term loan.

Test your knowledge

1 Debtors payment period =(£55,000/£390,000)×365 = 51 days

2 Cost of sales (60% x 600,000)=£360,000
Stock turnover =(£80,000/£360,000)×365 = 81 days

3 Creditors payment period = ((£251,000/£680,000)×365) = 135 days

4

Debtors payment period ((£11,500/£200,000)×365)	=	21 days
Stock turnover period ((£38,000/£200,000×62%)×365)	=	112 days
Creditors payment period (£31,500/£200,000×62%)×365)	=	(93 days)
Operating cycle		40 days

5 Any three of:
- Bank overdraft
- Short-term loan
- Commercial paper
- Debt factoring
- Invoice discounting
- Hire purchase
- Trade credit.

6 A fixed charge is where the security is a particular asset.
A floating charge is a charge on a certain group of assets of the business such as debtors or stock which will be continually fluctuating.

7 A finance lease is a lease where the user of the asset, the lessee, has the use and responsibilities of the asset over most of its useful economic life. An operating lease is any other type of lease but usually a shorter term lease of an asset for an element of its useful working life.

8 A sale and leaseback arrangement is where an organisation sells a major asset such as property back to a financial institution and then leases it back from them for a long period of time.

5

INVESTING SURPLUS FUNDS

INTRODUCTION

In the previous chapter we considered methods of raising finance if a shortfall of cash was highlighted in the cash budget. In this chapter we will consider the ways in which any cash surplus a business may have can be invested and the factors that should be considered before determining the best type of investment for the cash available.

KNOWLEDGE AND UNDERSTANDING

- Types of marketable security (Bills of Exchange, certificates of deposit, government securities, local authority short term loan); terms and conditions; risks (Element 15.2)
- Managing risk and exposure (Element 15.2)

CONTENTS

PERFORMANCE CRITERIA

- Invest surplus funds in marketable securities within defined financial authorisation limits (Element 15.2B)
- Ensure the organisation's financial regulations and security procedures are observed (Element 15.2C)

1 General requirements for investing

1.1 Introduction

Cash budgets, as we have seen, are meant to reveal, among other things, the amount of any surplus funds available to the company for short-term investment. Opportunities like this should always be taken; money invested just overnight will be worth more than money left idle. Surplus cash will therefore call for an investment decision. This should be based on general principles as well as factors specific to the particular circumstances. The general factors to consider are:

- Size of funds available for investment.
- Length of time for which funds are available.
- Certainty of surplus funds and accuracy of cash budget.
- Return on invested funds: Is it adequate? Does it compensate for the risk involved?
- Risk and variability of return from the investment if held for the full intended duration.
- Whether there is any possibility that the cash may be required prematurely to make unexpected payments and whether there would be any costs in the event of an early termination.
- Risks associated with early termination. A security which provides a fixed, risk-free return if held for the full term may prove risky if terminated early.
- The funds should be placed with creditworthy borrowers.
- Realisation. In some circumstances it may be important that the investment can be realised easily. It provides a company with a reserve, or safety margin, in its cash planning.

The overall aim should be to secure the maximum interest possible, consistent with a satisfactory level of risk and the required degree of liquidity. The investing company has to balance the expected interest with the risks involved.

The differences between the various forms of investment opportunities arise over rates of interest, periods to maturity, realisation and risk.

1.2 Main factors to consider

The three main factors that should be considered when determining how to deal with surplus funds are:

- risk
- return
- liquidity.

1.3 Risk and return

As a general rule risk and return are related. The higher the risk of an investment the higher will be its return. A business that has surplus funds to invest will wish those funds to earn a good profit or return but what is also paramount is the safety of the asset.

1.4 Risk

When cash is invested there are two potential risks. Firstly the risk that the value of the investment will fall, the capital risk, and secondly the risk that the return from the investment will be lower than expected due to changes in market rates.

EXAMPLE

A business has £10,000 of surplus cash to invest for a period of one month until it is needed to pay the quarterly VAT bill. The money could be paid into a bank deposit account earning 0.4% interest per month or it could be invested in shares purchased through a broker.

Consider the risks of these two options.

Solution

If the money is paid into the bank deposit account there is virtually no risk at all (provided that the bank is creditworthy!). The withdrawal in one month's time will total:

$$£10,000 + (0.4\% \times £10,000) = £10,040$$

The investment has earned £40 of income for the business.

If the £10,000 were to be invested in shares then in one month's time the share value may have increased to say £13,000, in which case the shares could be sold for that amount earning £3,000 of profit. However it is also possible that the share values have fallen and the shares can only be sold for £7,500 in one month's time meaning not only that a loss has been made but also that there is no longer enough cash available to pay the VAT bill.

1.5 Return and liquidity

When any surplus cash is invested it is important to ensure that it can be realised when needed. The ease of realisation will be reflected in the return that the investment gives. If the cash surplus is certain and the business is certain that it will not need the cash for a period then it will usually be able to earn a higher return than an investment where the cash can be realised immediately.

For example the interest earned on a bank deposit account which requires a month's notice for any withdrawal will be higher than the interest on a deposit account where the funds can be withdrawn at any time.

1.6 Treasury activities and risk

Many large companies have a separate treasury department which deals with investing of surplus funds and raising of finance. In smaller companies this role normally falls to the accounts department. Whoever is in charge of this function, care must be taken to ensure that although surplus cash is invested profitably, excessive risks are not taken. There are many highly speculative and highly risky financial instruments on the market which although they may reap very high returns can also have huge losses.

The aim of the treasury activities in a trading company is to earn a reasonable return on any surplus cash but not to speculate.

1.7 Organisational rules and procedures

Many companies will have regulations and procedures to ensure that the liquidity of the business is safeguarded. For example that a certain amount of cash must be available immediately at any point in time, that investments in certain types of instrument may be limited to a financial amount, that surplus funds might only be allowed to be invested in certain specified types of investment or that all investments must be convertible into cash within a certain number of days. These procedures, regulations and limits must be followed at all times.

▷ ACTIVITY 1

In the management of cash balances, surpluses may sometimes be forecast. When managing these surpluses, liquidity, safety and the rate of return should be taken into account.

(a) Describe what you understand by each of these three factors:
   (i) liquidity
   (ii) safety
   (iii) rate of return.
(b) Briefly explain which of these three factors you consider to be the most important, giving reasons for your choice.

[Answer on p.117]

▷ ACTIVITY 2

The benefits of good cash management to a company are:
(a) better control of financial risk
(b) opportunity for profit
(c) strengthened balance sheet
(d) increased confidence with customers, suppliers, banks and shareholders.
Explain how good cash management may realise two of these benefits.

[Answer on p.117]

2 Types of investment

2.1 Bank and building society deposit accounts

One of the safest and simplest forms of investment for surplus cash is to pay it into a high street bank or building society deposit account. There are a wide variety of such accounts available although the interest rate, particularly for small sums is generally quite low. There are high interest deposit accounts for larger amounts, for example provided that there is always a balance of, say, at least £5,000 in the account, and the interest rate on these is higher. Access to the cash is usually immediate and therefore useful if cash requirements are not known for certain.

For cash that is definitely not going to be required in the near future there are deposits that can be made for a fixed term of up to three months at a variable rate of interest which is linked to money market rates. This will normally yield a higher rate of return due to the lesser liquidity.

2.2 Government securities

DEFINITION

Government securities or gilt-edged securities are fixed interest securities issued by the Government and available for purchase.

Government securities are also known as gilt-edged securities or gilts and they are available for investment. They are normally fixed interest securities and they can be bought and sold through a broker. An example would be 5% Treasury 2016.

Government stocks are fairly low risk and very marketable ensuring that they are a popular form of investment for companies.

2.3 Pricing of gilts

On 26 January 20X6 the quoted price of 9% Treasury 20X8 was £111.63. This means that £100 of the gilts can be purchased for £111.63. The security will be redeemed in 20X8 at its nominal value of £100 and the closer the gilt gets to its maturity date the price will move towards £100.

When the gilt price is published in The Financial Times amongst other information the redemption yield is also published.

2.4 Redemption yield

DEFINITION

The redemption yield compares the interest payable to the date of redemption and the redemption value to the current price to give the overall return on the security.

The redemption yield can be calculated for any fixed interest security. It is a way of comparing different securities and also comparing the return to the return on other forms of investment.

The published redemption yield for 4¼% Treasury 2011 on 30 March 2007was 5.27%.

2.5 Interest yield

☐ DEFINITION

The interest yield or flat rate yield is simply the coupon rate of interest as a percentage of the current price of the gilt.

This shows the return on the gilt if it were bought today and held for a year whereas the redemption yield is the return throughout the whole life of the security.

Therefore the interest yield for 9% Treasury 20X8 on 26 January 20X6 would be:

$$(£9.00 / £111.63) \times 100 = 8.06\%$$

This figure for interest yield is also quoted in The Financial Times.

2.6 Treasury Bills

☐ DEFINITION

Treasury Bills are issued by the Bank of England on behalf of the UK government.

They are sold every Friday by auction to banks and Discount Houses. They are sold at a discount and repaid at face value at the end of the issue period, usually three or six months. The difference between the purchase price and the amount repaid represents the yield on the Bill.

○ EXAMPLE

What is the yield (expressed in annual terms) on a three-month Treasury Bill initially sold at a price of 98% of face value?

Solution

For an investment return of say £10,000, the buyer has only to pay £9,800. The profit on holding to maturity is £200, or as a percentage:

$$(£200/£9{,}800) \times 100 = 2.04\%$$

This percentage profit is made after 3 months.

This represents an annual yield of:

$$(1.0204)^4 - 1 = 8.41\%$$

2.7 Local Authority Bills

DEFINITION

These are Bills issued by individual local authorities and backed by the government.

As there is a less active market in local authority debt than gilts or Treasury Bills and their security is not considered to be quite as good as these, Local Authority Bills do tend to have higher yields than central government securities.

2.8 Sterling Commercial Paper (SCP)

DEFINITION

Sterling Commercial Paper refers to short-term promissory notes with a fixed maturity.

Companies with a high credit standing can issue these bills or 'commercial paper'. The fixed maturity date is normally between seven days and three months.

The market is controlled by the Bank of England which stipulates which companies can use this market: they must be publicly quoted (not necessarily in the UK) and have a balance sheet capital of at least £25m. The minimum denomination for SCP is £100,000. Obviously, companies can use SCP both to raise finance and as a short-term investment vehicle. The yield on commercial paper is rather higher than on public sector bills as the risk of default is higher.

2.9 Certificates of deposit

DEFINITION

A certificate of deposit (CD) is issued by a bank or building society which certifies that a certain sum, usually a minimum of £50,000, has been deposited with it to be repaid on a specific date.

The term can range from seven days to five years but is usually for six months. CDs are negotiable instruments, they can be bought and sold, therefore if the holder does not want to wait until the maturity date the CD can be sold in the money market.

CDs offer a good rate of interest and are highly marketable. The advantage to companies of investment in a CD is that they can be liquidated at any time at the current market rate. The market in CDs is large and active therefore they are an ideal method for investing large cash surpluses.

2.10 Bills of exchange

DEFINITION

A bill of exchange is 'an unconditional order in writing, addressed by one person to another, signed by the person giving it, requiring the person to whom it is addressed to pay on demand, or at a fixed determinable future time, a certain sum in money to, or to the order of, a specified person or to bearer'.

An example is given below:

> 1 January 20X9
>
> £5,000
>
> Six months after date pay to A Black or order the sum of five thousand pounds.
>
> C Blue
>
> To: B Green
> Sheffield

Here the bill is addressed by C Blue to B Green and requires him to pay A Black, or his order, £5,000 six months after the date of the bill, 1 January 20X9.

2.11 Trading of bills of exchange

Most bills of exchange are term bills which have a duration or maturity of between two weeks and six months and are of a value of up to £500,000 in any currency. Some bills are trade bills where one company draws a bill on another company. However the market in these is slim.

Bank bills however are bills of exchange drawn and payable by a bank, the most common of these are known as a banker's acceptance. There is an active market in such bills and a company with surplus cash could buy a bill of exchange at a discount and either hold it to maturity or sell it in the market before maturity, again at a discount. The difference between the price at which the bill is purchased and the price at which it is sold or it matures is the return to the investor.

3 Managing the cash balance

3.1 Regulations and procedures

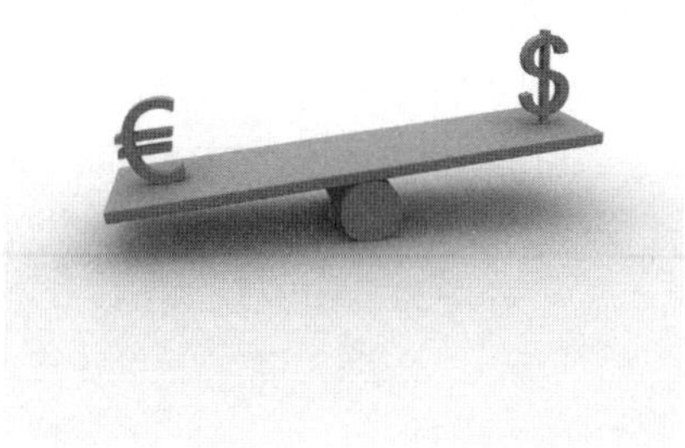

We have seen that the person responsible for managing the cash balances of a business needs to be aware of a great deal of information in order to decide how to best to do this.

That person must also have regard to the organisation's regulations and procedures. Some companies may have a policy of maintaining a minimum balance of, say, £50,000 of instantly available cash and a reserve of £100,000 available, say, within a month.

3.2 Monitoring and control

In order to manage the cash balance effectively, the treasury manager needs information about both the long-term and short-term cash flow figures. From the cash budget, the future can be predicted. However, the day-to-day balance needs to be monitored and controlled to ensure the actual balance approximates to the budgeted figures and is not in deficit.

The company's systems need to be looked at every day to ensure sufficient funds are available. The timing of the cash flows needs to be ascertained day by day to ensure money is banked quickly and prior to large cheques being written to suppliers, etc. Short-term daily cash flows are as important to the company's liquidity as the longer-term forecasts.

3.3 Cash not required

In some instances a significant cash surplus may arise for which a business has no foreseeable use. In such circumstances the cash should be returned to the shareholders by way of either a dividend or a share repurchase.

3.4 Investments and risk

We saw earlier in the chapter that there are two main types of risk with investments – capital risk and return risk. When investing in short-term investments it will be necessary to consider these risks and to take into account any expected changes in the economic and financial environment. Of particular concern will be anticipated changes in interest rates.

3.5 Fixed rate and variable rate investments

Some short-term investments will have variable rates of interest. For example, many bank deposit accounts have variable rates of interest which means that if the bank base rate goes up or down the interest earned on the deposit will also increase or decrease.

However, many other types of investment, such as fixed rate deposit accounts and gilt edged securities, are fixed rate investments. This means that if the general rate of interest changes there is no change in the interest paid on these investments. However, this does not mean that potential changes in interest rates can be ignored.

3.6 Effect on investments of changes in interest rates

If an investment is made in a fixed rate deposit account and interest rates were expected to change then this would have no effect on the amount deposited. The principal amount invested will always remain the same and this is the amount that will be repaid at the end of the term of the investment no matter what happens to interest rates.

However, an investment in fixed rate gilts is rather different. These are marketable securities and, as such, their market value will fluctuate with changes in underlying interest rates or the base rate. If a business has invested in gilts and the interest rate increases then the value of the gilt will fall in order to ensure that the yield is in line with general interest rates. Conversely, if the base rate of interest is decreased then the market value of the gilts will increase. Therefore, the person responsible for such investments should take account of expected changes in economic and financial conditions.

4 Dealing with cash

4.1 Introduction

At the start of this chapter it was argued that cash is an idle asset and ideally should be invested immediately to earn interest even if this is for a very short term, such as overnight. However, there are many businesses in the retail sector, or even manufacturing businesses with a retail outlet, which will necessarily have to deal with potentially large amounts of cash on a daily basis before it can be banked or otherwise invested.

4.2 Security of cash

Obviously cash is a highly risky asset to be holding on the business premises as it can so easily be misappropriated or stolen. Therefore, for any cash based business or part of a business there must be strict procedures and policies which must be followed to ensure that the cash and cheques taken from customers are secure and are banked as quickly as possible and intact.

4.3 Security procedures for cash

Any business dealing with cash must have basic security procedures in place. The main ones that must be followed are:

- **Physical safeguards.** The cash taken must at all times be kept safe and only accessible to authorised individuals. This means that cash should be kept under lock and key either in a cash box or in a lockable till. Only authorised individuals should have access to the keys.
- **Valid payment.** If cheques are accepted as payment then they must be supported by a valid cheque guarantee card. If credit cards are accepted, authorisation must be sought for payments which exceed the limit.
- Reconciliation. A list of all cash, cheques and credit card payments taken during the day must be kept and this must be reconciled at the end of the day to the amount of cash in the till or cash box. The list may be manual as each sale is made or may be automatically recorded on the till roll as each sale is rung in. The reconciliation should be carried out by someone other than the person responsible for making the sales. Any discrepancies between the amount of cash taken during the day and the amount left at the end of the day must be investigated.
- **Banking.** The receipts should be banked intact and promptly each day. This not only ensures the physical safety of the cash in the bank and that it cannot be used by employees for unauthorised purposes, but also that it is earning the business the maximum amount of interest in the bank account. All cash should be banked as soon as possible but if it is not to be banked until the following day, then either the cash must be left in a locked safe overnight or in the bank's overnight safe.
- **Recording.** The paying-in slip for the bank should be made out by someone other than the person paying the money into the bank and should be reconciled to the till records for the day.

▷ ACTIVITY 3

Task 1

Wilson Limited's long-term cash flow forecast to year ended 20X9 suggests a cash surplus of £1 million will be generated in 20X8 and £1.75 million in 20X9.

The company is considering its future cash management strategy and is considering four business strategies. For each of the following four scenarios, suggest what action you would take to manage the cash surplus and the reason for your recommendation.

(a) No further growth in Wilson Limited's existing business and no plans for further capital investment.

(b) Plans for an acquisition of a cycle parts manufacturer (value up to £5 million) when a suitable opportunity arises.

(c) Development in 20X8 and 20X9 of several new product lines requiring capital investment of £2.5 million.

(d) Phased development of two new product lines requiring capital investment of £1.25 million and the intention to acquire another cycle parts manufacturer (value up to £3 million) when a suitable opportunity arises.

Task 2

Identify three main factors to consider when investing a cash surplus and briefly explain their importance.

[Answer on p.118]

5 Test your knowledge

1 What are the three main factors to consider when deciding on the appropriateness of a short-term investment of surplus funds?

2 If a security is quoted 'xd' what does this mean?

3 If a 4% treasury bill can be purchased for £102.45 what is the interest yield?

4 What is the redemption yield of a fixed interest security?

5 What effect will an increase in the base rate of interest have on the market value of gilt edged securities?

[Answers on p.119]

6 Summary

If a business has a short-term surplus of funds then these should be invested rather than remaining as idle cash which is not earning any income for the business. The main factors to consider when determining the type of investment are the risk, return and liquidity of the investment. Typical suitable investments for short-term funds are bank and building society deposit accounts, government securities, local authority stocks, certificates of deposit, and bills of exchange.

If a business deals with cash sales then management should ensure that basic security measures for the cash are in place.

Answers to chapter activities & 'test your knowledge' questions

▷ ACTIVITY 1

(a) (i) *Liquidity*

The ability of a company to meet its debts as they fall due. The ability to change the liquidity profile (i.e. by selling investments) to meet unforeseen circumstances.

(ii) *Safety*

Investment of surplus cash must not be vulnerable to any unacceptable risk of loss through credit, market or exchange risk.

(iii) *Rate of return*

The return on the cash investment after taking into account transaction costs, management overheads and possible gains or losses on capital.

(b) Safety is the most important factor. Most short-term cash investments can be easily liquidated, even if at a discount. The difference between rates of return on high quality cash investments will be insignificant compared with the scale of loss encountered if there is loss of capital.

▷ ACTIVITY 2

(a) **Better control of financial risk**

By determining and maintaining the proper level of cash within a company in accordance with the organisation's financial procedures and within defined authorisation limits.

(b) **Opportunity for profit**

By reducing to a minimum the opportunity cost associated with maintaining cash balances in excess of a company's operating needs. Earnings (or surpluses) are improved by freeing up surplus cash for investment purposes while reducing interest charged through minimising borrowing.

(c) **Strengthened balance sheet**

By reducing or eliminating cash balances in excess of target balances and putting surplus cash to work by investing (e.g. in the overnight money market); by reducing or eliminating cash borrowing and keeping interest costs as low as possible.

(d) **Increased confidence with customers, suppliers, banks and shareholders**

By having access to funds to disburse to suppliers (creditors), banks (interest, fees and principal payments) and shareholders (dividends) when due. By providing good instructions to customers (debtors) to enable the organisation to convert receipts into usable bank deposits.

▷ ACTIVITY 3

Task 1

(a) **Action**

Pay shareholders an increased dividend or make an extraordinary dividend payment. Consider share repurchase (capital reduction).

Reason:

If no further investment opportunities are to be considered, surplus cash should be returned to shareholders to enable them to seek alternative opportunities. However the firm would be advised to maintain a small cash surplus.

(b) **Action**

Invest cash in bank deposits or marketable securities (e.g. CDs, commercial paper).

Reason:

To leave Wilson Limited with sufficient liquidity to help it make the acquisition, whilst receiving a market return on its cash investments.

(c) **Action**

Use cash to make the necessary capital investment in the new product lines.

Reason:

Unless the cash is likely to be needed for a specific reason (such as an acquisition when cash will be needed immediately) it is unlikely that Wilson Limited will receive a return on its cash investments equivalent to the cost of raising debt finance.

(d) **Action**

Hold the cash on short term deposit to make the acquisition; either borrow or raise additional equity finance.

Reason:

The cash will be required for the eventual acquisition at short notice. The new product lines should be easily financed using external funds.

Task 2

Safety	To ensure the securities invested in are of acceptable credit standing.
Liquidity	To ensure the securities have sufficient marketability to allow the maximum availability of funds.
Return	To ensure the securities invested in offer a good yield without unduly increasing risk or credit quality.

Test your knowledge

1
- Risk
- Return
- Liquidity

2 Ex-dividend – therefore the purchaser is not purchasing the right to the next interest payment.

3 (£4.00 / £102.45) ×100% = 3.9%

4 The yield over the whole life of the security to the redemption date.

5 An increase in the base rate of interest will lead to a fall in the market value of gilt edged securities.

6

GRANTING OF CREDIT

INTRODUCTION

Element 15.3 is about the granting of credit to customers. In this chapter we start by looking at some of the background knowledge that is required for this area of the syllabus. Then chapter then moves on the consider the entire process for the granting of credit from assessment of a potential credit customer through to either granting their credit request or refusing the request for credit.

KNOWLEDGE AND UNDERSTANDING

- Legal issues: basic contract; terms and conditions of contracts relating to the granting of credit; Data Protection legislation and credit control information
- Sources of credit status information
- External sources of information: banks, credit agencies and official publications
- Discounts for prompt payment

CONTENTS

PERFORMANCE CRITERIA

- Agree credit terms with customers in accordance with the organisation's policies — A 15.3
- Identify and use internal and external sources of information to evaluate the current credit status of customers and potential customers — B 15.3
- Open new accounts for those customers with an established credit status — C 15.3
- Ensure the reasons for refusing credit are discussed with customers in a tactful manner — D 15.3

1 Contract law

1.1 Introduction

Control of the credit given to a customer is important for any company. Most companies therefore appoint a credit controller whose responsibility is to give appropriate credit terms to customers and ensure these terms are kept. Debtors are an important part of working capital and careful management of this asset is required to maintain the company's liquidity.

First of all it is important to understand the legal background to contracts and credit arrangements.

1.2 Nature of a contract

The sale of goods and services is a type of contract and therefore the credit controller must ensure that each party abides by this contract.

DEFINITION

A contract is a legally binding agreement between two parties.

The law of contract is the branch of the civil law which determines whether or not a promise is legally binding (i.e. enforceable by a court of law).

1.3 The essential characteristics of a contract

There are seven fundamental requirements if a contract is to be valid:

- offer and acceptance (i.e. an agreement);
- the intention to create legal relations (i.e. the parties must be willing to submit to the authority of the law and be bound by their contracts);
- consideration, in that both parties must do, or promise to do, something as their side of the contract;
- written formalities must be observed in some situations;
- the parties must have the capacity, or ability, to contract and submit themselves to the authority of the law (children and mentally disordered people are restricted);
- the parties must genuinely consent to the terms of the contract in that they must not have been mistaken by the contract terms, or lied to in negotiations;
- the contract itself must be both legal and possible.

The key factors for Unit 15 are a basic understanding of offer, acceptance and consideration which will be considered below

1.4 Offer and acceptance

An offer may be addressed to a specific person, to a group of people or to the world at large. However, acceptance of the offer must be made specifically.

It is important to distinguish between an offer – which can be accepted by a mere act, express or implied of the other party, after which the contract is complete – and an invitation to treat where the resulting action of the other party is the offer. Advertisements, price tickets in shops etc are an invitation to treat. They are an invitation to the potential customer to make an offer.

Acceptance is the final expression of assent to the terms of the offer. To be effective, the acceptance must be made while the offer is still in force; it must be absolute, unqualified and communicated to the offeror by word or action.

Offer and acceptance constitute agreement.

1.5 Intention to create legal relations

If an offer is accepted, then an agreement is created but this agreement does not automatically become a contract. If one of the parties wishes to invoke the aid of the law in enforcing the terms of the agreement against the other party, he must show that there had been an intention by both parties that the agreement was to create legal relations.

There is a presumption in social or domestic agreements that legal relations are not intended. But in commercial agreements, it is generally assumed that relations are intended unless there is a clause in the agreement to the contrary.

1.6 Consideration

Before a simple binding contract exists, both parties must have agreed to provide something of value to the other. The price which each has to pay is termed the consideration and converts the mere promises of the parties into bargains enforceable by the courts.

DEFINITION

Consideration can be defined as 'some right, interest, profit or benefit accruing to one party, or some forbearance, detriment, loss or responsibility given, suffered or undertaken by the other'.

ACTIVITY 1

List the elements of a valid contract.

[Answer on p. 164]

2 The importance of debtors

2.1 The debtor balancing act

Debtors are people who owe you money, the almost inevitable consequence of trading. Very few business-to-business transactions are made for cash and increasingly fewer business-to-customer transactions are.

Debtor management principles involve a series of balancing acts. The following diagram should be remembered.

Balancing costs and benefits of debtors

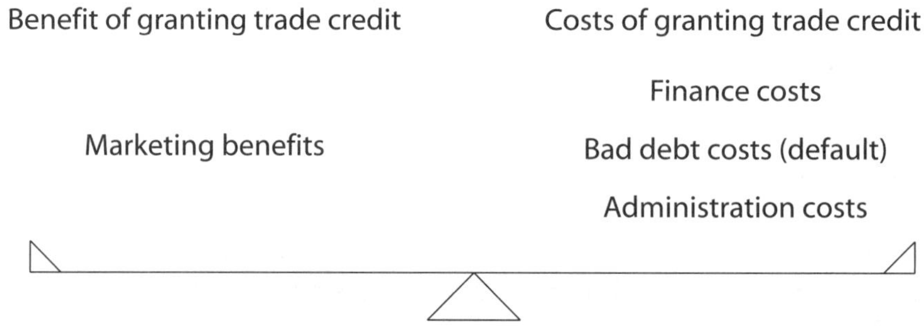

The main benefit to the company is that customers like to be given trade credit, rather than paying on delivery of goods. Thus, generous credit terms often have a beneficial impact on sales.

The main cost to the company of granting trade credit is the finance cost. Debtors on the balance sheet are a dead asset: they do not earn a return, compared to a company that demands cash on delivery. A company giving trade credit is effectively financing its debtor balances all year round in a similar manner to stock balances.

A company granting trade credit may suffer bad debts as customers go into liquidation before paying what is due. This cannot happen to a company giving no credit as cash is required on delivery.

If a company gives no credit its sales system will often be very simple to operate, and hence cheap. A business giving credit, by contrast, has more expensive recording and collection systems, hence much higher administrative expenses.

2.2 The credit cycle

The credit cycle is the time elapsing between the start of negotiating a sale and the collection of payment. During this period, a number of procedures are conducted which constitute a firm's credit policy.

The cycle starts with the decision as to whether or not to grant credit.

2.3 Customer credit

(a) Should credit be granted at all? Consider normal trade practice, but also consider leading a change. Advancing credit may stimulate sales.
(b) What is the true cost to the business of customer credit? This will be influenced by impact upon sales, risk of bad debts, cost of capital.

3 Credit terms

3.1 Introduction

As sales agreements are contracts, the credit terms are part of this contract. Credit terms have to be drawn up for a company and must take into account the need to maintain both the company's cash flow and a sensible profit margin on the goods sold.

These terms must be clearly understood by the customer and it is sensible to print these clearly on the invoice to the customer. The company must be prepared to enforce the terms if the customer is late paying the debt.

3.2 Types of credit terms

The most common types of credit term agreed between customer and supplier in the UK are as follows:
(a) **Cash with order** – This is effectively giving no credit, as no work on the order will happen until payment is received.
(b) **Cash before shipment** – This requires payment to be made before delivery and, while it safeguards cash receipts, if the customer refuses the goods at the last minute, a supplier could be left with bespoke articles which cannot easily be sold.
Cash on delivery is much the same in principle but depends on a trustworthy driver to collect the payment and the customer to pay with a bona fide cheque.
(c) **Load over load** is an agreement to pay for the last load before the next delivery is made.
(d) **Net monthly** requires payment of one month's deliveries to be made by the end of the following month. It is not always possible to post invoices exactly to the correct month and so month-end deliveries may not be paid for two months!
Net 30 days means payment 30 days after delivery and so brings forward the payment date on average 15 days earlier than a 'net monthly' agreement.
Net 14 days brings forward payment to 14 days after delivery while **Net 60 days/Net 90** days may be given if the market demands.

(e) **Stage-payments** allow for instalments of the expected total bill to be paid at agreed intervals. It is usual in certain trades (e.g. building and shipping) to make progress payments based on certified work during the course of the contract. Care needs to be taken when negotiating these terms and income matched with expenditure on the project; it is foolish to agree a down payment of 30% and the balance on completion if all the materials – constituting 70% of the final price – have to be paid for before the completion of the contract.

Whether the terms are agreed on a time basis as in (d) and (e) or on a delivery basis as in (a), (b) and (c), the terms must be clearly stated on the invoice and the accounting records must be able to identify customers who are late paying their debts.

3.3 Cash or settlement discounts

This style of discount is given for early payment of accounts by customers. For example, the normal credit period may be 90 days, but the company may be prepared to offer, say, 1% for payment within 45 days. This would be described as '1/45, net 90'.

The costs and benefits of a cash discount scheme are summarised below.

Benefits	Costs
Reduction in finance charges	Cost of discount (reduced revenue received)
Reduction in bad debts due to reduced collection period	Extra administrative costs
Improved customer relations and potential extra sales	Potential abuse of scheme (customer takes discount but does not pay early)

ACTIVITY 2

List four factors a firm would consider about a new customer that would influence the choice of credit terms offered.

[Answer on p. 164]

ACTIVITY 3

What is the true cost of giving a 5% prompt payment discount to customers who pay within 30 days rather than the usual 90 days?

[Answer on p. 164]

4 Payment methods

4.1 Introduction

A variety of payment methods are available in the UK for credit customers. The choice between them depends upon:

(a) the user (business or personal)

(b) the frequency of the payment (regular or one-off)

(c) convenience, and

(d) cost.

4.2 Cash

Some customers still pay by cash. Although this is an instantaneous payment, with no delays attached to drawing the money, it involves cumbersome visits to the bank to deposit the money and it is sometimes hard to allocate the money to a specific invoice in the accounts.

4.3 Cheque

Many customers still pay by cheques (or banker's drafts for very high value transactions) which pass through a clearing system to transfer the money from the customer's to the supplier's bank account.
Cheques take three days to clear through the system.

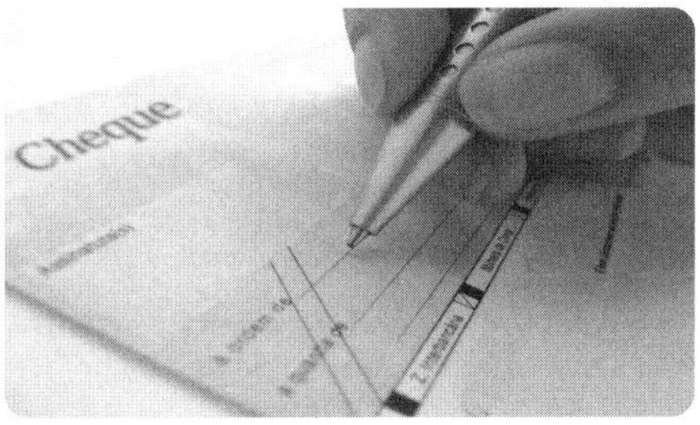

4.4 Cheque crossings

DEFINITION

A cheque crossing is two vertical lines on the face of a cheque with or without some additional words.

Cheques can have a number of different types of crossing and you need to be aware of the meaning of these.

A general crossing is two vertical lines on the face of the cheque. This crossing instructs the paying bank to make payment only to another bank.

A special crossing is where the name of the collecting bank is written across the cheque. The cheque can then only be paid to the bank stated.

When 'not negotiable' is written between the lines of the crossing this means that in a case of fraud the person given the cheque has no better rights to it than the person who gave it to them. Therefore if A steals a cheque and gives it to B in payment for goods, if the cheque has a not negotiable crossing then B has no right to the cheque.

If 'account payee' is written across the cheque crossing this is an instruction to the collecting bank that the cheque must only be paid into the bank account of the original payee.

Most pre-printed cheques these days have the account payee crossing.

4.5 Dates on cheques

If cheques are received as payment from debtors then it is important that the date is checked.

If the cheque is dated more than six months ago then the banks will view it as a stale cheque and will return it unpaid.

If the cheque is post-dated, i.e. dated after today's date, then technically it cannot be paid into the bank until the date shown on the cheque.

4.6 Stopped cheque

A customer can stop payment of a cheque after it has been written and sent out by instructing its bank in writing not to pay the cheque unless by using the related cheque guarantee card the bank is committed to honour the cheque.

4.7 Cheque guarantee card

If a cheque guarantee card is used when payment is made then the bank is committed to pay the cheque even if this results in an unauthorised overdraft.

4.8 High value payments

DEFINITION

The Clearing House Automated Payments System (CHAPS) is an electronic, inter-bank, on-line, real-time credit clearing system for guaranteed same-day value sterling payments.

It is a system which has grown rapidly because of its nationwide electronic access capability, its ability to handle large volumes and its relatively low operating costs. The system allows for payments to be transmitted (on a real-time basis) from one bank branch to another. Settlement is effected electronically after the cut-off time each day across settlement members' accounts at the Bank of England. Such transactions are irrevocable and unconditional from the time they enter the system and consequently high levels of security are maintained.

4.9 Bulk electronic clearing

Most items of low value and of a repetitive nature (wages, other credit transfers, direct debits) are dealt with through the BACS system. Settlements occur after three days and are effected by payment instructions submitted via magnetic media or by a direct telecommunications link to the BACS centre. There the items are sorted and instructions sent out to clearing banks' and building societies' computer centres. The cost of BACS is significantly less than other methods.

4.10 Direct debit

A direct debit allows the supplier to obtain payment direct from the customer's bank on presentation either of manually prepared direct debit vouchers or a computer magnetic tape. It is a system which deals equally well with regular or irregular amounts but, although it offers considerable administrative savings, the supplier may find that dealing with dishonoured payments is very time-consuming and considerable effort is required to set up direct debit payments.

4.11 Credit cards

A customer effectively borrows money from a credit card company to pay the supplier; the supplier pays a fee (up to 4% of the transaction value) to operate the system.

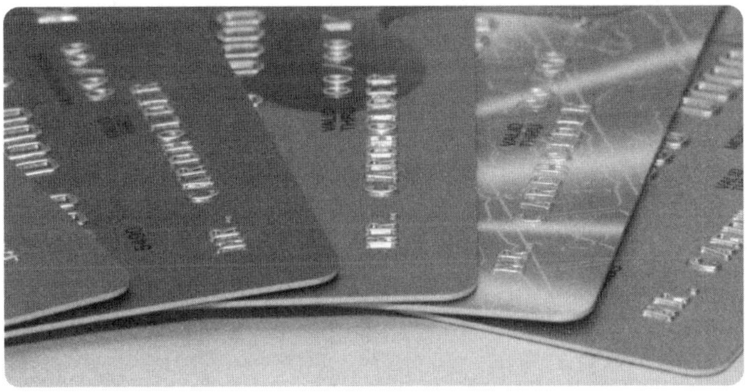

4.12 Debit cards

Here, the customer allows the supplier to transfer money directly from his account to the supplier's account. It is an alternative to paying by cash or writing a cheque and is becoming increasingly popular.

▷ ACTIVITY 4

You have recently been appointed to a position in the cash management section of the accounting department at Stenwater Limited, a marine construction contracting company based in Aberdeen. The company was formed by the merger of two local companies 18 months ago and it has been experiencing some administrative difficulties following the rapid expansion of business.

From your work so far, you are aware that Stenwater's procedures for managing the cash collection process are rather basic and some improvements could be made.

(a) No procedures exist to ensure that delays do not occur in Stenwater Limited's internal handling procedures. Suggest ONE way in which funds could be delayed within Stenwater before they are paid into the bank.

(b) Most customers pay directly to Stenwater's bankers by BACS. What payment instructions must you send to these customers? Suggest FIVE items.

[Answer on p. 164]

5 Data Protection Act

5.1 Introduction

Due to the growth in the use of computer technology the Data Protection Act 1998 was introduced to make certain restrictions on the use of data about individuals and the use of personal data. It is likely that your organisation will hold computer data about credit customers and therefore you need to be aware of the broad outlines of the Act. However it is important to realise that the Act relates to data held about individuals not about organisations so will only be relevant to non-corporate customers or to data about individuals who belong to a customer organisation.

5.2 Definitions

Personal data is information held about an individual, not only factual information but also expressions of opinion about that individual.

Data users are individuals or organisations who use personal data.

A computer bureau is an individual or organisation which processes personal data for data users or allows data users to process personal data on its equipment.

5.3 Main provisions of the Act

- All data users and computer bureaux have to register with the Data Protection Registrar – the data user must then only hold data and use data for the purposes which are registered.
- Processing of personal data is forbidden except in the following circumstances:
  - with the consent of the individual
  - due to a legal obligation
  - due to a contractual obligation
  - due to a contractual arrangement
  - in the public interest
  - to protect the vital interests of the individual.
- If data is obtained from a third party the data subject must be given:
  - the identity of the controller of the data
  - the purposes for which the data is being processed
  - the data that will be disclosed and to whom.
- Data subjects have the right to a copy of the data held, the right to know why the data is being processed and the logic behind the processing.
- Data subjects may seek compensation through the courts for damage or distress caused by the loss, destruction, inaccuracy or unauthorised disclosure of personal data.
- Data subjects can apply to the courts or Registrar for inaccurate data to be corrected or removed from the data user's files.

6 Granting of credit

6.1 Introduction

Giving a customer credit terms for payment is always a risk and all companies try to reduce this risk and potential bad debt problems.

There are various ways of obtaining information about customers both from one's own experience and from external sources and references. All available information needs to be collected and assimilated so that appropriate credit terms can be given to the customer. Once agreed, these terms will then form the basis of the contract of sale between the two parties and trading can proceed smoothly.

One of the first steps is to appoint a credit manager or a senior person to take responsibility for the granting of credit terms.

6.2 The credit manager

The purpose of the credit manager in a company is to protect the company's investment in debtors. This entails ensuring appropriate credit terms are negotiated with customers and are then adhered to. The manager usually reports to the finance director or financial controller; sometimes, however, he may be found within the sales/marketing area. Wherever the manager is placed, it is important that he is aware of the sales and marketing opportunities and constraints, as well as confident that the cash flow of the business is not disrupted by inappropriate financial terms.

6.3 Company policy

The credit manager needs to ascertain the basis of the company's credit terms. This may have been decided upon by the finance director, be documented and so merely require implementing. However, most companies are not so well organised and a pattern of credit terms has to be developed by the credit controller in consultation with his superior and the sales department. This has the advantage of allowing a flexible method to develop which can cater for differing situations. But in a large organisation this can lead to uncertainty and areas of doubt and it may be sensible to establish written guidelines and terms of reference. In order to do this, it is necessary to establish two key points – the nature of the market and the authority of the credit manager.

6.4 Nature of the market

Consideration needs to be given to any seasonal fluctuations, the expected level of sales, the marketing strategy and the policies of competitors. It is easy to set standards but, if this results in the loss of trade and goodwill, the company will not flourish. So the credit manager must try to keep debtors low without losing business.

6.5 Authority of the credit manager

It must be clear who establishes the credit terms: the sales manager or the credit manager, or both in consultation – in which case, their joint policy must be clearly documented to avoid any misunderstandings. Also, the credit manager needs to establish whether he has the authority to accept or reject new customers or new orders. The business will be handicapped if there is constant resentment or a feeling of interference by the credit and sales departments, in each other's work and authority. Ideally, this will not arise if good communications are present and each department liaises with the other.

▷ ACTIVITY 5

Mark Middleton, the UK Marketing Manager, made the following comments to you on credit policies. Draft notes to reply to Mark when you next see him at the weekly credit management and marketing management meeting.

(a) **The period and amount of credit to be granted**
'I do not understand why we need an internal policy to regulate the amounts of credit we provide to our customers. Most pay regularly anyway and, when there is a problem, one of my sales staff can always move things along. These policies just create inflexibility and frankly I can do without the interference.'

(b) **The frequency with which accounts are monitored**
'You say you review accounts every quarter. Given that you monitor credit limits continuously, what sort of things are included in your review?'

(c) **The discount structure to be applied**
'Of course I understand why we give discounts for prompt payment. But what factors do we take into account when deciding what discount to give?'

[Answer on p. 165]

6.6 Cost of credit

The company has to consider the total credit it can afford to offer customers. It is important that this global figure is discussed and the overall effect of granting credit is assessed in the light of company profitability, cash flow, asset usage and interest costs.

Most companies will offer credit to customers because, if all other companies in the market offer such terms, they are unlikely to build up a large customer base without offering comparable terms.

The cost of offering credit must be considered.

O EXAMPLE

Z buys an item for £20 on 1 January 20X6 and pays the company one year later on 31 December 20X6.

The company earns a profit of £4 on each unit sold, i.e. a profit margin of 20% on sales price.

The company has an overdraft, paying interest at 10%.

What profit does the company make from the sale of the unit after allowing for the cost of credit?

Solution

	£
Net profit on sales	4
Less: Interest on overdraft (20 (Note) x 10%)	(2)
Real profit after credit period costs	2

(Note: sales revenue = $£4 \times \frac{100}{20} = £20$)

So the granting of one year's credit has reduced the company's profit margin by 50% which is a substantial cost to the company. A year's credit is probably longer than most companies would grant but even a two-month credit period costs a company a substantial percentage of the profit margin, i.e.:

	£
Net profit on sales	4.00
Less: Interest on overdraft (using simple interest) 20 x 10% x (2/12)	(0.33)
Real profit after credit period costs	3.67

i.e. (33p/400p) x 100% = 8.25% of the profit is lost.

In other words, it costs the company 8.25% to offer two months' credit to its customers.

If interest rates increase, then the cost of credit will also increase. The main board of directors needs to consider these facts when agreeing credit terms with the credit manager.

6.7 Evaluating a customer's credit status

The correct evaluation of credit risk is the most difficult and the most vital part of the credit manager's role. Regrettably, the credit manager is sometimes merely regarded as a 'credit controller' and the evaluation of the credit risk is left to the sales department, so ignoring the potential contribution to profits which a trained credit manager can make.

It may be tempting to select safe customers who will pay promptly, but this will restrict the company's market share and hence its profit share. In order to maximise profits, it is necessary to sell to 'risky' customers and it is the process of evaluating this risk that is now considered. It is not only new accounts that need to be considered, the credit manager needs constantly to review his established customer base to ensure that they continue to be a safe risk and have not slipped with their payments. Where danger signals are spotted, prompt action is required in consultation with the sales department to decide on future strategy as to whether to continue with sales, restrict sales or even cease trading with the customer.

Remember that if one is dealing with a major customer there are many points to consider and one needs to balance the risk of non-payment against other factors such as the stoppage of production and the laying off of workers.

6.8 Sources of information

There are many sources of information from which an assessment can be made regarding the risk of non-payment by a debtor. These can be split into two types:

(a) **external sources** – from outside publications, statistics and institutions, and
(b) **internal sources** – derived from the company's own database, analysis of accounts and direct contacts with the customer.

7 External sources of information about customers

7.1 Trade references

Traditionally, creditworthiness has been checked by asking the customer to supply trade references from two other suppliers. As it can be assumed that customers will not quote suppliers likely to give a bad report, it is unwise to rely on this procedure alone. Beware of companies that pay their two referee suppliers promptly, but pay all other suppliers late. Used in conjunction with other information, this procedure however may be helpful.

Trade reference requests should be made formally and should ask for credit terms. Often a standard form can be used requesting:

- the exact name of the potential customer
- the usual credit terms offered
- the expected level of business
- names and addresses of two trade referees.

From this information, the credit manager can contact the trade referees and ensure the potential customer can pay on time and adhere to agreed credit terms.

EXAMPLE

You are the credit controller for John James Ltd and you are considering a request from Donald & Sons who wish to trade on credit with your company. You are considering offering them a credit limit of £20,000 with payment terms of payment within 30 days of the invoice date. You have a standard form for trade references and Donald & Sons have provided you with the name and address of another supplier of theirs, Priory Trading, to whom you have sent the standard trade reference form. The reply you receive is given below.

What, if any, conclusions could you draw from the trade reference?

John James Ltd
4 The Parade
York
YK4 6TP

PRIVATE AND CONFIDENTIAL
Credit Controller
Priory Trading
44 Kiln Terrace
York YK3 4XS

10 May 20X5

Dear Sir or Madam

We recently received a request from Donald & Sons, a customer of ours, who gave yourselves as a reference. I would be grateful if you could assist us by answering the following questions and returning them in the stamped addressed envelope provided.

1 How long have Donald & Sons been trading with you?

2 years months

2 When Donald & Sons opened an account with you, did the company supply you with suitable trade and credit references?

YES / (NO)

3 What are your normal credit terms for Donald & Sons?
Amount: £10,000

Terms: Cash Weekly (Monthly) Other (please detail below)

4 Does Donald & Sons make payments in accordance with your terms?

(YES) / NO / SLOW PAYER

5 Have you ever had to suspend credit facilities to Donald & Sons?

YES / NO

If Yes, when?

6 Please supply any other information which you consider relevant.

Thank you for your help.

Yours faithfully

B Down

Brian Down

Credit Controller

Solution

The information provided in the trade reference looks positive in that Priory Trading offer monthly payment terms which appear to have been adhered to. However, the amount of credit they offer is only £10,000 whereas Donald & Sons have applied to you for credit of £20,000.

However, in conjunction with perhaps another trade reference and other internal and external information about Donald & Sons, this trade reference may give you some confidence in the company.

7.2 Bank references

It is usual to take up bank references at the same time as trade references. Requests to the bank need to be precise, detailing the amount of credit you envisage giving the customer and the credit period. Bank replies are usually structured in one of three ways:

(1) an unqualified, positive assurance

(2) a general indication that the firm is operating normally

(3) a guarded statement, indicating that 'capital is fully employed' or 'we are unable to speak for your figures'.

It is always useful to speak to the bank on the telephone as more information may be conveyed via word of mouth. However, a reference of the latter type should put the credit manager on guard.

EXAMPLE

You are the credit controller for John James Ltd and you are considering a request from Donald & Sons who wish to trade on credit with your company. You are considering offering them a credit limit of £20,000 with payment terms of payment within 30 days of the invoice date.

You have written to Donald & Sons' bank, Northern Bank, asking for a reference having specified that you are considering a credit limit of £20,000. The bank's reply is given below.

What, if any, conclusions could you draw from the bank reference?

Northern Bank plc

Doncaster Branch
501 High Street
Doncaster DN3 4XL

Credit Controller
John James Ltd
4 The Parade
York YK4 6TP

19 May 20X5

Dear Sir or Madam

Reference: Donald & Sons

I refer to your letter dated 10 May 20X5 enquiring about the creditworthiness of the above. In our view, Donald & Sons is reasonably constituted and should prove good for your figures.

Yours faithfully

G Donarski

Gerald Donarski

Manager

Solution

This is not the very highest quality reference that could be received from a bank, but it is fairly positive and in the absence of any other negative information should make the credit controller reasonably confident about extending credit to Donald & Sons.

7.3 Credit agency references

Credit agencies are not covered by the Data Protection Act but by the Consumer Credit Act 1974 which actually gives stronger protection in terms of the handling of information.

One of the most widely used registers is that of Dun & Bradstreet. It summarises data for around 200,000 firms in Great Britain and Northern Ireland, including the name, address, date of formation, nominal and issued share capital, existing mortgages and charges, proprietors and associates, credit rating and Dun & Bradstreet rating.

The vital piece of information for the credit manager is the credit rating which indicates the average amount of credit to the firm. This helps the credit manager to assess the relative size of the proposed credit limit to the potential customer. If this is much greater than the average listed, it would be advisable to undertake further investigations.

7.4 Using credit agency reports

The usefulness of a report from an agency depends on the skill and competence of the agency. A specialised agency for the particular industry concerned can normally offer more detached information, but the credit manager needs to research the agency carefully. If he is satisfied that:

- they have experienced, trained staff,
- the report is based on up-to-date information, and
- they produce reports for other reputable firms,

then confidence may be placed in their findings.

The questions of cost and speed of reporting should not be considered as agencies who offer low-cost reports are immediately suspect. Worthwhile reports cannot be produced cheaply and, although speed is important, it is very difficult to specify minimum reporting periods for gathering information from so many different sources.

7.5 Contents of credit agency reports

The credit manager should look for the following contents in the report on the potential customer:

- name and address; associated companies with names and addresses
- name of proprietors, partners and/or directors
- amount of authorised and issued share capital
- description of the customer's activities
- latest balance sheet and profit and loss and trading account
- a list of secured charges and mortgages
- name and address of its financial advisers, bankers
- payment pattern/experience from other suppliers
- a recommended credit limit based on the findings in the report.

7.6 Problems with credit agency reports

The problems with agency reports are as follows:

- New companies have no track record. It is therefore very difficult to form a judgement.
- It takes time for current information to be analysed and fed into computer/ appraisal systems. It is possible for very relevant information (such as the collapse of a major customer) not to be in a report.
- Suppliers' references may be too old to be of value.

7.7 Historical financial information

Extel provide a summary of the last three years' balance sheets and details of profits, turnover, taxation, dividends, earnings per share and equity capital for up to ten years. The usefulness of this is that all the information is on two pages and easy to access in a filing system. Other providers of such information on computer are Bloomberg, Reuters and FT.

7.8 Press reports

The press provide an up-to-date commentary on the situation within local and national companies. If the proposed customer is a big national company, reading The Financial Times enables the credit manager to keep up-to-date with half-yearly reports, comments on the customer as well as keeping abreast of industry trends and problems. Smaller more local companies are commented upon in regional and local papers.

7.9 Trade journals

Often produced weekly or monthly, trade journals are another valuable source of information and commentary on trends and results.

▷ ACTIVITY 6

A new customer, Rioch, cannot supply two years' trading accounts, having only traded for 14 months. You are supplied with an unaudited set of accounts for the past year and the names of a bank referee and two trade referees. Each of the trade references is favourable. You are, however, concerned at the lack of depth in the company's trading performance.

The managing director has decided Rioch is a valuable new customer and should be granted credit. What three conditions do you suggest?

[Answer on p. 165]

▷ ACTIVITY 7

Bank references are commonly used to assess a customer's creditworthiness. When writing references, identify two parties to whom the bank owes a duty of care. Briefly explain the reasons for this duty.

[Answer on p. 165]

8 Internal sources of information about customers

8.1 Sales representatives' knowledge

A company's sales representatives will have first hand information on existing customers and may have met or known of potential customers, all of which is useful to the credit manager.

It is beneficial to the credit manager to train the sales staff to observe and listen for information on customers' ability to pay by finding out:

- the level of activity at the factory
- the impression/competence of the customer's staff and premises
- the names of other suppliers
- future plans of the customer/client,

and any other information possible.

This provides more background information to analyse alongside other facts, though the credit manager would need to be mindful of the sales representatives' optimism!

8.2 Analysis of accounts

One of the most useful sources of information are the annual accounts of the customer (if it is a company). From these, various statistics can be calculated to help to analyse the company's situation. However, it must be remembered that the financial accounts only give historic data and it is often the case that the most recent accounts available from companies are at least 12 months out of date.

Whatever accounts are produced for examination, it is necessary to respect the confidential nature of the documents and the credit manager must exercise due care in this regard.

Before examining the various accounting ratios in detail, it is important to remember that:

(a) an opinion cannot be formed from one year's statistics alone – it is more useful to develop trends for several years/months before concluding;
(b) it is helpful to be able to compare the company's statistics with other companies in the same industrial sector – hopefully the company concerned will be better than average;
(c) the accounts may be distorted due to inter-company transactions, group funding etc and so an opinion can only be formed by looking at the accounts for the whole group;
(d) statistics are only statistics! It is very easy in recessionary or inflationary times for the position of a company to change very quickly from profitable to loss making, so the credit manager must not become blinded by numbers alone.

8.3 Main aspects to consider

There are three aspects of a company's performance that the credit manager should consider.

- **Solvency** – the ability of the company to pay its debts from its current assets, i.e. there are sufficient liquid resources.
- **Profitability** – this is obviously important as, in the long run, an unprofitable company will not survive.
- **Gearing or capital ratios** – these are concerned with the ratio of risk capital (equity) to loan capital.

EXAMPLE

The following illustration demonstrates the important ratios with which you need to be familiar when assessing credit risk – the risk that the customer will not pay!

JG Limited
Summarised balance sheet at 31 December 20X1

	£000	£000
Fixed assets, at cost, less depreciation		2,600
Current assets		
Stocks	600	
Debtors	900	
Balance at bank	100	
	1,600	
Creditors: Amounts falling due within one year	(800)	
		800
		3,400
Creditors: Amounts falling due after more than one year		
Debenture stock		(1,400)
		2,000
Capital and reserves		
Ordinary share capital (£1 shares)		1,000
Preference share capital		200
Profit and loss account		800
		2,000

Summarised profit and loss account for the year ended 31 December 20X1

	£000
Turnover	6,000
Cost of sales	(4,000)
Gross profit	2,000
Operating expenses	(1,660)

Net trading profit	340
Debenture interest	(74)
Profit before tax	266
Taxation	(106)
	160
Preference dividend	(10)
Profit available for ordinary shareholders	150

Note that cost of sales and operating expenses include £600,000 of depreciation charges.

Solution

Solvency ratios

- **Current ratio**

This is a common method of analysing working capital (net current assets) and is generally accepted as the measure of short-term solvency. It indicates the extent to which the claims of short-term creditors are covered by assets that are expected to be converted to cash in a period roughly corresponding to the maturity of the claims.

$$\text{Current ratio} = \frac{\text{Current assets}}{\text{Current liabilities}} = \frac{£}{£} \text{ ——— } = \text{(fill in the figures yourself)}$$

- Acid test ratio

Known as the quick ratio, this is calculated in the same way as for the current ratio but stocks are excluded from current assets.

$$\text{Current ratio} = \frac{\text{Current assets - stock}}{\text{Current liabilities}} = \frac{£}{£} \text{ ——— } =$$

This ratio is a much better test of the immediate solvency of a business because of the length of time necessary to convert stocks into cash (via sales and debtors).

Although increasing liquid resources more usually indicate favourable trading, it could be that funds are not being used to their best advantage (e.g. a large unused cash balance).

- **No credit interval**

This is the business's debtors plus cash plus short-term investments compared to the daily operating expenses, exluding depreciation.

$$\text{No credit interval} = \frac{\text{Debtors + cash + short - term investments}}{\text{Daily operating expenses excluding depreciation}} = \frac{£}{£}$$

This ratio shows the number of days that the organisation could survive by paying its regular day-to-day expenses from cash, debtors and short-term investments. Depreciation is excluded as this is not a cash expense. It therefore indicated liquidity and the safety margin the business has.

- **Debtor days**

Also known as the debtors' ratio

$$\text{Average collection period} = \frac{\text{Debtors}}{\text{Sales}} \times 365 = \frac{£}{£} \times 365 =$$

This indicates the time scale over which the company receives cash from its credit customers. This is not directly relevant to the decision whether or not to grant credit but it can give useful information about how the company operates.

- **Creditor days**

Also known as the creditors' ratio

$$\text{Average payment period} = \frac{\text{Creditors}}{\text{Costs of sales}} \times 365 = \frac{£}{£} \times 365 =$$

This is directly relevant to the decision whether or not to grant credit as it indicates the general time scale over which the company pays its current credit suppliers.

Profitability ratios

- **Return on capital employed (return on assets)**

Capital employed is normally measured as capital and reserves plus long-term liabilities (or, alternatively, Fixed Assets plus Current Assets minus Current Liabilities); it represents the long-term investment in the business.

Return on capital employed is frequently regarded as the best measure of profitability, indicating how successful a business is in utilising its assets. This ratio is only meaningful when the true values of assets are known and used in the formula.

$$\text{Return on capital employed} = \frac{\text{Profit before interest and taxation}}{\text{Capital employed}} \times 100$$

$$= \frac{\pounds\qquad\qquad}{\pounds\qquad\qquad} \times 100$$

A low return on capital employed is caused by either a low profit margin or a low asset turnover or both. These two factors are measured as follows:

- **Net profit margin (on sales)**

$$\text{Margin} = \frac{\text{Net profit before interest and taxation}}{\text{Turnover}} \times 100$$

$$= \frac{\pounds\qquad\qquad}{\pounds\qquad\qquad} \times 100$$

A low margin indicates low selling prices or high costs or both. Comparative analysis will reveal the level of prices and costs in relation to competitors.

- **Asset turnover**

This will show how fully a company is utilising its assets.

$$\text{Asset turnover} = \frac{\text{Turnover}}{\text{Capital employed}}$$

$$= \frac{\pounds\qquad\qquad}{\pounds\qquad\qquad}$$

A low turnover shows that a company is not generating a sufficient volume of business for the size of the asset investment. This may be remedied by increasing sales or by disposing of some of the assets or both.

- **Gross profit margin**

This ratio isolates the pure 'nuts and bolts' of a business, i.e. ignoring indirect expenses and sundry income.

$$\text{Margin} = \frac{\text{Gross profit}}{\text{Sales}} \times 100$$

$$= \frac{\pounds\qquad\qquad}{\pounds\qquad\qquad}$$

A low margin indicates a similar position to a low net profit margin, but the causes can be traced more readily to trends in sales and cost of sales.

- **Stock turnover**

This ratio indicates whether a business's stocks are justified in relation to its sales. If stock turnover falls, this may indicate excess stocks or sluggish sales.

$$\text{Stock turnover} = \frac{\text{Cost of sales}}{\text{Stock}}$$

$$= \frac{£\_\_\_\_\_\_}{£}$$

Gearing ratios

Here we are trying to assess the amount of long-term capital in the company's capital structure as this can be an element of the riskiness of a company.

$$\text{Borrowing ratio (gearing ratio)} = \frac{\text{Loan capital}}{\text{Capital employed}} \times 100$$

$$= \frac{\text{Loans}}{\text{Share capital + Reserves + Preference shares + Loans}} \times 100$$

$$= \frac{£\_\_\_\_\_\_}{£} \times 100$$

Interest cover

This measures the ratio of the profit before interest to the interest charge itself.

$$\text{Interest cover} = \frac{\text{Profit before interest}}{\text{Interest charge}} = \frac{£\_\_\_\_\_\_}{£}$$

This gives an indication of how easily the company can maintain payments of its loan and debenture interest and therefore gives additional information about the riskiness of the company.

Answers

Before you look any further, make sure you have written down an answer for every ratio.

Current ratio

$$\frac{1,600}{800} = 2$$

Acid test ratio

$$\frac{1,600 - 600}{800} = 1.25$$

No credit interval

$$\frac{900 + 100}{(4,000 + 1,660 - 600) / 365} = 72 \text{ days}$$

Debtors' days

$$\frac{900}{6,000} \times 365 = 55 \text{ days}$$

Creditors' days

$$\frac{800}{4,000} \times 365 = 73 \text{ days}$$

Return on capital employed

$$\frac{340}{2,000 + 1,400} \times 100 = 10\%$$

Net profit margin

$$\frac{340}{6,000} \times 100 = 5.67\%$$

Asset turnover

$$\frac{6,000}{3,400} = 1.76 \text{ times}$$

Gross profit margin

$$\frac{2{,}000}{6{,}000} \times 100 = 33.33\%$$

Gearing ratio

$$\frac{1{,}400}{2{,}000 + 1{,}400} \times 100 = 41\%$$

Stock turnover

$$\frac{4{,}000}{600} = 6.67$$

Interest cover

$$\frac{340}{74} = 4.6 \text{ times}$$

▷ ACTIVITY 8

Summarised balance sheet at 31 December 20X1

	£000	£000	£000
Fixed assets, at cost, less depreciation			2,500
Current assets			
Stocks		900	
Debtors		800	
Balance at bank		300	
		2,000	
Creditors: Amounts falling due within one year			
Trade creditors	700		
Accrued charges	300		
		(1,000)	
			1,000
			3,500
Creditors: Amounts falling due after more than one year			
10% debentures			(1,500)
			2,000
Capital and reserves			
Ordinary shares (£1 shares)			1,000
Preference shares			250
General reserve		600	
Profit and loss account		150	
			750
			2,000

Profit and loss account for year ended 31 December 20X1

	£000	£000
Turnover		6,000
Cost of sales		
Stock at 1 January	500	
Purchases	4,000	
	4,500	
Less: stock at 31 December 20X1	(900)	
		(3,600)
Gross profit		2,400
Administrative expenses and distribution costs		(1,830)
Trading profit		570
Debenture interest		(150)
Profit before tax		420
Taxation		(210)
		210
Preference dividend		(10)
Profit available for ordinary shareholders		200

Required

Calculate as many useful ratios as possible from the information above.

[Answer on p. 166]

9 Interpretation of ratios

9.1 The current ratio

$$\frac{\text{Current assets}}{\text{Current liabilities}}$$

The aim is to ensure that current liabilities can be met as they fall due. Sometimes, textbooks suggest that if a business's current ratio is below a certain level (which is usually given as between 1.5 and 2), the business should become seriously concerned. This should not be taken to be a strict rule, because:

(a) current liabilities include the bank overdraft which, in practice, is not repayable within one year (technically, of course, repayable on demand)

(b) different types of industry will have different typical current ratios. For example a supermarket will have high creditor levels and high stocks but very few debtors. Whereas a manufacuring business will not only have high creditor and stock levels but also significant levels of debtors.

9.2 Debtor days

$$\frac{\text{Debtors}}{\text{Credit sales}} \times 365$$

- Accounts do not show the split between cash and credit sales. This means that assumptions have to be made (e.g. all sales on credit) that may distort the result.
- Seasonality may also distort the result.

9.3 Return on capital employed (ROCE)

$$\frac{\text{Profit before interest tax}}{\text{Capital employed}}$$

The aim is to see how effectively the business is using the money invested in it.

Care should be taken with the interpretation of this ratio for the following reasons:

- it is based upon the balance sheet values of the net assets rather than the true market value
- as the balance sheet values are based upon historical cost then the age structure of the assets of the business can also affect the return on capital employed.
- Often new investment does not bring immediate profits. This may be for a number of reasons. It may take time for the company's employees to learn how to use the new equipment. Alternatively it may take the company time to obtain enough orders to use the new facilities to the full. (This may result in a temporary reduction in the ROCE.)

9.4 Gross and net profit margins

$$\text{Gross profit margin(GPM)} = \frac{\text{Gross profit}}{\text{Sales}} \quad \text{Net profit margin(NPM)} = \frac{\text{Net profit}}{\text{Sales}}$$

Looking at these two ratios together can determine whether a fall in the gross profit margin can be explained by a misclassification of cost rather than by deteriorating trade success.

	20X1	20X0
	£	£
Sales	100	100
Cost of sales	(85)	(80)
Gross profit	15	20
Overheads	(5)	(10)
Net profit	10	10
GPM	15%	20%
NPM	10%	10%

The fact that the net profit margin has remained constant while the gross profit margin has fallen would lead us to check that our costs had been properly classified.

This is an illustration of using more than one ratio to guide our thoughts.

9.5 Stock turnover

$$\frac{\text{Cost of sales}}{\text{Stock}}$$

This ratio provides an excellent example of the need to investigate the circumstances behind the figures.

	20X1	20X0
Z Limited's stock turnover	5	10

Interpretation one: A poor performance by Z Limited. It is holding too much stock and some of it may be obsolete or unsaleable.

Interpretation two: Z Limited management has shown commendable foresight in building up its stocks to meet the extra demand that will arise from 20X2's new advertising campaign.

We cannot determine which interpretation, if either, is correct without further information. The contrasting nature of the two explanations simply illustrates the fact that the ratio provides no answers; it simply raises questions.

9.6 Gearing ratio

The greater the extent to which a company is financed by debt, the greater is the risk of investing in it.

From a lender's point of view, the more debt there is, the less likely that money will be recovered if the company goes into liquidation.

From a shareholder's point of view, the more debt there is, the greater the variability of return.

EXAMPLE

Walthamstow Limited and Hackney Limited are identical companies except that Hackney Limited has £50,000 of debenture finance with interest at 10% per annum.
In 20X0 trading profits for both companies are £100,000.
In 20X1 they fall by 50% to £50,000.

Calculate the fall in profit available to shareholders in both companies.

Solution

In the case of Walthamstow Limited, this means that the profits available to the shareholders fall by 50% from £100,000 to £50,000.

In the case of Hackney, the fall is from £95,000* to £45,000*, a fall of 53%.

In both cases, the more debt there is the riskier the investment.
* Profit available to shareholders = Trading profit minus interest

Exactly what constitutes a long-term loan is open to discussion. Many writers argue that bank overdrafts and preference shares should be included as both have characteristics similar to long-term loans. For simulation purposes, you should either exclude these items or give a brief explanation as to why you are treating them as long-term loans.

9.7 Interest cover

The purpose of the assessment of the customer's financial statements is to determine the likelihood that they will pay their trade debts on time. If a company has long-term loan capital in its capital structure, then the interest on this must be paid thereby reducing the profits available to make other payments such as those to trade creditors. Therefore the interest cover is additional evidence of the risk associated with the company.

▷ ACTIVITY 9

The draft accounts of Falcon Limited for the years ended 30 June 20X3 and 30 June 20X2 are as follows.

	20X3		20X2	
	£	£	£	£
Balance sheets				
Freehold premises at cost		125,000		75,000
Plant at cost	210,000		125,000	
Less: Depreciation	(80,000)		(55,000)	
		130,000		70,000
Debtors		80,000		60,000
Stock		120,000		100,000
		455,000		305,000
£1 ordinary shares		100,000		50,000
Trade creditors		45,000		30,000
7% debentures		50,000		50,000
Bank overdraft		15,000		5,000
Revenue reserves		135,000		120,000
Share premium account		90,000		35,000
Current taxation		20,000		15,000
		455,000		305,000
Profit and loss accounts				
Sales		525,000		425,000
Trading profit		78,500		61,000
Less:Depreciation	25,000		20,000	
Debenture interest	3,500		3,500	
Corporation tax	20,000		15,000	
Dividends paid	15,000		10,000	
		(63,500)		(48,500)
Added to reserves		15,000		12,500

Required

By means of ratio analysis, draw as many conclusions as you can from these accounts.

[Answer on p. 167]

10 Refusal of credit

10.1 Introduction

In many cases, once the credit manager has carried out checks on a new potential customer such as bank references, trade references, credit agency reports and analysis of financial statements, then a decision will be made to grant the customer credit and the terms of payment will be communicated to the new customer. We have already seen that it is important that these terms of payment are made quite clear on all documentation which is sent to the customer such as invoices, statements, reminders, etc.

However, in some cases, the credit manager may decide that it is not possible to trade with a new potential customer on credit terms.

10.2 Possible reasons for refusal of credit

The decision to refuse to grant credit to a new customer is a big decision for the credit manager as the business will not wish to lose this potential customer's business, but the credit manager will have taken a view that the risk of non-payment from the customer is too high for credit terms to be granted.

Refusal of credit does not necessarily mean that the potential customer's business is bad or is likely not to survive, it simply means that on the evidence available to the credit manager the risk of non-payment is too high for the company to take the risk.

There are a variety of reasons why a credit manager may decide against granting of credit which include the following:

- a non-committal or poor bank reference
- poor trade references
- concerns about the validity of any trade references submitted
- adverse press comment about the potential customer
- poor credit agency report
- indications of business weakness from analysis of the financial statements
- lack of historical financial statements due to being a recently started company.

The credit manager will consider all of the evidence available about a potential customer and the reason for the refusal of credit may be due to a single factor noted above or a combination of factors.

10.3 Communication of refusal of credit

If credit is not to be granted to a potential customer then this must be communicated to the customer in a tactful and diplomatic manner. The reasons for the refusal of credit must be politely explained and any future actions required from the potential customer should also be made quite clear. The credit manager, whilst not wishing to grant credit to the customer at the current time, equally does not necessarily want to lose the potential business of this customer.

10.4 Trading on cash terms

In almost all cases where credit is to be refused to a potential customer, the company should make it quite clear that they would be happy to trade with the customer on cash terms. This may be acceptable to the customer, although not desirable, and the business will not be lost.

10.5 Future re-assessment of creditworthiness

In some cases, although the granting of credit to the new customer has been refused now, it may be that the credit manager wishes to encourage the customer to apply for credit terms in the future. For example, with a newly formed company there may be little external information on which the credit manager can rely at the current time but if financial statements and references can be provided in the future then the decision as to whether or not to trade on credit terms in future can be re-assessed.

10.6 Telephone or letter?

In most cases it may be most appropriate to communicate the reasons for the refusal of credit initially in a letter. However, in such a letter the credit manager may suggest that a further telephone call might be appropriate in order to discuss the matter and any future actions that may be necessary.

EXAMPLE

You are the credit manager for Howard Ltd and your name is Belinda Sean. You have recently been assessing requests for credit from three potential new customers.

Kenwick Partners – they have requested to purchase goods from you, would like a £5,000 credit limit and 60 days' credit. You asked for trade references and bank references and financial statements for the last three years. They have provided you with a bank reference which states that 'the partnership appears to be well constituted but we cannot necessarily speak for your figures due to the length of time that the partnership has been in operation'. They have also provided one trade reference which is satisfactory from a company which allows Kenwick £2,000 of credit on 30-day terms. However, the partnership has only been in operation for nine months and therefore they have not been able to provide you with any financial statements.

Fisher Ltd – this company has requested credit limit of £5,000 from your company and 30 days' credit. Two trade references have been provided (but no bank reference), along with the last set of published financial statements which include the previous years' comparative figures. The trade references appeared satisfactory although one is from Barnaby & Sons and it has been noted that the managing director of Fisher Ltd is Mr R Barnaby. Analysis of the financial statements has indicated a decrease in profitability during the last year, a high level of gearing and low liquidity ratios.

Jacob Enterprises Ltd – this company is requesting 30 days of credit and a credit limit of £4,000. They have provided their balance sheet at their last year end which was four months ago and the profit and loss account for the year to that date. The financial statements indicate fairly low levels of profitability but there is nothing to compare the figures to. The bank reference is satisfactory but of the two trade references one has only been trading with Jacob Enterprises for two months.

You are to draft suitable letters to each potential customer.

Solution

HOWARD LTD
Dene Court
Dene Park
Hereford
HF3 9RT

Finance Director
Kenwick Partners
Kenwick House
Green Land
Watnall

Dear Sir

Re: Request for credit facilities

Thank you for your enquiry regarding the provision of credit facilities by us for £5,000 of credit on 60 day terms. We have taken up your trade and bank references which you kindly sent details of.

We have some concerns about offering credit at this early stage of your business as there are, as yet, no financial statements for your business that we can examine. Therefore, at this stage I am unable to confirm whether we can provide you with credit facilities.

We would of course be delighted to trade with you on cash terms until we have had an opportunity to examine your first year's trading figures. Therefore, please send us a copy of your first year financial statements when they are available and in the meantime contact us if you would like to start trading on a cash basis.

Thank you for your interest in our company.

Yours sincerely

Belinda Sean

Belinda Sean
Credit Manager

HOWARD LTD
Dene Court
Dene Park
Hereford
HF3 9RT

Finance Director
Fisher Ltd
Farm Road Industrial Part
Fordtown

Dear Sir

Re: Request for credit facilities

Thank you for your enquiry regarding the provision of credit facilities by us for £5,000 of credit on 30 day terms. We have taken up your trade references and examined your latest set of financial statements.

We are unfortunately concerned about your levels of profitability in the most recent year and also have some concerns about one of the trade references from Barnaby & Sons.

On balance we are not in a position to grant your request for trade credit at the current time, although we would of course be delighted to trade with you on a cash basis. If you do not wish to trade on this basis and would like to enquire about credit terms in the future then we would be delighted to examine your current year's financial statements when they are available.

Thank you for your interest in our company.

Yours sincerely

Belinda Sean

Belinda Sean
Credit Manager

HOWARD LTD
Dene Court
Dene Park
Hereford
HF3 9RT

Finance Director
Jacob Enterprises Ltd
White Hill
Blacktown

Dear Sir

Re: Request for credit facilities

Thank you for your enquiry regarding the provision of credit facilities by us for £4,000 of credit on 30 day terms. We have taken up your trade references and examined your latest set of financial statements.

We have some concerns about your level of profitability and would like the opportunity to examine your balance sheets and profit and loss accounts for the two previous years. As one of your trade references has only been trading with you for two months, we would request details of a further supplier that we could contact for a trade reference.

At this stage I am unable to confirm whether we can provide you with a credit facility but will reconsider the situation when we receive your financial statements and additional trade reference.

Thank you for your interest in our company and in the meantime we would of course be delighted to trade with you on a cash terms basis.

Yours sincerely

Belinda Sean

Belinda Sean
Credit Manager

10.7 Trial period for credit

In some cases there may be some concerns about the information available about a potential new customer, but perhaps not enough of a concern to refuse to grant credit. In such circumstances it might be appropriate to grant a degree of credit to the customer on a trial basis with review of the situation at some point in the future.

For example, if a potential customer's trade references show that in one case although the customer has been given 30 days of credit they generally take 60 days to pay, then your company may offer them a fairly low credit limit on 30-day terms and monitor the situation for, say, six months when the situation will be re-assessed.

EXAMPLE

You are again the credit manager for Howard Ltd and your name is Belinda Sean. You have been assessing the financial statements for Reed & Sons who have requested £6,000 of credit on 60-day terms. You also have received a satisfactory bank reference and trade references.

Your analysis of the 20X3 and 20X2 financial statements show the following picture:

	20X3	20X2
Gross profit margin	28%	30%
Net profit margin	4%	3%
Interest cover	1.5 times	0.9 times
Current ratio	1.3 times	0.8 times

You are to draft a suitable letter to Reed & Sons dealing with their request for credit facilities.

Solution

HOWARD LTD
Dene Court
Dene Park
Hereford
HF3 9RT

Finance Director
Reed & Sons
Ghyll Farm Development
Steel Cross

Dear Sir

Re: Request for credit facilities

Thank you for your enquiry regarding the provision of credit facilities by us for £6,000 of credit on 60 day terms. We have taken up your bank and trade references and examined your latest set of financial statements.

Although your references are satisfactory, we have some concerns about your profitability and liquidity. Clearly, your overall profitability and liquidity position have improved since 20X2 but their levels are still lower than we would normally accept in order to grant a credit facility.

However, due to your bank and trade references, we would be happy to offer you a credit facility for six months at the end of which period the movement on your account would be reviewed and the position re-assessed. The credit limit that we could offer you would initially be £2,000 and the payment terms would be strictly 30 days from the invoice date.

Thank you for your interest in our company and we look forward to trading with you on the basis set out above.

Yours sincerely

Belinda Sean

Belinda Sean
Credit Manager

11 Test your knowledge

1 What are the seven essential elements of a contract?

2 'Consideration need not be adequate but must be sufficient'. What is meant by this statement?

3 If credit terms are stated as 'net monthly', what does this mean?

4 A business has normal credit terms of 60 days but offers a settlement discount of 3% for payment within 14 days. What is the annual cost of this discount?

5 If a cheque has 'account payee' written between parallel lines on the face of it, what does this mean?

6 Today's date is 14 June and a cheque has been received dated 18 June. What type of cheque is this?

7 What is a direct debit payment?

8 How is the current ratio calculated?

9 Why is the acid test ratio sometimes used instead of the current ratio?

10 How is return on capital employed calculated if a business has a long-term loan as well as owners' capital?

[Answers on p.170]

12 Summary

In this chapter we have considered the question of whether to grant credit to a customer and how much credit to grant. The sale of goods on credit to a customer is a contract and therefore you need to be aware of the legal background in terms of the general nature of contract law. You must also be aware of the basic provisions of the Data Protection Act.

The decision as to whether to grant credit should be based upon external information such as references and also internal information created from ratio analysis of a customer's financial statements. After all of this information has been considered, a final decision can be made as to whether or not to grant the customer credit terms.

If credit is to be refused to a potential customer or a compromise agreement reached, then this must be communicated to the customer in a polite and tactful but firm manner. You will not wish to lose the potential business of this customer, therefore an offer to trade on a cash basis and any requirements for a potential future credit relationship should be fully explained.

Answers to chapter activities & 'test your knowledge' questions

▷ ACTIVITY 1

(1) Offer and acceptance
(2) Intention to create legal relations
(3) Consideration
(4) Legality (i.e. any formalities observed)
(5) Capacity
(6) Genuine consent
(7) The contract is both legal and possible

▷ ACTIVITY 2

(1) The normal practices of the trade. It is difficult to offer terms very different from competitors and still retain a market share.
(2) The nature of the product. An oil rig would be paid for in instalments over several years while perishable products would have a very short credit period.
(3) The size of the order. Firms purchasing hundreds of items are worthy of credit terms while other customers who buy single items may not warrant any credit period.
(4) Risk of customer not paying. The greater the risk of non-payment, the shorter the credit period should be.
Further point:
(5) The amount of working capital available to finance debtors.

▷ ACTIVITY 3

The supplier gains 60 days' use of the amount due at a cost of 5%, i.e. an annual rate of:

$(5/(100-5)) \times (365/(90-30)) \times 100\% = 32\%$.

This discount rate is unlikely to be worthwhile in the UK.

▷ ACTIVITY 4

(a) One of the following:
- Cheques sent to wrong person in the organisation.
- Cheques held by an individual before they are banked.
- Cheques NOT paid into the bank daily.

(b)
- Bank name
- Bank address
- Sort code
- Account name
- Account number

▷ ACTIVITY 5

The answer should make mention of the following points.

(a) The period and amount of credit to be granted

- The need for organisational policies (including legal issues, the company's Memorandum and Articles of Association).
- The need to establish credit limits for every customer so that the organisation can manage its credit exposure to individual customers.
- To prevent erosion of profit margins through the financing of late payments.
- The dangers of breaching the organisation's financial procedures and authorisation limits.

(b) The frequency with which accounts are monitored

- If credit limits have been breached (monitored daily).
- The age analysis of transactions with the customer.
- Average periods of credit taken.
- Any doubtful debts.
- The economic and competitive environment.
- The recommendation of changes to the period and amount of credit to be granted.

(c) The discount structure to be applied

- The profitability of the transaction.
- Cost of financing (interest rates).
- Credit quality.
- Value of the relationship with the customer.

▷ ACTIVITY 6

- Reduced credit limit
- Reduced collection period
- Offer incentives for prompt payment

▷ ACTIVITY 7

(i) To the customer – the bank has a duty not to give an adverse opinion without justification. The bank has a confidential relationship with the customer.

(ii) To the enquirer – a bank can be considered negligent (and liable for damages) if the information it gives is misleading *(Hedley Byrne and Company Limited vs Heller & Partners Limited 1964)*.

ACTIVITY 8

Return on capital employed	(570 / 3,500) x 100	= 16.3%
Net profit on sales	(570 / 6,000) x 100	= 9.5%
Asset turnover	6,000 / 3,500	= 1.7 times
Current ratio	2,000 / 1,000	= 2:1
Acid test ratio	1,100 / 1,000	= 1.1:1
Stock to net current assets	(900 / 1,000) x 100	= 90%
Debtor days	(800 / 6,000) x 365	= 49 days
Creditor days	(700 / 3,600) x 365	= 71 days
Rate of stock turnover	3,600 / 900	= 4 times
Gearing ratio (including preference shares)	((1,500 + 250) / 3,500) x 100	= 50%
Interest cover (including preference divi)	570 / (150 + 10)	= 3.6 times

▷ ACTIVITY 9

As a first step, you should have redrafted accounts into a presentable form to throw out the figures you need.

Balance sheets

	20X3		20X2	
	£	£	£	£
Fixed assets				
Premises		125,000		75,000
Plant		130,000		70,000
		255,000		145,000
Current assets				
Stock	120,000		100,000	
Debtors	80,000		60,000	
	200,000		160,000	
Creditors: Amounts falling due within one year				
Creditors	45,000		30,000	
Overdraft	15,000		5,000	
Taxation	20,000		15,000	
	80,000		50,000	
Net current assets		120,000		110,000
		375,000		255,000
Creditors: Amounts falling due after more than one year				
7% Debentures		(50,000)		(50,000)
		325,000		205,000
Capital and reserves				
£1 ordinary shares		100,000		50,000
Share premium account		90,000		35,000
Profit and loss account		135,000		120,000
		325,000		205,000

Profit and loss accounts

	20X3	20X2
	£	£
Turnover	525,000	425,000
Trading profit	53,500	41,000
Debenture interest	(3,500)	(3,500)
Profit before tax	50,000	37,500
Tax	(20,000)	(15,000)
Profit after tax	30,000	22,500
Dividends	(15,000)	(10,000)
Retained profit	15,000	12,500

(a) **Return on capital employed**

20X3: (53,500 / 375,000) x 100 = 14.27%

20X2: (41,000 / 255,000) x 100 = 16.08%

(b) **Profit margin**

20X3: (53,500 / 525,000) x 100 = 10.19%

20X2: (41,000 / 425,000) x 100 = 9.65%

(c) **Asset turnover rate**

20X3: 525,000 / 375,000 = 1.4

20X2: 425,000 / 255,000 = 1.67

(d) **Stock turnover rate** (based on turnover as no cost of sales figure is known)

20X3: 525,000 / 120,000 = 4.38

20X2: 425,000 / 100,000 = 4.25

(e) **Current ratio**

20X3: 200,000 / 80,000 = 2.5

20X2: 160,000 / 50,000 = 3.2

(f) **Acid test ratio**

20X3: 80,000 / 80,000 = 1.0

20X2: 60,000 / 50,000 = 1.2

(g) **Debtor days**

20X3: (80,000 / 525,000) x 365= 56 days

20X2: (60,000 / 425,000) x 365 = 52 days

(h) **Borrowing ratio**

20X3: (50,000 / 375,000) x 100 = 13.33%

20X2: (50,000 / 255,000) x 100 = 19.6%

Comments

- Profitability. The return on capital employed has worsened and this is as a result of less efficient use of assets. (The asset turnover has deteriorated whereas the profit margin has improved.) If we look at the assets individually, the stock turnover and the debtors turnover should not have caused any overall reduction of the asset turnover; the major change appears to have occurred in the fixed assets where at some point during the year, extra capital has been raised for a major investment in fixed assets. If these assets were purchased towards the end of the year, then this would have made the figure for assets at the year end unrepresentative of the assets used throughout the year. If we take the average of the beginning and year end assets, the return on capital employed is 16.98%. Therefore, before we can draw any firm conclusions about the performance of the company, we need further information about the purchase of the fixed assets.

- Liquidity. The ratios used to measure liquidity have also worsened during the year. This is mostly due to a large increase in the overdraft, perhaps to part-finance the purchase of the fixed assets. Once again, it is necessary to establish whether the year end picture is really representative of the year as a whole before coming to any firm conclusions.

- Finance. The borrowing ratio has been reduced over the year due entirely to the large amount of share capital raised to finance the purchase of the fixed assets.

Test your knowledge

1
- Offer
- Acceptance
- Intention to create legal relations
- Consideration
- Capacity of parties
- Genuine consent
- Legality and possibility

2 Consideration must have some value and be capable in law of being regarded as consideration.

3 Payment for one month's deliveries should be made by the end of the following month.

4 Cost of discount = (3/ (100 – 3)) x (365 / (60 – 14)) x 100 = 24.5%.

5 The cheque must only be paid into the bank account of the original payee.

6 A post-dated cheque.

7 A direct debit allows the supplier to obtain payment directly from the customer's bank account.

8 Current assets / current liabilities.

9 The acid test ratio excludes stock which are the least liquid current assets and therefore can be seen as a better test of liquidity.

10 (Profit before interest and taxation / capital plus long-term liabilities) x 100

7

MANAGING DEBTORS

INTRODUCTION

Element 15.4 concerns the monitoring and control of the collection of debts. In this chapter we shall consider the procedures that must be carried out on a regular basis to monitor the position of credit customers. We shall also be considering the approach to take when there are problems with the collection of debts from credit customers.

KNOWLEDGE AND UNDERSTANDING

- Interpretation and use of credit control information (Elements 15.3 and 15.4)
- Methods of analysing information on debtors; age analysis of debtors; average periods of credit given and received; incidence of bad and doubtful debts (Element 15.4)

CONTENTS

PERFORMANCE CRITERIA

- Monitor information relating to the current state of debtors' accounts regularly and take appropriate action (Element 15.4A)
- Send information regarding significant outstanding accounts and potential bad debts promptly to relevant individuals within the organisation (Element 15.4B)
- Ensure discussions and negotiations with debtors are conducted courteously and achieve the desired results (Element 15.4C)
- Base recommendations to write off bad and doubtful debts on a realistic analysis of all known factors (Element 15.4E)

1 Analysis of debtors

1.1 Introduction

Having agreed credit terms with a customer, the credit manager needs to monitor the debtors' ledger regularly to ensure that customers are abiding by their credit agreements. Those who fail to meet the terms have to be investigated and the causes of the failure established. Close liaison is required with other departments in the company to ensure a consistent approach is adopted towards the customer.

The credit manager needs accurate and up-to-date information to check that debts are recoverable and customers are keeping to their credit terms.

1.2 Sales ledger information

Most companies obtain information from the sales ledger where each sale is recorded and all payments from customers are noted.

All entries in the sales ledger must be identifiable and traceable back to delivery note/payment. At the end of each month, the total debtors' figure in the nominal ledger should be calculated as follows.

Balance at last month end		X
Add:	Net invoiced sales during month	X
Less:	Cash received from debtors	(X)
	Discounts allowed to customers	(X)
Debtor balance at month end		X

This balance should be reconciled to the total of the balances on the individual debtors' accounts in the sales ledger and any differences resolved.

Although the credit manager may not have responsibility for the production of the debtors' listing, he will still be concerned if it is inaccurate or does not reconcile. Effective monitoring of debtor balances can only occur if the accounts information is correct.

1.3 The sales ledger system

All internally produced entries to the ledger – invoices, credit notes, receipts, contra items and journal items – must have the correct customer reference in order to be posted to the correct account. So all departments who raise such items must have up-to-date lists of customer codes to avoid mistakes.

1.4 Invoices

The invoice design is also important to the credit manager. Invoices should clearly state:
(a) customer's order number
(b) the address to which payment should be sent
(c) terms of payment
(d) invoice number, date and customer's account number,
in order to ensure speedy settlement.

1.5 Receipts

The cashier will be responsible for receiving, recording and banking cash receipts, cheques, direct debits, etc.
(a) The daily receipts need to be entered into the computer speedily to establish the credit balance of each customer, which will dictate when the next orders can be despatched.
(b) In large organisations, large receipts should be noted separately (e.g. amounts over £5,000) and the credit manager should be allowed to read these entries before other smaller items.
(c) The cashier should inform the credit manager immediately of any dishonoured cheques received from customers i.e. cheques returned by the bank once they have been paid in.
(d) Payments from customers need to be reconciled quickly and allocated promptly to each debtor's account within the accounting system. Delay could cause problems to go unnoticed for some time and consequently affect the cash flow.

1.6 Other management data

As well as the sales ledger system, the credit manager will keep a file of customer names and addresses. This may be kept on a computer database or in a manual card index, to suit the personal preference of the manager.

The filing system is vital to ensure up-to-date names and addresses are available. This information must be kept secure and it is advisable to restrict access to this data. Normally the information can only be amended or added to by the credit department, who likewise are responsible for issuing new account numbers.

The type of information stored would include:
(a) statement address
(b) credit limit
(c) risk category
(d) payment terms
(e) regional or branch office code.

1.7 Analysed information

Computer systems are used to produce various reports to aid the credit manager. Although these same reports can be produced manually, this takes much longer and is generally not cost effective.

1.8 Statements and invoices

Invoices can be produced, perhaps twice a month, requesting payment from customers. At the end of each month, it is also useful to send statements to customers to draw their attention to unpaid items and to ensure that the outstanding balance is agreed between the two parties.

Statements, like invoices, must be clear so that customers can easily see the outstanding balance due.

1.9 Aged analysis of debtors

DEFINITION

The aged analysis of debtors analyses the balance due from each debtor according to the amount of time that each individual invoice has been outstanding.

The debtors' age analysis is a useful report for the credit manager. It allows speedy perusal of old/slow paying debtors which facilitates prompt action.

The report is usually produced at the end of each month alongside the monthly statements. It splits the total outstanding balance into differing age categories, for example:

(a) amounts less than one month old
(b) amounts between one and two months old
(c) amounts between two and three months old
(d) amounts over three months old.

It is also useful to print the customer's credit limit alongside this information.

1.10 Monitoring debt collection

The credit manager should closely monitor the collection of debts. Since this is of such fundamental importance to the cash flow, it is a regular if not daily task. It is important for all the departments in the company to pool their collective knowledge.

The credit manager needs to warn the sales department of:

(a) customers who are building up a significant outstanding account
(b) customers who have not paid for a long period of time
(c) customers whose cheques have been dishonoured by their bank.

Liaison between the two should warn the sales department that the customer may be having problems and be wary on the next visit of any further signs of this.

1.11 Analysis of the aged debtors listing

The regular review of the aged debtor analysis should highlight the following potential problems:

- credit limit exceeded
- slow payers
- recent debts cleared but older outstanding amount
- old amounts outstanding and no current trading.

Each of these will be considered in turn.

1.12 Credit limited exceeded

If a customer's account balance shows that their credit limit has been exceeded then this must be investigated.

This is sometimes due to a lack of communication between the sales department and the sales ledger department. However, before a new sale on credit is agreed with a credit customer, it should be standard practice to ensure that this new sale will not mean that the customer has exceeded the agreed credit limit.

If a customer is highlighted in the aged debtor listing as having exceeded their credit limit then normally the customer should be told that no further sales will be made to them until at least some of the outstanding balances have been repaid. However, in some circumstances, liaison between the sales ledger and the sales department may result in an increase in the customer's credit limit if they have a good payment record and are simply increasing their trade with our company rather than just delaying payment of the amounts due.

1.13 Slow payers

Some businesses can be identified from the aged debtor listing as being slow payers as they always have amounts outstanding for, say, 31 to 60 days and 61 to 90 days as well as current amounts. In these cases consideration should be given to methods of encouraging the customer to pay earlier. This could be in the form of a letter from the finance director or perhaps more successfully the offer of a settlement discount for earlier payment.

1.14 Recent debts cleared but older outstanding amount

If a customer is generally a regular payer and the most recent debts have been cleared but there is still an outstanding older amount then this will normally indicate either a query over the amount outstanding or a problem with the recording of invoices, credit notes or payments received.

If there appears to be no communication with the debtor about a queried invoice that would account for the old debt outstanding then the invoice postings, credit note postings and payments received from that debtor should be checked to ensure that there have been no errors which have resulted in the recording of this outstanding amount. If there appear to be no errors then the debtor should be contacted in order to find out what the problem is concerning payment of this particular amount.

1.15 Old amounts outstanding and no current trading

This is probably the most concerning situation for a credit manager. In this case it would appear that the debtor is no longer buying from us but still owes us money from previous purchases. In this case the debtor should be contacted immediately and payment sought. If no contact can be made with the debtor or there is a genuine problem with payment, such as bankruptcy or liquidation, consideration should be given to writing off the debt as bad (see later in the chapter).

EXAMPLE

Wood Limited
Debtors' age analysis at 31.12.X1

Account No	Name	Credit limit	Total	Up to 30 days	31-60 days	61-90 days	Over 90 days
		£	£	£	£	£	£
A001	ABC Limited	10,000	9,580	9,500	–	80	–
A002	DEF Limited	20,000	400	400	–	–	–
A003	GHI Limited	15,000	14,000	10,000	3,000	1,000	–
A004	JKL Limited	2,500	2,500	–	–	2,000	500
A005	MNO Limited	3,500	4,000	1,500	2,500	–	–
.	.	.	.	.	.	.	.
.	.	.	.	.	.	.	.
Total			30,480	21,400	5,500	3,080	500
%			100	70.2	18.0	10.2	1.6

Solution

Taking each debtor in turn we will consider what information the aged debt analysis has provided and what further action might be taken.

ABC Ltd	The vast majority of this debt is current therefore there may be some dispute over the £80 over 60 days old which should be investigated.
DEF Ltd	There would appear to be no problems with this account.
GHI Ltd	This would appear to be a slow payer and encouragement should be given to pay the older debts.
JKL Ltd	This debtor is a concern. There has been no trading with this customer in the last two months and their full credit limit has been used and is still outstanding after 61 and 90 days.
MNO Ltd	This debtor has been allowed to exceed the credit limit set by £500. The reason for this should be investigated and either supplies should be stopped until some of the outstanding balance has been cleared or the credit limit should be re-assessed.

The percentage of each ageing of total debtors is also useful information for the credit manager as any increase in the older debtors percentage would be a cause for concern.

▷ ACTIVITY 1

Goldie plc is reviewing its credit granting procedures and has produced a trade debtors analysis by industry. This is shown below.

Industry	Current credit utilisation £ million	% of total debtors	Annual sales £ million	As a % of total sales
Building	22,352	26.22	145,875	28.40
Construction	15,584	18.29	109,008	21.23
Property	14,568	17.10	99,876	19.45
Electricals	12,568	14.75	81,635	15.90
Engineering	9,584	11.25	43,214	8.42
Water utilities	3,225	3.78	13,587	2.65
Electricity utilities	3,158	3.71	6,785	1.32
Gas utilities	2,587	3.04	4,596	0.90
Motor trades	1,589	1.86	8,875	1.73
Total	85,215	100.00	513,451	100.00

(a) Why is a trade debtors analysis valuable? List two reasons.

(b) Making use of the analysis, prepare a written analysis of Goldie plc's credit exposure for inclusion in its monthly management report. This analysis should also consider the implications for Goldie plc's future credit policy.

[Answer on p.191]

1.16 The role of the computer

The debtors' analysis can be produced by computer and the format adapted to suit the company. For example:

(a) the computer could just list all debtors with amounts due over 90 days, thereby enabling oldest debts to be chased first of all

(b) the computer can compare total balances due with the credit limits and print out a list of customers who have exceeded their limits.

Other information

A computer can be programmed to extract different information and analysis as required. For instance:

(a) The credit controller could merely print out an aged analysis of debtors above a particular amount. This could be useful in very large companies with thousands of debtors. The credit manager can then direct efforts to collect in material large amounts first, then consider the smaller outstanding amounts.

(b) The credit controller could use the computer to print reminder letters to customers. The computer can be programmed to print name, address, a standard letter and the outstanding amount due.

(c) The computer can also be used to calculate ratios for the credit manager.

1.17 Debtors and creditors payment periods

As discussed in the previous chapter, knowing the average time debtors take to pay is helpful in monitoring payment terms. With a computer, this statistic can be calculated for each customer, or for different groups of customers as well as a global figure for all debtors.

Likewise, on the purchase side, the computer can calculate the number of days credit being taken by the company.

We have seen that it is desirable for the debtors' collection period to be shorter than the creditors' payment period. This way the company collects what is due before it has to pay out to its own creditors. However, with a competitive market it is not always possible to arrange the cash flows so advantageously. Nevertheless, the ratios should not be too different to avoid a negative cash flow.

▷ ACTIVITY 2

Task 1

You are working in Wilson Limited's credit control section. The Sales Manager has asked for your views on the credit status of four organisations to whom Wilson Limited supplies goods. Using the extracts from the aged analysis of debtors given below, analyse these four accounts and write a memorandum to the Sales Manager.

Your memorandum should:

- provide an opinion of the creditworthiness of the customer and the status of the account
- suggest how the account should be managed in future.

Customer name and address	Current month £	Total due £	Up to 30 days £	Up to 60 days £	Up to 90 days £	Over 90 days £
Megacorp plc						
Oakham, Rutland	10,000	72,540	11,250	12,250	15,500	23,540
Credit limit	85,000			Terms of sale: 60 days net		
Goodfellows Cycles						
Limited, Manchester	9,500	24,000	9,500			5,000
Credit limit	50,000			Terms of sale: 30 days net		
Hooper-bikes						
Limited, Sheffield	5,000	26,750	6,250	4,875	5,275	5,350
Credit limit	25,000			Terms of sale: 60 days net		
Dynamo Cycles						
Limited, Nottingham	4,500	7,250	2,750			
Credit limit	7,500			Terms of sale: 30 days net		

Task 2

To improve Wilson Limited's credit control procedures you have been asked by the Credit Manager, in your position as Credit Analyst, to design a standard form to be sent to a potential customer's trade referees. Draft a suitable form.

[Answer on p.192]

1.18 Updating the aged debtor analysis

The aged debtor analysis can be prepared by updating the previous analysis for any invoices issued in the period and any cash received in the period. The monthly balance, if still remaining unpaid, must then move into the column representing one month further outstanding. For example, if an invoice in the 'up to 30 days' column is not paid in the following month then it moves into the '31 to 60 days' column.

EXAMPLE

Given below is an extract from the aged debtor analysis for a company at 30 April 20X4:

Account	Name	Credit limit £	Total £	Up to 30 days £	31 – 60 days £	61 – 90 days £	> 90 days £
0001	Ace Partners	6,000	4,800	2,100 inv 0257	1,700 inv 0244	1,000 inv 0211	
0002	Aflek Ltd	10,000	8,850	4,550 inv 0259	4,000 inv 0247		300 inv 0196
0003	Amber Ltd	5,000	2,400	2,400 inv 0252			

During the month of May 20X4 the following transactions took place with these debtors:

Ace Partners	Invoice 0269 issued for £1,800
	Paid invoice 0211
Aflek Ltd	Invoice 0266 issued for £1,300
	Paid half of invoice 0247
Amber Ltd	Invoice 0273 issued for £2,200

Update the aged debtor analysis to reflect the transactions in May 20X4.

Solution

Account	Name	Credit limit £	Total £	Up to 30 days £	31 – 60 days £	61 – 90 days £	> 90 days £
0001	Ace Partners	6,000	5,600	1,800 inv 0269	2,100 inv 0257	1,700 inv 0244	
0002	Aflek Ltd	10,000	8,150	1,300 inv 0266	4,550 inv 0259	2,000 inv 0247	300 inv 0196
0003	Amber Ltd	5,000	4,600	2,200 inv 0273	2,400 inv 0252		

2 Debt collection procedures

2.1 Introduction

The collection of cash starts by sending invoices and statements. It is helpful to file a goods received note in the credit management system as this helps credit controllers to substantiate claims of delivery. These notes must be diligently filed, having been signed by the recipient, dated and pre-numbered, and matched with invoices.

Many customers do not pay their invoices promptly and a polite reminder is often needed. Other customers require more than a gentle reminder and it may be necessary to take legal action to obtain payment from certain buyers.

It is important to have a planned approach to non-payment problems to ensure that the company's cash flow is not severely affected. The following sequence of events should be effective.

(1) The problem must be identified, in terms of the value of unpaid accounts, the number and age.

(2) This problem must then be broken down into manageable units and individuals given responsibility to collect in the debts from each unit.

(3) A plan of action must be agreed. This may include visiting, phoning, faxing, emailing, sending reminders and other suitable techniques to encourage payment.

(4) The results of these actions must be monitored and reported to managers who can take more serious steps of a legal nature if necessary.

2.2 The action plan for debt collection

A possible timescale might be as follows:

	Date
Customer places order	1 January
Credit limit is checked	2/3 January
Delivery note raised and goods are delivered	8 January
Invoice raised	15 January
Statement of all invoices	31 January
Follow up procedures	1-14 February
Cash received from customer	15 February

2.3 Methods of encouraging payment

The length of follow-up period will depend on whether the customer has merely overlooked payment or is trying to extend credit terms further. Consequently, the follow-up period may go on for several months during which time the following procedures will be used to persuade the customer to pay the bill:

- visits
- telephone calls
- collection letter
- re-scheduling.

2.4 Visits to debtors

Visits to debtors are helpful in assessing their ability to pay and secondly in sorting out any administrative problems. Establishing good relations with key personnel is always helpful in ensuring positive action and it clears the way for easier communication if problems or uncertainties arise.

However, these visits need careful planning to bring constructive attention to queried invoices and a follow-up visit may be necessary to resolve the problems. Visiting may be the only practical way of resolving queries on an account with hundreds of entries as long involved letters or telephone calls are too cumbersome to sort out a large problem. If the customer refuses to co-operate and does nothing to investigate problems, then the whole process can be very frustrating and the credit controller will need to employ much tact and diplomacy to make the visit worthwhile.

It is therefore advisable to do the following:

- plan the meeting by making an appointment to see someone in authority
- prepare the facts of the case carefully prior to the meeting, possibly by summarising the last six months' transactions and taking back-up schedules of the details
- make the most of the visit to get a general impression of the state of the factory, stock levels and staff attitudes
- ascertain why the account has become overdue and try to identify what steps the client is taking to avoid a repetition of the problems
- conduct the meeting firmly and politely whilst remaining responsive to problems and queries.

2.5 Telephone calls

Telephone calls are a quick way of making personal contact and of obtaining an immediate response. It is also a much quicker method than visiting customers; however, to be effective, the same approach needs to be adopted:

- planning and preparation
- contacting the right person with sufficient authority to act
- adopting the right tone to persuade the customer to pay
- concluding the call with an agreed plan.

Clients may employ delaying tactics, such as asking for copy invoices, which must be supplied promptly, but the caller must be receptive to signs of possible problems, e.g.:

- the customer says he is unable to pay or promises to send part-payment
- payments become later and later each month
- promises are persistently broken
- contra claims are made
- agreed points/plans are ignored and promises are broken.

In these cases, it is often advisable for the credit manager to take control and try to resolve the situation, for it may require legal action to obtain payment.

2.6 Collection letters

Collection letters are a quick and relatively easy way of contacting overdue debtors.

Each letter must convey the salient points, namely that:

- the debtor is late in paying
- the debtor is in breach of his credit terms
- payment is therefore due immediately.

A final reminder may be sent out if there is no response to the first. There is often little point in pursuing the debtor with many letters and sometimes a threat of legal action will result in prompt payment.

If further action is threatened, then the company must be prepared to carry out the threat whether it be to instruct solicitors, put the account out for collection or stop supplies.

2.7 First reminder letter

The first reminder letter is designed to point out the facts, the amount outstanding and as a reminder or encouragement to pay the amount due very soon. As with all letters to customers, it must be courteous and succinct as well as firm.

The first reminder letter will be sent out when the debts are a certain amount overdue. The timescale of the reminder letter will depend upon company policy towards debt collection but might be sent out 7 days after a debt becomes overdue. Therefore, if an invoice is sent to a customer with 30-day credit terms then the first reminder letter will be sent out 37 days after the invoice was sent out.

The first reminder letter will normally be sent to the person with day-to-day responsibility for payment of creditors rather than more senior management.
An example of a first reminder letter is given below:

HOWARD LTD
Dene Court
Dene Park
Hereford
HF3 9RT

Date: 6 April 20X4
Accounts Payable Manager
Westrope Ltd
White Hill
Stone Cross
Account no: **021547**

Dear Sir

Further to our invoices detailed below, I do not appear to have received payment. I trust that this is an oversight and that you will arrange for immediate payment to be made. If you are withholding payment for any reason, please contact me urgently and I will be pleased to assist you.

Invoice no	**Terms**	**Due date**	**Amount**
			£

If you have already made payment please advise me and accept my apology for having troubled you.

Yours faithfully

Janet Bernard
Credit Control Manager

2.8 Final reminder letter

If there is no response from the initial reminder letter then there will tend to be little point in sending a second reminder letter. However, in some instances a telephone call at this stage is useful to clear up any misunderstanding and to assess whether further action is required.

The options for a company are to put the debt into the hands of a debt collector, to take the company to court for payment or to suspend any further sales to the company until payment is received. Whatever action the company decides to take, a final reminder letter must be sent to the customer detailing this action if payment is not received.

At this stage the final reminder letter will normally be sent to a senior member of the management team such as the chief accountant or finance director.

An example of each type of final reminder letter is given below.

2.9 Debt collectors

HOWARD LTD
Dene Court
Dene Park
Hereford
HF3 9RT

Date: 12 April 20X4
Finance Director
Westrope Ltd
White Hill
Stone Cross
Account no: **021547**

Dear Sir

Further to our invoices detailed below and the reminder letter dated 6 April 20X4, I do not appear to have received payment. If you are withholding payment for any reason, please contact me urgently and I will be pleased to assist you.

Invoice no	**Terms**	**Due date**	**Amount**
			£

I regret that unless payment is received within the next seven days I will have no alternative but to put the collection of the amounts due into the hands of a third party.

If you have already made the payment please advise me and accept my apology for having troubled you.

Yours faithfully

Janet Bernard
Credit Control Manager

2.10 Legal action

HOWARD LTD
Dene Court
Dene Park
Hereford
HF3 9RT

Date: 12 April 20X4
Finance Director
Westrope Ltd
White Hill
Stone Cross
Account no: **021547**
Total amount outstanding: **£2,279.50**

Dear Sir

Despite the previous reminders and telephone calls we have still not received your payment in settlement of the above account total. You have promised payment on a number of occasions but no payment has been received to date.

We regret that due to the above we have no alternative but to consider the Small Claim procedure in the County Court in order to recover the sum outstanding. Prior to us taking such action we would however wish to give you one final opportunity to make payment. We will therefore delay submission of the claim to the County Court for a period of seven days from the date of this letter in the hope that the account is settled. We will not enter into further correspondence regarding this matter other than through the County Court.

Please note that if we are forced to take legal action you may become liable for the costs of such action which, if successful, may affect your future credit rating.

Yours faithfully

Janet Bernard
Credit Control Manager

2.11 Stopping sales

HOWARD LTD
Dene Court
Dene Park
Hereford
HF3 9RT

Date: 12 April 20X4
Finance Director
Westrope Ltd
White Hill
Stone Cross
Account no: **021547**

Dear Sir

Further to our invoices detailed below, I do not appear to have received payment. I trust that this is an oversight and that you will arrange for immediate payment to be made. If you are withholding payment for any reason, please contact me urgently and I will be pleased to assist you.

Invoice no	**Terms**	**Due date**	**Amount**
			£

I regret that unless payment is received within the next seven days I will have no alternative but to stop any further sales on credit to you until the amount owing is cleared in full. If you have made payment please advise me and accept my apology for having troubled you.

Yours faithfully

Janet Bernard
Credit Control Manager

2.12 Time period

The follow-up period may take several months, during which time the company is effectively losing interest on the outstanding amount. If the debt can only be recovered through the courts, the time delay will be extended even further.

This whole procedure is speeded up if a factor is employed. Factors will chase outstanding debts much more aggressively than the company is likely to do and so reduce the payment period (this is discussed further in the next chapter).

2.13 Courtesy and tact

Throughout all the negotiations with customers, it is important to remember that the aim is to persuade them to pay their bill. A firm approach is needed in all dealings to ensure this message is understood. Credit controllers should act with authority as late payment is in breach of the credit terms.

However, unhelpful comments which annoy and irritate the customer do not smooth the wheels of communication and are likely to hinder rather than help the proceedings. It is therefore important that people with good interpersonal skills communicate with the customer to avoid unnecessary acrimony.

It is also important that pursuit of the customer is discreet and confidential. Broadcasting to the business community that a certain business is not paying its bills can have severe effects on that business, and may even result in libel writs.

▷ ACTIVITY 3

You have recently joined the accounting department of Barnaby Soft Drinks Limited as an accounting technician. Barnaby is a family-owned business based in New Cross, South East London. It has traded now for 14 years and produces a range of still and fizzy drinks which it markets from a range of retail outlets it owns in the capital. The soft drinks sector is noted for providing its shareholders with a steady cash flow and stable profits.

Recently, Barnaby has signed agreements with a number of distributors to market its products nationwide. But, since signing these agreements, Barnaby's cash flow has been affected because these credit sales now represent 35% of its turnover (as opposed to 5% before the new marketing agreements). The remainder of its sales are cash sales to customers at its own retail outlets.

Barnaby has operated successfully without a formal credit policy or credit control function since the start of trading. Its new marketing strategy has provided good growth and improved profitability. However, the finance director has recently had to negotiate an extended overdraft facility and is concerned that the latest cash flow forecast has many associated uncertainties. Some of Barnaby's larger customers have been taking over 80 days (as opposed to 30 days according to the terms of sale) to settle their accounts.

(a) What is meant by the term 'credit policy'?

(b) Outline in a brief memorandum to the finance director the key features that should be contained in a credit policy.

(c) To cope with the additional volume of sales, Barnaby has invested in a new sales accounting system. Every month (and as required) an aged analysis of debtors report will be produced, itemised by customer. The consultants installing the system have asked what you would like to see from such a report.
Design a suitable report.

(d) The finance director has heard that a lot of collection delays relate to customer queries.
   (i) How might customer queries cause difficulties when collecting amounts due from trade debtors?
   (ii) Describe two features that are desirable in a policy of managing customer queries.

[Answer on p.194]

▷ ACTIVITY 4

Peter Honey & Sons Limited is a well established chain of book shops in the West Midlands of England. It can trace its origins back to 1762 when it first started to distribute literature and periodicals from its first premises, still in existence, in Dudley High Street. It caters for a wide market, including the general public (adults and a wide selection of children's books), technical publications for libraries and businesses, academic (there are now 15 colleges in the area) and a new computer-based publishing section.

In the past 12 months, both the academic and computer-based publishing sections have seen rapid growth. Peter Honey & Sons Limited now has branches at all higher educational establishments in the area (including two opened at the new universities of Solihull Metropolitan University and the University of Walsall) and has established outlets for its computer-based publishing section at five of its shops. Traditionally, 90% of Peter Honey & Sons Limited's sales were for cash (or cheque or credit card) over the counter at its outlets. However, the growth of its academic section has meant that a substantial number of books are despatched to academic staff on approval (i.e. to be paid for later or returned) or sold on credit to the libraries of the institutions. This has been a particular problem for Peter Honey & Sons Limited, as although the new universities in the area have expanded their library stock in response to rapid growth in student numbers, these establishments have encountered many problems with their financial control systems, leaving Peter Honey & Sons Limited with a growing days' sales outstanding ratio for these customers.

The computer-based publishing section has encountered similar problems, with many sales now made on credit to commercial and industrial customers wishing to publish trade catalogues and promotional material on CD-ROM.

Whilst these two new markets have provided Peter Honey & Sons Limited with sales growth and improved profit margins (particularly with the computer-based publishing business), it has created other problems. Peter Honey & Sons Limited now has a growing trade debtor balance, and an ever larger overdraft.

Peter Honey & Sons Limited has recently employed a new Finance Director who in turn has employed you as the Credit Controller for the company. She feels that the company's procedures for deciding terms of sales are adequate, but its credit collection procedures are in need of a complete overhaul.

(a) Define the following terms, mentioned in the case study above:
   (i) days' sales outstanding
   (ii) terms of sale.

(b) The Finance Director has made an initial review of the credit collection process and has decided that, as part of it, a proper system of sending out collection (or reminder) letters to credit customers should be put in place.

   You have been asked to design a reminder letter system to suit the particular circumstances of Peter Honey & Sons Limited.

   Write a memorandum to the Finance Director outlining how your proposed system will operate and the type of letters to be despatched. Your answer should describe the whole of the reminder system and explain the rationale for the operations. Do not include drafts of the reminder letters.

(c) Design three different suitable reminder letters to be used for THREE different situations. Highlight the circumstances in which they would be used.

(d) Suggest two other ways in which customers may be contacted (other than by letter) to facilitate debt collection and briefly describe the advantages of each.

[Answer on p.195]

3 Test your knowledge

1 What document would be sent to each debtor at the end of each month outlining any unpaid amounts?

2 As well as the ageing of each debtor's debts what other information can usefully be shown on an aged debt analysis?

3 If a debt has not been paid by a customer what methods are available to encourage payment of the debt?

[Answers on p.198]

4 Summary

Once trade credit is allowed to customers it is vital for the cash flow of the business that the debtors' position is regularly monitored One of the most useful analyses is an aged debtors listing which can be used to identify customers that may need chasing for payment. Once these customers have been identified there are a variety of ways in which they can be encouraged to pay – personal visits, telephone calls and reminder letters. At all times the customer should be treated firmly but with courtesy, tact and respect. If a debt is overdue it is normal practice to send a first reminder letter followed up at a later date with a final reminder letter detailing the action that will now be taken if payment is not received.

Answers to chapter activities & 'test your knowledge' questions

▷ ACTIVITY 1

(a) (i) Provides a guide to the company of its exposure to particular industries (company will have an opinion on the industry risk).

(ii) Provides an analysis of the relative importance of each sector to the company and their granting of credit.

(b) *Presentation*:

Answers should be written in sentences and in a manner that suggests they form part of a monthly management report.

Good answers might note:

- The large exposure to the building, property and construction sectors (62%) which is notoriously cyclical and prone to any down-turn in the economic cycle.
- The excessive use of credit by these companies.
- The company's view about the prospects for the property, building and construction industry.
- Is it worth continuing to grant such credit to these sectors to sustain sales?
- Patterns of credit payment record for these sectors.
- Why is relatively low utilisation made of credit by the utility sectors, traditionally regarded as low-risk, low volatility sectors?

▷ ACTIVITY 2

Task 1

MEMORANDUM

To: Sales Manager Date: XX-XX-XX
From: Credit Controller
Subject: Credit status of organisations

Megacorp plc

Megacorp enjoys a high credit limit from our company. However the company is a poor payer and abuses the 60 days net terms of sale. Ways in which the account might be managed in the future include:

- The use of discounts for early payment or cash sale.
- Develop a better relationship with the customer to ensure prompt payment.
- Consider ways of providing a better service to Megacorp to facilitate prompt payment.

Goodfellows Cycles Limited

Goodfellows enjoys a relatively high level of credit from our company, of which it does not make excessive use. It is a prompt payer, with the exception of £5,000 which has been outstanding for over 90 days. Ways in which the account might be managed in the future include:

- Settlement of the £5,000 due over 90 days. This possibly relates to a single item, on which there may be a customer query outstanding.
- Find ways of selling more goods to this customer.
- Develop better ways of managing customer queries.

Hooper-bikes Limited

Hooper-bikes enjoys a medium sized credit limit from our company, which it has abused in recent months. Also it has exceeded its credit limit and urgent action needs to be taken to bring this account to order. Future action should include the following.

- Ensuring Hooper-bikes reduces outstanding amounts below the available credit limit.
- Considering reducing the credit limit.
- Considering ways of improving Hooper-bikes' payment record.
- Considering reducing sales to Hooper-bikes.

Dynamo Cycles Limited

Dynamo Cycles enjoys only a modest credit limit from our company and has a good payment record. In the future we could consider the following.

- Increasing sales to Dynamo.
- Increasing Dynamo Cycles' credit limit.

Task 2

WILSON LIMITED TRADE REFERENCE FORM
STRICTLY CONFIDENTIAL

To: Name of Trade Referee

Address of Trade Referee

Name of Potential Customer

1	How long have you traded with this firm?	.... months*
		.... years*
		Many years*
2	How much credit do you usually allow?	£
3	What are your payment terms?	Pro-forma*
		Monthly*
		.... days*
4	Are payments generally made to your satisfaction?	To terms*
		Up to 1 month late*
		More than one month late*
		Very slow/irregular*

5 Any other information will be appreciated
....
....
....
....
....
....

Signed .... Date ....

*please delete where inapplicable.

▷ ACTIVITY 3

(a) A policy that defines, amongst other things, the terms and conditions under which the company grants, controls and monitors credit, decides settlement terms and how it liaises with customers in the credit process.

(b) The memorandum should refer to:

- the procedures for granting credit, including such matters as how customers are evaluated for credit (using bank and trade references, historical financial information, press reports, trade journals, credit agency references)
- who may grant credit, authorise limits
- the determination of settlement terms
- procedures for monitoring credit
- the relationship between the credit control and marketing functions.

(c)

Barnaby Soft Drinks Limited
Aged analysis of debtors

Customer name	*Sales ledger ref*	*Credit limit*	*Total*	*1–30 days*	*31–60 days*	*61–90 days*	*90+*	*Other*

The 'Other' column may include such answers as 'Debit notes' and 'Unreconciled cash'. Other acceptable column headings would include 'Current' and 'Risk category'.

(d) (i) Customers may be unable to reconcile the information provided within the invoice to their own records, or be dissatisfied with the delivery of goods or the level of service they are receiving.

(ii) Mention **two** of:

- a policy of developing a relationship with the customer's administrative staff
- understanding customers' administration procedures
- monitor customer queries
- develop a courteous and firm approach when dealing with all customers.

▷ ACTIVITY 4

(a) The trade debtors' balance expressing the number of days is calculated as follows:

Days' sales outstanding = (Total debtors / Sales) x 365 days
Terms of sale – the payment (and/or credit) terms offered to customers.

(b) The answer should be set out in the form of a memorandum and written in appropriate language. The answer might include the following as elements of a collection system:

The purpose of the system
The purpose of a reminder letter is to initiate action, i.e. remind the individual/organisation that payment is outstanding and to set in motion the process for collecting the debt, perhaps involving a debt collection agency or court action.

The number of letters to be sent
The number of reminder letters that should be sent out should be low, a first and then a final, should be adequate.

The frequency and timing of the letters
The first reminder letter should be sent out around 14 days after due date. This allows a period of grace for any payments that have just failed to have been received after the due date and allows the supplier to update their accounting system. The second (or final) reminder should be sent a further 14 days after the first reminder.

The content of the letters
All letters should be polite, brief and concise. The first reminder should be addressed to the Accounts Payable Manager (preferably by name), subsequent (or final) reminders should be addressed to the Chief Accountant/Company Secretary/Finance Director to advise the possibility of serious action.

The design of the letters
Letters should be designed so they can be produced quickly, ie preferably a standard letter produced by the company's computerised accounting system. Other means could include faxing the letters directly, with final letters being addressed personally to the Chief Accountant/Company Secretary/Finance Director.

(c)

First Reminder

Peter Honey & Sons Limited,
212 Dudley High Street,
Dudley,
West Midlands

Date:
Attention: **Accounts Payable Manager**

Dear Sirs

We have not received payment for your September account, value £156.98, which was due at the end of October.

Your prompt attention to this will be appreciated.

Yours faithfully

[Name]
Circumstance in which it might be used: As a first reminder

Final Reminder

Peter Honey & Sons Limited,
212 Dudley High Street,
Dudley,
West Midlands

Date:
Attention: **Chief Accountant**

Dear Sirs

FINAL NOTICE – £156.98

We cannot trace any response to our previous reminders about this account. We are not aware of any reason why it should not be paid and we must demand you settle the account WITHIN SEVEN DAYS.

Failure to pay will result in the account being placed in other hands for collection without further reference to you.

Yours faithfully

[Name]
Circumstance in which it might be used: As a final reminder

Part Payment Letter

Peter Honey & Sons Limited,
212 Dudley High Street,
Dudley,
West Midlands

Date:
Attention: **Accounts Payable Manager**

Dear Sirs

Thank you for your payment of £100.

This clears the overdue account referenced in our recent letter, leaving a balance of £56.98.

Your attention to this will be appreciated and we look forward to receiving a further cheque from you.

Yours faithfully

[Name]
Circumstance in which it might be used: As a part payment letter

(d) Any two required from:

Telephone
Enables the credit control staff to make personal contact with the customer's sales ledger department. May assist with understanding if any problems are created by the invoicing process with the customer. May enable the credit control staff to understand if there is any problem with the goods or service provided (ie inadequate service, faulty products, etc).

Facsimile/email
Suggests a sense of urgency.

Personal visit
Usually by sales staff or possibly by a credit analyst. Again enables company to make personal contact with the client to see if there are any problems. Can also encourage sales staff to take a more active role in the credit collection process.

Test your knowledge

1 Statement

2
- Customer account code
- Customer credit limit
- Terms e.g. cash/settlement discounts

3
- Personal visit
- Telephone call
- Collection letters
- Final reminder

8

COLLECTION OF DEBTS

INTRODUCTION

In this final chapter, we will consider how to deal with situations where credit customers are not paying the debts that are due. This chapter considers various alternative methods of debt collection, the legal situation regarding collection of debts due and the procedure for writing off bad debts.

KNOWLEDGE AND UNDERSTANDING

- Legal issues: remedies for breach of contract (Element 15.4)
- Legal and administrative procedures for the collection of debts (Element 15.4)
- The effect of bankruptcy and insolvency on organisations (Element 15.4)
- Methods of collection (Element 15.4)
- Factoring arrangements (Element 15.4)
- Debt insurance (Element 15.4)
- Evaluation of different collection methods (Element 15.4)

CONTENTS

PERFORMANCE CRITERIA

- Ensure discussions and negotiations with debtors are conducted courteously and achieve the desired results (Element 15.4C)
- Use debt recovery methods appropriate to the circumstances of individual cases and in accordance with the organisation's procedures (Element 15.4D)
- Base recommendations to write off bad and doubtful debts on a realistic analysis of all known factors (Element 15.4E)

1 Collection of debts

1.1 Introduction

In most cases with good credit control procedures (as discussed in the previous chapters) monies will be received from credit customers sometimes after encouragement such as reminder letters or telephone calls. However there will no doubt be some cases in which either the debt is never collected and has to be written off or the business has to resort to legal procedures to obtain payment. Before we consider these matters there are other methods that a business can use to minimise the possibility of either of these two occurrences.

1.2 Factoring arrangements

DEFINITION

Factoring involves the use of a factoring company to provide sales ledger services, finance and in some cases protection against bad debts in return for a fee.

A company may wish to farm out the collection of its debts through a factoring arrangement. This relieves the company of the burden of maintaining a detailed credit control system.

A factoring arrangement can be taken out with a factoring company (the 'factor'). Factoring companies are generally controlled by the clearing banks which gives considerable credence to the industry.

1.3 Options available

The factoring arrangement usually allows for the following.

(a) Administration of the sales ledger and credit control functions. The factor takes over all operations on the credit side from credit approval to collecting the cash. This facility only leaves the client the work of raising invoices and clearing disputes, as the factoring company effectively runs the sales ledger. The customer has little need for a sophisticated computer system; the cost of such a scheme is between 0.75% and 3% of turnover.

(b) Finance. If the company requires cash immediately, the factoring company may provide up to 85% of the value of the debt immediately. This is effectively a cash advance and usually costs slightly more than bank borrowing rates. However, the payment is certain and allows for a determined cash flow.

(c) Credit protection. This can be provided by the factor to cover against bad debts. If the factoring agreement is 'without recourse' then the factor bears the risk of any debtors that do not pay. If the agreement is 'with recourse' then the customer will have to repay to the factor any monies advanced for the debt that is bad.

1.4 Advantages of debt factoring

Factoring is particularly useful in the early stages of development when a company is sufficiently large to need to devote attention to debtors but not yet large enough to warrant employing a full-time credit manager.

The advantages of debt factoring are as follows.

- The company need no longer incur the costs of employing its own debt collection staff.
- Because the factor can act for several companies concurrently, the client will benefit from the economies of scale of such an organisation and the factor's fees are reduced.
- The cash flow advantages that ensue from a regular predetermined cash inflow should reduce the company's financing charges.

One of the main disadvantages of factoring is that control of debtors is surrendered to the factor which may displease customers or give the impression of liquidity problems in the company.

1.5 Invoice discounting

Invoice discounting is the purchase of invoices from a company, but, unlike debt factoring, the invoice discounter does not take over control of debt collection. The invoice discounter solely supplies an advance of cash.

The main advantage of this system is that debtors remain unaware of the arrangement.

From the invoice discounter's point of view, this method of advancing money on debts is more risky than debt factoring, for the discounter does not control debt collection and relies on the company to collect the debt for them. Therefore such a service may only be available to companies with reliable, well established collection procedures.

EXAMPLE

Ant Limited has problems collecting debts from debtors and consequently has an overdraft of £300,000. Debtors take on average three months to pay and have an average value of £300,000.

The bank charges interest on the overdraft at 9.5% per annum. The company is considering three options in its attempt to reduce costs.
Which is the cheaper option over a year?

(1) Using a debt factor who will charge 2.25% of the book value of each debt for immediate payment of the full invoice.
(2) Using an invoice discounting firm who will agree to advance 60% of each debt immediately, for a 4% fee on the amount advanced.
(3) Offering a 5% discount for immediate payment from customers of whom 50% are expected to take up the discount.

Solution

Annual sales	£300,000 x (12/3)	£1,200,000
Present cost	£300,000 x 9.5%	£28,500 pa
Option 1 Cost		£
Debt factor charge per annum	1,200,000 x 2.25%	27,000 pa
Option 2 Cost		£
Invoice discounting charge per annum	1,200,000 x 60% x 4%	28,800
Interest on remaining 40% who still take three months' credit	1,200,000 x 40% x (3/12) x 9.5%	11,400
Total		40,200
Option 3 Cost		£
Discounts	1,200,000 x 5% x 50%	30,000
Interest on remaining 50% who do not take up the discount	1,200,000 x 50% x (3/12) x 9.5%	14,250
Total		44,250 pa

The present situation costs £28,500 per annum. The cheapest of the three options is Option 1 which involves employing a debt factor, so reducing the cost by £1,500 per annum to £27,000 per annum.

The saving is not very large and the company must consider the potential loss of goodwill if debts are collected by a third party.

▷ ACTIVITY 1

What are the main advantages of a factoring company?

[Answer on p.214]

1.6 Debt insurance

Debt insurance is a method of guarding against unexpected failures. Credit management is still required but it is a way of safeguarding one's cash flow. It may be particularly useful when a company deals with one or two major customers and is therefore dependent upon them.

Debt insurance or credit insurance is obtained through a broker who establishes terms and an agreement between the insured and the underwriter. The broker receives a commission for his work and, if he negotiates the policy well, will be able to renew it in the following year.

The types of cover available fall into four main categories:
(a) whole turnover
(b) datum line
(c) catastrophe
(d) specific account
allowing the insured to insure different types of debts.

1.7 Selecting the correct policy

Each company will have its own system of credit control and its own pattern of sales/debtors. Entire turnover policies are available to cover all possible bad debts, usually with a de minimis limit, but these are often very expensive. A more specific policy can be taken out, such as a datum line policy, which covers customers whose indebtedness exceeds an agreed amount.

Alternatively, a policy-holder may decide to exclude certain large customers in whom he has full confidence and so the policy becomes quite specific in its nature with only certain individual accounts insured.

1.8 Terms of the policy

Most policies insure between 75% and 90% of agreed sales.

The premium is negotiable between the parties.

A credit limit will need to be agreed for each customer. This is sometimes a difficult part to negotiate as the insured may well require a higher level of credit to cover the expected trade with the customer than the underwriter is prepared to accept. Trading above the agreed limit may invalidate the policy; but having to restrict sales to the customer may lose goodwill. A good relationship with the underwriter may help to solve this problem.

1.9 Pre-shipment insurance

Pre-shipment insurance is available to cover work-in-progress losses or losses of finished goods. It offers protection for orders cancelled at the last minute where there is no alternative buyer and only scrap value is obtainable.

1.10 Catastrophe policies

The main features of catastrophe policies are as follows:

(a) the insured agrees to bear the first £1,000, say, of the loss due to the catastrophe

(b) above this aggregate limit the cover will reimburse a specified percentage of the loss

(c) this policy is not normally suitable for small companies.

Credit insurance is a means of protecting against bad debts; however, it is usually a costly way of obtaining security and many companies may decide to bear the cost of bad debts themselves when they are confident that this is less expensive than the insurance premium.

▷ ACTIVITY 2

BarCo Ltd is re-considering its methods of managing debtors. These include:

(a) credit insurance through a whole turnover policy

(b) factoring.

Write a memorandum to the managing director outlining your understanding of how each of these two methods may improve credit control.

Your note should describe briefly the principles involved in each method, who will be involved in its operation, the effect on customer relationships, the impact on cash flow and the effect on the company's financial statements.

[Answer on p.215]

1.11 Stopping supplies

Stopping supplies is one way of preventing a problem escalating with an overdue debtor. The credit manager must protect the company's investment and minimise the chance of a bad debt.

There are various reasons for non-payment of debts: the customer may be unable to pay, be inefficient, or be dissatisfied.

- If the customer is unable to pay the supplier must safeguard his own position and ceasing to supply will prevent the debt increasing; however, the customer may claim he is able to trade out of the problem for which purpose he needs continuing supplies. The supplier needs to be quite convinced of this before releasing more goods.
- Inefficiencies may be quickly resolved by the prospect of a stoppage in supplies and this is often a useful jolt to rectify the position. If there is dissatisfaction over the supply of goods, however, stopping supplies is unlikely to resolve the problem.
- Customers who deliberately fail to pay need to be dropped from the sales ledger. Although there is often great reluctance to do this – particularly in small firms where there is a fear of losing business – it is the only answer.

1.12 Collection agencies

A collection agency can be appointed to collect debts. Various types of agency exist but they can generally be split into three types:

(a) **trade associations** are usually non-profit making bodies who charge an annual membership fee and a percentage of the monies recovered

(b) **voucher agencies** sell books of collection vouchers to client companies who are entitled to complete a voucher for any outstanding debt and send it to the agency

(c) **commercial agencies** who usually work on a 'no-collection, no-charge' basis.

Collection agencies have the advantage of relieving the credit manager of the time-consuming work of chasing customers. A good agency will be specialised in tracing debtors who have disappeared, and will often have legal expertise. The charge is reasonable compared with the cost of employing another member of staff.

However, if the credit manager has a good efficient staff they may be able to do the work and so save the costs of an agency. Customers rarely respond well to outside agencies whose sole aim is to obtain payment of a debt and goodwill can easily be lost by such steps.

It is usually sensible to check that the agency:

(a) is of good standing in the locality

(b) is licensed for debt collection under the Consumer Credit Act 1974

(c) is financially sound

(d) uses an audited client trust account with its bank

(e) reports regularly to the company and returns payments promptly.

▷ ACTIVITY 3

Collection agencies exist to assist companies with collecting debts. Typically a commercial agency will charge a proportion of the debt collected, with no charge if no collection is made.

When approaching a credit collection agency, what points would you look for from such an agency? List three items.

[Answer on p.216]

▷ ACTIVITY 4

(a) For many small companies, factoring proves an attractive alternative to bank lending. Typically, bank lenders are concerned with the state of a company's balance sheet. What element of a company's balance sheet do factors consider when advancing funds?

(b) Factoring and discounting have experienced steady growth in recent years. List three services provided by factors and discounters.

[Answer on p.216]

2 Legal action

2.1 Introduction

Legal action can be taken to force an overdue debtor to pay its debts. Before commencing, it is wise to ensure that:

(a) the debt is not disputed

(b) the name and trading style of the debtor is accurate ie sole trader, partnership or company, and

(c) the customer has sufficient assets to pay the bill.

2.2 Remedies for breach of contract

This section examines the legal remedies that may be available to any injured party as a result of the breach of a contract. We shall be paying particular attention to the remedies that are of use to an unpaid creditor/supplier.

In such a situation, the injured party may have one or more of the following remedies.

(a) He may recover damages for any loss suffered as a result of the breach by bringing an action for damages for breach of contract.

(b) If the breach consists of the other party's failure to pay a debt (i.e. the contractually agreed price or other remuneration due under the contract), the appropriate course for the injured party is to bring an action for the agreed sum to recover that amount, rather than an action for damages.

2.3 How to bring a dispute to court

If threats of legal action are carried out for a debtor who has not paid then the initial step is to instruct a solicitor. The solicitor will require details of the goods or services provided, the date the liability arose, the exact name and trading status of the debtor, any background information such as disputes in the past and a copy of any invoices that are unpaid.

In some cases after the solicitor has got involved there may be a negotiated settlement between the creditor and debtor as the debtor does not want to run the risk of going to court. However in other situations the case will be taken to court.

2.4 Appropriate courts

If the claim is for less than £3,000 then the claim will be made in the Small Claims Court. Any claims for less than £25,000 will normally be dealt with in the County Court and for claims higher than this, the High Court.

2.5 Procedure

The appropriate court, once it has received all of the paperwork will issue a summons to the debtor requiring an acknowledgement of service of the summons. If the debtor does not reply then the judgement will go against him. The debtor may admit the claim and perhaps offer to pay by instalments. If the creditor does not accept this then the court will determine a suitable method of paying off the debt.

Once the court order has been made then the money must be collected and there are a number of methods of achieving this.

2.6 The seizure of goods

Seizing goods is effective against businesses with valuable items in their offices, such as computers. The court bailiff is given a 'warrant of execution'. He will seize the goods and sell them by public auction with the proceeds paid to the creditor.

2.7 Attachment of earnings order

An attachment of earnings order ensures that the creditor is paid directly by the debtor's employer out of his/her pay packet.

This is only available against individual debtors who are in employment and is usually very unsuccessful as the court needs to determine the 'protected' earnings of the individual and the debtor's employer needs to co-operate fully. Such a person is likely to change employment frequently which creates further complications in tracing them and taking out fresh attachment orders.

2.8 Garnishee order

A garnishee order allows the creditor to be paid directly by a debtor of the offending company i.e., a third party who also owes the defaulting company money.

2.9 Administrative order

Where a debtor has a number of debts totalling less than £5,000 then the debtor might make regular payments into court and the court distributes them to the creditors on a pro rata basis.

2.10 Charging order

The court can order a charge on the debtor's property and if the debt is not paid within six months the creditor has the right to have the property sold.

2.11 Bankruptcy notice (against a partner or individual)

A bankruptcy notice is usually very effective as few people like to go out of business.

However, if the business is on the verge of bankruptcy and a bankruptcy order is issued, then the official receiver will distribute the assets in the following order:

(a) secured creditors
(b) bankruptcy costs
(c) preferential creditors (such as HM Revenue and Customs, DSS)
(d) unsecured creditors
(e) deferred creditors
(f) the bankrupt.

As an unsecured creditor, the supplier is a long way down the list of payments and even in a bankruptcy may not receive the money owed.

For a bankruptcy order to succeed the debt must be in excess of £750, it must be unsecured and the debtor must be domiciled in the UK.

2.12 Consequences of a petition for bankruptcy

The consequences of a petition for bankruptcy against a debtor are:

- if the debtor pays money to any other creditors or disposes of any property then these transactions are void
- any other legal proceedings relating to the debtor's property or debts are suspended
- an interim receiver is appointed to protect the estate.

2.13 Consequences of a bankruptcy order

The consequences of a bankruptcy order are:

- the official receiver takes control of the assets of the business
- a statement of the assets and liabilities is drawn up – this is known as a statement of affairs
- the receiver summons a meeting of creditors within 12 weeks of the bankruptcy order
- the creditors appoint a trustee in bankruptcy
- the assets of the business are realised and distribution is made to the various creditors in the order given above.

2.14 Liquidation (or winding-up) of a company

A company cannot be dissolved until it is removed from the register of companies, which requires the correct legal procedures to be completed. This means that its assets must be realised (converted into cash) and then applied in payment of its debts (in due order) and any surplus distributed among its members according to their entitlement.

The process commences with a court order or by the members passing a resolution to wind the company up. If a creditor for more than £750 serves a statutory demand for payment at the registered office of the company and the company neglects for three weeks to pay the debt or to secure or compound it to the creditor's reasonable satisfaction, then the company is deemed unable to pay its debts.

2.15 Steps in a liquidation

The following steps will then be taken:

(a) ascertaining that the company is unable to pay its debts
(b) petition for winding up
(c) winding-up order
(d) meeting of creditors
(e) statement of affairs
(f) appointment of liquidator
(g) administration of the company's estate
(h) payment of creditors

2.16 Payment in a liquidation

The order of pay-off of the company's debts is as follows:

(a) secured creditors, excluding holders of floating charges
(b) liquidation costs
(c) preferential creditors (e.g. HM Revenue and Customs, and PAYE, VAT and National Insurance)
(d) holders of floating charges
(e) unsecured creditors
(f) shareholders.

3 Writing off bad debts

3.1 Specific provision for doubtful debts

DEFINITION

A specific provision for doubtful debts is a provision against a particular debt owed as there is concern than it may not be paid in full.

As soon as there is a problem with a debtor which indicates he may be unable to pay a debt, it is prudent to provide against the debt. A specific provision can be set up for debts and a list is compiled of:

(a) invoices disputed
(b) invoices with warranty claims
(c) part-payment invoices
(d) old invoices
(e) suspense account items,

and the total figure forms part of the specific provision and is written off against the year's profit.

3.2 General provision

DEFINITION

A general provision is a further provision against normally a percentage of remaining debts which reflects the fact that some debts may not be paid in full.

In addition, a further general provision may also be sensible. Often a percentage of debtors (after the specific provision) is written off each year as a prudent exercise, say 1% of outstanding debtors. This percentage will be based on the credit manager's experience of the business, the economic environment and previous years' figures.

3.3 Accounting for provisions for doubtful debts

The specific and general provisions together form the total bad and doubtful debt provision which is credited in the balance sheet against debtors. This provision is an accounting entry only and does not represent any movement in the cash position.

3.4 Bad debts

DEFINITION

A bad debt is a debt which the credit manager is fairly certain will never be received from the customer.

Unlike a provision for doubtful debts a bad debt will have an effect on the cash flow, as this represents income which is no longer realisable. For example suppose that a debtor company has gone into liquidation and the final dividend (say 40p in the £) has been paid to creditors, the balancing 60% of the debt has to be written off. This occurs both in the accounts and in the cash flow. The latter will need to be adjusted and, if the debt is large, the credit manager will need to consider the effect on the overall cash balance and take the necessary adjusting steps.

3.5 Assessing bad debts

As the person dealing with the accounts of debtors and analysing the aged debtors analysis, you are in a position to be able to assess potential bad debts. You should ensure that when doing this you use all available information. This might include the following:

- evidence of long outstanding debts from the aged debt analysis
- a one-off outstanding debt when more recent debts have been cleared
- correspondence with debtors
- outstanding older debts and no current business with the customer
- press comment
- information from the sales team.

3.6 Communicating potential bad debts

If you believe that a debt is bad or perhaps doubtful then it will normally not be your decision to actually write the debt off or provide against it. This will normally be the decision of a more senior person in the accounting function. Therefore, if you have information about potential bad or doubtful debts then all of this information should be communicated clearly to the relevant person within the accounting function.

3.7 Incidence of bad debts

It can be argued that a high level of bad debts in an organisation is an indicator of poor credit control, although there could obviously be other reasons such as the general economic climate. A high level of bad debts could be an indication of:

- sales being made to high risk customers
- poor assessment of creditworthiness
- lack of useful information for checking on creditworthiness
- weak sales ledger accounting
- poor follow up procedures for outstanding debts.

Therefore a useful indicator or ratio can be the amount of bad debts in a period as a percentage of the total debtors at the end of the period. It might also be useful to calculate a similar ratio for the percentage of doubtful debts to total debtors.

EXAMPLE

A business has the following balances at the end of March and end of June.

	March	June
	£	£
Debtors	158,700	176,200
Bad debts expense	4,700	6,300
Provision for doubtful debts	3,200	3,100

Calculate the percentage of bad debts to total debtors and the percentage of the provision for doubtful debts to total debtors. What, if anything, does this tell you?

Solution

	March	June
Bad debts/total debtors =	(4,700/158,700) x 100	(6,300/176,200) x 100
=	3.0%	= 3.6%
Provision/total debtors =	(3,200/158,700) x 100	(3,100/176,200) x 100
=	2.0%	= 1.8%

The bad debts percentage has increased but the provision percentage has decreased. This might indicate a worsening in credit control or perhaps that a number of previously doubtful debts have now been written off as bad.

ACTIVITY 5

(a) What is the main drawback associated with using published reports and accounts for credit control information?

(b) Using the courts to recover bad debts is costly and time consuming. Describe THREE methods of enforcing a judgement in the county courts.

[Answer on p.216]

ACTIVITY 6

Identify the two main purposes of bankruptcy procedures from the viewpoint of the debtor and creditor(s).

[Answer on p.217]

4 Test your knowledge

1 What services are normally provided by a factoring service?

2 What are the main advantages of a factoring arrangement?

3 What is without recourse debt factoring?

4 How does invoice discounting differ from factoring?

5 What are the four main types of credit insurance cover available?

6 What is a garnishee order?

7 What are the consequences of a bankruptcy order?

8 What are the steps in a liquidation?

9 What is the difference between a specific provision and a general provision for doubtful debts?

10 Does a bad debt have an effect on cash flow?

[Answers on p.217]

5 Summary

There are a variety of methods for collection of debts which may help businesses in different circumstances. Factoring arrangements can relieve a business of having to collect its own debts and can also be useful for cash flow purposes if funds are advanced and the debts are collected by the factor. Invoice discounting also allows money to be advanced to the business but still the business has the job of collecting their own debts. Debt insurance is a way of guarding against the non-payment of debts but is often a fairly expensive option. A collection agency can be used for collection of debts but this often has an adverse effect on the goodwill of the business. As a final resort a business can bring legal action to recover its debts, usually in the County Court or the High Court. If an individual is made bankrupt or a company goes into liquidation, then the unsecured creditors are some of the last to be paid and may well receive only a small amount of that which is owed to them or possibly none at all.

Finally, if there is concern over the recoverability of debts then a specific doubtful debt provision should be set up in the accounting records and possibly a general provision as well. If a debt is never going to be received then it should be written off as a bad debt expense in the accounting records and the cash flow forecasts should be reviewed.

Answers to chapter activities & 'test your knowledge' questions

▷ ACTIVITY 1

Advantages of factoring

- It provides an additional source of working capital.
- It is a flexible method. Unlike a bank loan or overdraft which may need to be renegotiated if business volumes grow, a factoring facility grows in line with the turnover.
- A factor is likely to invoice more funds against invoices than a bank manager. Bank managers may advance up to 50% of the value of invoices, but a factor will usually be willing to advance up to 80% of the value immediately with the remainder minus fees and interest when the clients settle their bills.
- For small companies, when financial controls are not highly developed, factoring may prove the answer. The factor can take over the handling of the client's sales ledger, including chasing up slow payers, providing cash against invoices and also, if needed, arranging credit insurance.

▷ ACTIVITY 2

MEMORANDUM

To: Managing Director Date:
From: Accounting Technician
Subject: Alternatives to improve credit control

Introduction

Although I have limited experience of operating any of the schemes you mention in your recent memorandum, my understanding of how each would work is as follows:

Credit insurance

Particularly useful where the size of an individual customer is such that his default would jeopardise the existence of our company.

Insurance cover will be provided by a member of the British Insurance and Investment Brokers Association (BIBA) or their sub-division, the UK Credit Insurance Brokers Committee.

There will be no effect on customer relationships as customers will be unaware that our company is insured.

Cash flow will be affected only by payment of an annual insurance premium. There will be no effect on the company's financial statements.

Factoring

Factoring is not a means of credit insurance but a means of improving the collection process at a cost. The service does not remove the need for credit control but does remove the need to operate a sales ledger and the normal debt collection process, thus reducing our costs.

We prepare invoices and receive advances against them. In the event of a bad debt, however, the factor will return the invoice to us to take further proceedings, legal or otherwise. Essentially, factoring is secured borrowing with trade debtors as security.

Companies use factoring to assist cash flow, to simplify the work done by their accounting departments and to bring instant expertise in operating collection procedures.

▷ ACTIVITY 3

Any three from:

- Well-known and respected locally
- Financially sound
- Operates a trust account with its bank that is regularly audited and will pay the client promptly
- Licensed under the Consumer Credit Act 1974.

▷ ACTIVITY 4

(a) The book debt of the company.

(b) Three of:

- Maintenance of the sales ledger
- Collection of accounts receivable
- Bad debt provision
- Finance.

▷ ACTIVITY 5

(a) Such historic reports are likely to be out of date, therefore the customer's credit status could have changed dramatically since the date of the accounts; financial ratios calculated even on recent accounts show credit problems often too late for an analyst to act on; aggregation within the group could mean important credit information is lost.

(b) Three of:

- 'Warrant of execution' whereby a court orders an enforcement officer or bailiff to seize and sell by public auction goods belonging to the debtor.
- A 'charging order' which a creditor can obtain on a debtor's property, for example, their house. If the debtor later sells the property they are assured of receiving some of the proceeds.
- An 'attachment of earnings order' which will oblige a debtor's employer to deduct a sum of money from the debtor's wages or salary.
- A 'garnishee order' enabling money owed to the debtor by a third party (the garnishee), frequently a bank or building society, to be held for the benefit of the creditor.
- An 'administrative order' whereby a debtor with multiple debts not exceeding £5,000 (at least one of which is a judgement debt that they are unable to settle immediately) would be able to discharge all obligations by making regular payments into court. These are distributed amongst creditors on a pro-rata basis.
- Petition for bankruptcy in a designated court or the High Court.

ACTIVITY 6

The procedures have two main purposes:

(a) the equitable distribution of assets

(b) a new start for the debtor.

Test your knowledge

1
- Administration of the sales ledger and credit control functions
- Finance
- Credit protection

2
- No need to incur debt collection costs
- Benefit from factor's economies of scale
- Cash flow advantages

3 The factor bears the risk of any bad debts.

4 Invoice discounting is the purchase of invoices from a customer but the invoice discounter does not take over control of the debt collection.

5
- Whole turnover
- Datum line
- Catastrophe
- Specific account

6 A court order where the business is paid by a debtor of the offending company directly.

7
- Official receiver takes control of the assets of the business
- Statement of assets and liabilities is drawn up
- Receiver summons a meeting of creditors within 12 weeks
- Creditors appoint a trustee in bankruptcy
- Assets of the business are realised and distribution is made to creditors

8
- Ascertain that the company is unable to pay its debts
- Petition for winding up
- Winding up order
- Meeting of creditors
- Statement of affairs drawn up
- Appointment of liquidator
- Administration of company's estate
- Dividend

9 A specific provision for doubtful debts is against a particular debt which is in doubt whereas a general provision is against a percentage of total debtors based upon past experience.

10 Yes - the amount of the bad debt written off will be cash flow that was expected but will not be received.

KEY TECHNIQUES QUESTION BANK

Chapter 1
Cash budgets

▷ ACTIVITY 1

The following data and estimates are available for ABC Ltd for June, July and August:

	June	July	August
	£	£	£
Sales	45,000	50,000	60,000
Wages	12,000	13,000	14,500
Overheads	8,500	9,500	9,000

The following information is available regarding direct materials:

	June	July	August	September
	£	£	£	£
Opening stock	5,000	3,500	6,000	4,000
Material usage	8,000	9,000	10,000	
Closing stock	3,500	6,000	4,000	

Notes:

(1) 10% of sales are for cash, the balance is received the following month. The amount to be received in June for May's sales is £29,500.

(2) Wages are paid in the month they are incurred.

(3) Overheads include £1,500 per month for depreciation. Overheads are settled the month following. £6,500 is to be paid in June for May's overheads.

(4) Purchases of direct materials are paid for in the month purchased.

(5) The opening cash balance in June is £11,750.

(6) A tax bill of £25,000 is to be paid in July.

Task

(a) Calculate the amount of direct material purchases in EACH of the months of June, July and August.

(b) Prepare cash budgets for June, July and August.

(c) Describe briefly the advantages of preparing cash budgets.

▷ ACTIVITY 2

From the following statements, prepare a month-by-month cash budget for the six months to 31 December.

(a) **Revenue budget (i.e. trading and profit and loss account)**

Six months to 31 December (all revenue/costs accrue evenly over the six months)

	£000	£000
Sales (cash received one month in arrears)		1,200
Cost of sales:		
Paid one month in arrear	900	
Paid in month of purchase	144	
Depreciation	72	
		1,116
Budgeted profit		84

(b) **Capital budget**

	£000	£000
Payments for new plant:		
July	12	
August	25	
September	13	
November	50	
		100
Increase in stocks, payable August		20
		120
Receipts: New issue of share capital (October)		30

(c) **Balance sheet**

	Actual 1 July £000
Assets side:	
Fixed assets	720
Stocks	100
Debtors	210
Cash	40
	1,070
Liabilities side:	
Capital and reserves	856
Taxation (payable December)	30
Creditors – trade	160
Dividends (payable August)	24
	1,070

▷ ACTIVITY 3

XYZ Ltd has the following forecast sales at list price for the nine months to 29 February 20X2:

June	£40,000	September	£48,000	December	£44,000
July	£44,000	October	£40,000	January	£42,000
August	£50,000	November	£45,000	February	£50,000

60% of the company's sales are on credit, payable in the month after sale. Cash sales attract a 5% discount off list price.

Purchases amount to 40% of selling price, and these are paid for two months after delivery.

Stock is maintained at a level equal to 50% of the following month's sales except that in November stock is to be increased by £2,000 (at cost prices) to ensure that XYZ Ltd has a safety stock during the period when its major supplier shuts down. This safety stock will be released in March.

Wages comprise a fixed sum of £2,000 per month plus a variable element equal to 10% of sales; these are payable in the month they are incurred.

Fixed costs amount to £7,500 per month, payable one month in arrears, of which £1,500 is depreciation.

XYZ Ltd has capital expenditure/receipts scheduled as follows:

	£
Acquisitions:	
September	15,000
November	10,000
February	4,000
Disposal:	
October	8,000

Corporation tax, payable in November, amounts to £44,000.

The bank balance on 1 September 20X1 is expected to be £5,000.

Task

(a) Prepare a cashflow forecast for XYZ Ltd for EACH of the six months from September 20X1 to February 20X2, using a row and column format.

(b) Explain clearly, using your answer to (a) above, how a spreadsheet may be used to assist in the preparation of cash forecasts.

Chapter 2
Forecasting and monitoring cash flows

▷ ACTIVITY 4

The managers of a company are preparing revenue plans for the last quarter of Year 4, and for the first three quarters of Year 5. The data below refer to one of the main products:

Revenue	April–June Quarter 1 £000	July–September Quarter 2 £000	October–December Quarter 3 £000	January–March Quarter 4 £000
Year 1	49	37	58	67
Year 2	50	38	59	68
Year 3	51	40	60	70
Year 4	50	42	61	–

Task

(a) Calculate the four-quarterly moving average trend for this set of data.
(b) Calculate the seasonal factors.

ACTIVITY 5

You have been given the following cash flow report, comparing actual cash flows with the cash budget for the period January to March.

	January		February		March	
	Budget	Actual	Budget	Actual	Budget	Actual
	£	£	£	£	£	£
Cash receipts						
Cash sales	6,000	4,500	6,000	5,900	8,000	7,500
Cash from debtors	29,000	28,500	30,000	28,000	32,000	29,000
Total receipts	35,000	33,000	36,000	33,900	40,000	36,500
Cash payments						
Payments for materials	15,000	15,500	18,000	18,000	20,000	19,500
Wages and salaries	8,000	8,600	9,000	8,800	10,000	9,800
Overhead expenses paid	7,000	7,200	8,000	7,900	8,000	8,000
Capital expenditure	–	1,000	2,000	2,400	–	2,000
Interest on loan	–	–	–	–	4,000	4,000
Total payments	30,000	32,300	37,000	37,100	42,000	43,300
Cash receipts less payments	5,000	700	(1,000)	(3,200)	(2,000)	(6,800)
Opening cash balance	6,000	6,000	11,000	6,700	10,000	3,500
Closing cash balance	11,000	6,700	10,000	3,500	8,000	(3,300)

Your company currently has a bank overdraft limit with its bank of £5,000.

Task

Prepare a memo for your supervisor, Ann Drew, identifying the problems that appear to have arisen with cash flows, in comparison with the budget, and suggest any suitable measures that should be taken.

Chapter 4
Raising finance

▷ ACTIVITY 6

Your business is well-established and has a good relationship with its bank. It now wishes to arrange a loan of £500,000, and you have been asked to discuss terms with the bank.

What terms might you wish to negotiate in order to try to obtain the 'best deal' possible for the loan?

▷ ACTIVITY 7

An important method of finance provided by the UK banking system is the overdraft. List THREE features of an overdraft facility.

Chapter 5
Investing surplus funds

▷ ACTIVITY 8

Task 1
Briefly describe what is meant by the term 'marketable security'.

Task 2
Give TWO examples of a marketable security used in liquidity management.

Task 3
A key feature of a bank overdraft is the uncommitted nature of the funds. When can a bank ask for such a facility to be repaid?

▷ ACTIVITY 9

An issue of 4% Treasury Stock has a current market price of 94.00. The stock has exactly three years to redemption, when it will be redeemed at par.

Tasks
1 Calculate the current interest yield on the stock.
2 Calculate an approximate redemption yield.

Chapter 6
Granting of credit

▷ ACTIVITY 10

You are in the process of arranging the granting of credit to a potential customer. As part of this process you are preparing a detailed ratio analysis based on that company's last three years' annual accounts. You prepare a similar analysis for every new customer the company does business with. Suggest THREE reasons why such an analysis may be helpful.

▷ ACTIVITY 11

In gathering credit information on a potential client, identify TWO sources of internal credit information and TWO sources of external information.

▷ ACTIVITY 12

DATA

Salon Select Limited supplies hairdressing consumables to the hairdressing business in Scotland and North East England from its base in Glasgow. Salon Select has been approached by Crocodile Cuts, which operates a chain of hairdressers, to supply goods for its five shops. Crocodile Cuts has asked for credit of £20,000 on 60 days' terms and has supplied a bank reference and two trade references. You have written to the bank and the trade referees and their responses are enclosed.

Strathclyde Bank plc

Argyle Street Branch
501 Argyle Street
Glasgow G2 7LT

Credit Controller
Salon Select Limited
1 Weaver Street
Glasgow Gl 9OP
19 May 20X5

Dear Sir or Madam,

Reference: Crocodile Cuts Limited

I refer to your letter dated 10 May 20X5 enquiring about the creditworthiness of the above. In our view, Crocodile Cuts is reasonably constituted and should prove good for your figures.

Yours faithfully

G Donarski

Gerald Donarski
Manager

Salon Select Limited
1 Weaver Street
Glasgow
G1 9OP

PRIVATE AND CONFIDENTIAL
Credit Controller
Black Fred - The Barber's Friend Limited
27 Westminster Terrace
Glasgow G3 4EF

10 May 20X5

Dear Sir or Madam

We recently received a request from Crocodile Cuts Limited, a customer of ours, who gave yourselves as a reference. I would be grateful if you could assist us by answering the following questions and returning them in the stamped addressed envelope provided.

1 How long have Crocodile Cuts been trading with you?

2 years months

2 When Crocodile Cuts opened an account with you, did the company supply you with suitable trade and credit references?

YES / (NO)

3 What are your normal credit terms for Crocodile Cuts?

Amount: £10,000

Terms: Cash Weekly (Monthly) Other (please detail below)

4 Does Crocodile Cuts make payments in accordance with your terms?

(YES) / NO / SLOWPAYER

5 Have you ever had to suspend credit facilities to Crocodile Cuts?

YES / (NO)

If YES, when?

6 Please supply any other information which you consider relevant.

Thank you for your help.

Yours faithfully

B Diamond

Bruce Diamond
Credit Controller

Salon Select Limited
1 Weaver Street
Glasgow
G1 9OP

PRIVATE AND CONFIDENTIAL
Credit Controller
John Mathieson
19 St Mary's Court
Hyndland
Glasgow G11 7UN

10 May 20X5

Dear Sir or Madam

We recently received a request from Crocodile Cuts Limited, a customer of ours, who gave yourselves as a reference. I would be grateful if you could assist us by answering the following questions and returning them in the stamped addressed envelope provided.

1 How long have Crocodile Cuts been trading with you?

3 years months

2 When Crocodile Cuts opened an account with you, did the company supply you with suitable trade and credit references?

YES / NO (circled)

3 What are your normal credit terms for Crocodile Cuts?
Amount: N/A

Terms: Cash Weekly Monthly (circled) Other (please detail below)

4 Does Crocodile Cuts make payments in accordance with your terms?

YES / NO / SLOWPAYER N/A

5 Have you ever had to suspend credit facilities to Crocodile Cuts?

YES / NO N/A
If YES, when?

6 Please supply any other information which you consider relevant.

We have been supplied by Crocodile Cuts now for 3 years and we are very happy with them.

Thank you for your help.

Yours faithfully
B Diamond
Bruce Diamond
Credit Controller

Tasks

1 Study the two references above and consider Crocodile Cuts' request. Recommend how Salon Select should proceed.

2 What other information could Salon Select seek on Crocodile Cuts and how would it use this information? Identify two other items and how they would be used.

3 Credit rating agencies provide information about businesses to enable their creditworthiness to be evaluated by a supplier. The information supplied by such agencies could be categorised as legal data, commercial data and credit data.

   Describe two items of information you might expect to find in each of these categories in a typical agency report:

   (a) legal data
   (b) commercial data
   (c) credit data.

4 As most of the information provided by Credit Reference Agencies is publicly available, why do you think companies use them?

▷ ACTIVITY 13

A new customer, Crust Limited, has asked your company for credit terms. Your company has a policy of carrying out an analysis of a customer's financial statements as a part of an internal credit checking exercise, before deciding whether to agree to granting credit.

Task

You have been given the financial statements of Crust Limited (extracts shown below) and you are required to calculate the following financial ratios for the past two years:

(a) The ratio of working capital to total assets.

(b) The no credit interval. This is the ratio of liquid assets (debtors plus short-term investments plus cash) to daily cash operating expenses. Assume a 365-day year.

(c) The ratio of retained earnings to total assets

(d) The ratio of earnings before interest and taxation to interest charges plus annual loan repayments.

Note: Earnings is a term that can be taken to mean 'profit'.

Extracts of accounts of Crust Limited

	Current year	Previous year
	£	£
Sales	3,100,000	3,350,000
Cash operating expenses	2,400,000	2,700,000
Profit before interest and taxation	105,000	53,000
Interest charges	4,000	3,000
Fixed assets	310,000	367,000
Current assets		
Stock	62,000	66,000
Debtors	75,000	86,000
Cash and short-term investments	30,000	8,000
	167,000	160,000
Current liabilities		
Bank overdraft	5,000	28,000
Trade creditors	70,000	75,000
Other creditors	2,000	12,000
	77,000	115,000
Total assets less current liabilities	400,000	412,000
Bank loans	40,000	30,000
Total assets less total liabilities	360,000	382,000
Called up share capital	100,000	100,000
Profit and loss reserves		
Brought forward	225,000	260,000
Retained for the year	35,000	22,000
	360,000	382,000

Note: Last year, bank loan repayments totalled £10,000.

Chapter 7
Managing debtors

▷ ACTIVITY 14

Stoneybridge Limited has trade debtors at the end of November 20X5 of £52,000. Average daily credit sales are £2,500. Calculate the debtor collection period in days.

▷ ACTIVITY 15

A company is concerned about the size of its debtors and its cash flows. It therefore decides to offer a 'prompt payment discount' of 1.5% for payment within 14 days. Without the discount, customers take 60 days' credit.

Task

Calculate the cost of offering the discount, as an annual interest percentage.

▷ ACTIVITY 16

Task 1

An extract from EKAT's aged debtor analysis as at 30 April 20X7 is shown on the next page, followed by a proforma aged debtor analysis for May. You should assume the date is 3 June 20X7. Use the information below on transactions which took place during May to complete the May aged debtor analysis.

Customer	**Information**
Gartcosh	Paid invoice K449 £9,000. Invoice K496 remains unpaid. Invoice K521 £5,000 issued.
Strathaven	Paid invoice K495 £7,000. Invoice K511 £6,600 issued.
Coatbridge	Paid invoice K323 £3,000. Invoice K411 remains unpaid. Invoice K502 £2,775 issued.
New Mains	Invoices K289 £8,000 and K487 £2,000 remain unpaid. Invoice K508 £4,000 issued.
Castlemilk	Paid invoice K442 £4,000. Invoice K472 £11,000 remains unpaid.
Rutherglen	Invoice K481 £1,000 remains unpaid.
Cambuslang	Invoice K204 £1,500 remains unpaid.
Easterhouse	Paid invoice K331 £10,000. Invoice K392 £13,000 remains unpaid. Invoice K510 £3,000 issued.
Airdrie	Paid half invoice K234, balance remains unpaid.
Stewartfield	Paid invoice K382 £3,000. Invoice K513 £5,000 issued.

EKAT Aged Debtors Analysis – 30 April 20X7. Credit terms: 30 days

Customer name and ref	Total amount	Invoices not yet due	Outstanding 1 month	Outstanding 2 months	Outstanding 3 months	Outstanding > 3 months	Action 1 Statement 2 1st reminder 3 2nd reminder 4 Telephone call 5 Warning letter 6 Recovery action implemented					
							1	2	3	4	5	6
Gartcosh	£14,000		£5,000 K496	£9,000 K449			03-Mar K449 03-Apr K496	03-Apr K449				
Strathaven	£7,000		£7,000 K495				03-Apr K495					
Coatbridge	£6,000			£3,000 K411	£3,000 K323		03-Feb K323 03- Mar K411	03- Mar K323 03- Apr K411				
New Mains	£10,000		£2,000 K487			£8,000 K289	03- Jan K289 03-Apr K487	03- Feb K289	03-Mar K289	03-Apr K289		
Castlemilk	£15,000		£11,000 K472	£4,000 K442			03-Mar K442 03-Apr K472	03-Apr K442				
Rutherglen	£1,000		£1,000 K481				03-Apr K481					
Cambuslang	£1,500					£1,500 K204	03-Dec K204	03-Jan K204	03-Feb K204	03-Mar K204	03-Apr K204	
Easterhouse	£23,000		£13,000 K392	£10,000 K331			03-Feb K331 03-Apr K392	03-Mar K331				
Airdrie	£5,500				£5,500 K234		03-Feb K234	03-Mar K234	03-Apr K234			
Stewartfield	£3,000			£3,000 K382			03-Mar K382	03-Apr K382				
TOTALS	£86,000		£39,000	£29,000	£8,500	£9,500						

EKAT Aged Debtors Analysis – 31 May 20X7. Credit terms: 30 days

Customer name and ref	Total amount	Invoices not yet due	Outstanding 1 month	Outstanding 2 months	Outstanding 3 months	Outstanding > 3 months	Action 1 Statement 2 1st reminder 3 2nd reminder 4 Telephone call 5 Warning letter 6 Recovery action implemented					
							1	2	3	4	5	6
Gartcosh												
Strathaven												
Coatbridge												
New Mains												
Castlemilk												
Rutherglen												
Cambuslang												
Easterhouse												
Airdrie												
Stewartfield												
TOTALS												

Task 2

For each customer, outline briefly how that account should be managed.

- Gartcosh a medium-sized, regular customer
- Coatbridge a large, major customer
- New Mains a medium-sized, regular customer
- Cambuslang a small and irregular customer
- Airdrie a large and irregular customer

Task 3

EKAT grants credit terms of 60 days net to its major customers, but offers an early settlement discount of 2.5% for payment within seven days.
What is the cost of this discount?

Task 4

Why might EKAT choose to offer its major customers such a generous discount? Identify two reasons.

Chapter 8
Collection of debts

▷ ACTIVITY 17

Collection agencies exist to assist companies with collecting debts. Typically a commercial agency will charge a proportion of the debt collected, with no charge if no collection is made.

When approaching a credit collection agency, what points would you look for from such an agency? List THREE items.

▷ ACTIVITY 18

The outstanding balances on a company's sales ledger total £125,000, representing three months' sales. A factor will operate the ledger on a non-recourse basis, for an annual charge of 2% of turnover. There is a danger of loss of business if it is generally known that the firm is using a factor: annual sales could fall by £30,000 and annual cash profits are 50% of sales. Using the factor would generate annual administration savings of £20,000. Bad debts currently run at 3% of turnover.

Task

Assess whether it is financially worth using the factor. For the purpose of this activity, you should ignore interest costs.

▷ ACTIVITY 19

A company has monthly credit sales of £200,000, and it gives customers 60 days' credit. All customers take the full credit allowed. It has bad debts each year amounting to about 2.5% of sales turnover. It operates with a bank overdraft and pays interest at 8% on its overdraft balance.

The company's management is considering whether to use a factor to collect its debts, under a non-recourse factoring arrangement. A factor has indicated that it will take over the administration of the sales ledger and debt collection for a fee of 2% of annual credit sales turnover. This would save the company internal operating costs of £30,000 each year.

The factor would also charge 1.5% of turnover for credit insurance.
The factor will advance 80% of the value of invoices as soon as they are sent out, and charge interest at 7.75%.

If the services of the factor are used, it is anticipated that there will be no change in annual sales turnover and no change in the collection period of 60 days.

Task

Assess the financial consequences of using the factor for non-recourse factoring and factor finance.

PRACTICE SIMULATION QUESTIONS

Data and tasks

Instructions

This simulation is designed to test your ability to operate a cash management and credit control system.

The situation is set out overleaf.

The tasks for you to perform are detailed on the pages that follow.

Please write your answers in the Answer Book provided where indicated to do so.

You are allowed four hours to complete your work.

A high level of accuracy is required. Check your work carefully before handing it in.

Correcting fluid may be used but it should be used in moderation. Any errors should be crossed out neatly and clearly. The use of pencils for your written answers is not acceptable.

You should read the whole simulation before commencing work so as to gain an overall picture of what is required.

The situation

Your name is Jaymini Patel and you work as an accounts clerk for Blether Telecom. The company is an independent telephone brokerage for fixed telephones. It claims to offer customers savings of up to 30% of national and international calls. The system works by re-programming a customer's switchboard, enabling Blether Telecom to switch between the different telecommunications carriers according to which operator is offering the best deal that month.

Personnel involved in the scenario

Accounts Clerk:	Yourself, Jaymini Patel
Cash Manager:	Douglas Gulland
Credit Controller:	Millie Will
Financial Controller:	Firdu Gomal

Tasks to be performed

Control cash receipts and payments

1. Refer to the budget data sheet in the data that follows. The date is 1 December 20X7. You are required to use this information to produce a cash forecast for Blether Telecom for the period to 31 March 20X8. The cash forecast should clearly show the opening and closing cash position for each month, as well as the net cash flow for the period. It might help you to complete a table of estimated call volumes before calculating revenues and costs. Proformas for both the forecast and the table are provided in the Answer Book.
2. Analyse the cash flow forecast prepared in Task 1. Briefly describe how the forecast cash position should be managed. Also identify three legitimate measures that Blether Telecom can take to improve the cash position, giving a reason for each.
3. What other cash flow items have been possibly excluded from this cash flow forecast? Identify four items and, for each one, an appropriate individual in the organisation (not necessarily named in the scenario) who could provide this information.

Manage cash balances

4. Consider the cash flow forecast produced in Task 1. Identify the control action required (if any), and the timing of that action, in respect of this forecast. Write your answer in the form of an email note to Douglas Gulland.
5. It is likely that within 18 months, Blether Telecom will be forecasting a cash surplus. As a growing organisation, Blether Telecom has already negotiated short-term borrowing facilities but has little experience of investing cash. Douglas Gulland has asked you to prepare a presentation for the benefit of the senior management group. The presentation should include the following:
   - introduction: why a policy for managing investments is required
   - the main criteria to be considered when investing cash
   - the main types of cash investments available, and a brief description of each
   - the main types of marketable securities suitable for short-term investment
   - summary: an outline policy for Blether Telecom.

   Your presentation should be prepared in note form, outlining the relevant details for each of the points. You should prepare notes for a presentation to last no more than ten minutes.

Grant credit

6 A new customer, MetalBash plc, wishes to contract with Blether Telecom to provide its telephone services. It wishes to do this on 60 days' credit. Blether Telecom's credit policy requires a satisfactory credit analysis based on the potential customer's trading record. An extract from MetalBash's accounts for the four years to 31.03.X7 is reproduced on page 241. Using these accounts calculate the following ratios for the three years to 31.03.X7:

- working capital : total assets
- no credit interval (debtors plus cash and short-term investments : daily operating expenses, excluding depreciation)
- retained earnings : total assets
- earnings before interest and taxation : interest charges plus annual repayment of loans.

Insert the ratios in the table in the Answer Book.

7 Write a brief memo to Millie Will to identify:

- the meaning and purpose of the ratios
- the trends in these four ratios for the three years to 31 March 20X7
- Whether Blether Telecom should grant credit and/or trade with MetalBash.

Write your memo on the memo form in the Answer Book.

8 After completing your credit review, and discussing the position with Millie Will, MetalBash have telephoned you to establish whether you will be granting them credit. How will you respond?

Collection of debts

9 An extract from Blether Telecom's aged analysis of debtors as at 31 October 20X7 is shown on page 242. Update the analysis as at 30 November 20X7, including the transactions shown on page 242. Use the proforma analysis in the Answer Book.

Each of the five customers is profiled briefly on page 242. For each of the five debtors, outline an appropriate action to manage the account.

10 John Chancer, a sole trader, has traded with Blether Telecom for four months but has not paid for any of the calls made. Total debts stand at £861.00. Millie Will has suggested that Blether Telecom have Chancer declared bankrupt, but is not sure how effective this action might be. You are scheduled to meet Millie later that week. Write notes for her attention covering the following points:

- the conditions necessary for a petition for bankruptcy to succeed
- the consequences of a petition and a bankruptcy order
- the order in which Chancer's debts will be paid
- whether Blether Telecom should write this off as a bad debt.

BLETHER TELECOM
BUDGET DATA SHEET

Revenue:

National call (peak)	£0.048 per minute
National call (off peak)	£0.021 per minute
International call (peak)	£0.105 per minute (average rate)
International call (off peak)	£0.078 per minute (average rate)

Call volume (previous three months):

Type of call	Sep 20X7 (minutes)	Oct 20X7 (minutes)	Nov 20X7 (minutes)
National call (peak)	1,195,687	1,203,360	1,231,049
National call (off-peak)	30,651	30,914	31,982
International call (peak)	295,999	296,771	319,754
International call (off-peak)	14,478	14,637	15,980
Total	1,536,815	1,545,682	1,598,765

Projected call mix in the period to March 20X8 (based on average over previous 12 months):

Type of call	Percentage share of call volume
National call (peak)	78%
National call (off-peak)	2%
International call (peak)	19%
International call (off-peak)	1%
Total	100%

Note: assume call mix will be as above to March 20X8.

Projected growth rates (straight-line) in call volumes over the next four months:

Month	Dec	Jan	Feb	Mar
Cumulative Growth rate (%)	2	5	9	11

(i.e. all based on November volume)

Assume the mix of call volumes is unchanged.

Direct costs:

Type of call	Cost to Blether Telecom per minute
National call (peak)	0.031
National call (off-peak)	0.014
International call (peak)	0.067
International call (off-peak)	0.050

Overheads

- Staff costs, £13,350 per month, with a rise of 3.5 per cent in March.
- Marketing costs, £5,000 per month. In addition a targeted advertising campaign will be undertaken in the next six months, with costs of £22,000 paid in March.
- Other overheads of £9,000 per month are incurred. This includes depreciation of £3,000 per month and a provision for doubtful debts of £200 per month.
- Premises costs are paid for by direct debit each month and average £9,350 per month.

Other payments

- A tax bill of £8,500 is payable in December.
- Dividend payment of £8,000 is to be paid in March.
- Interest is payable on a loan of £275,000 at a rate of 9% per annum, with one year's interest paid in February.

Working capital management

- Customers are billed monthly, with payment being made (on average) 60 days in arrears.
- Blether Telecom pays the operating companies supplying the communications monthly, 30 days in arrears.
- The cash balance at bank on 31 October 20X7 was £51,784.

MetalBash plc

Extract from report and accounts for four years ending 31 March 20X4, 20X5, 20X6 and 20X7

Extract Profit and loss account

	20X4	20X5	20X6	20X7
	£000	£000	£000	£000
Turnover	5,981,000	6,041,000	6,343,000	6,660,000
Operating expenses (excluding depreciation)	28,700	31,511	33,010	37,384
Earnings before interest and taxation	415,000	284,000	285,500	205,500
Interest charges	76,500	63,472	59,775	79,240

Balance sheet

	£000	£000	£000	£000
Fixed assets				
Intangible	140,000	160,000	200,000	246,000
Tangible	1,980,000	2,060,000	2,072,000	2,359,000
Investments			20,000	20,000
	2,120,000	2,220,000	2,292,000	2,625,000
Current assets				
Stocks	802,000	864,000	908,000	958,000
Debtors	2,541,000	2,658,000	3,170,000	3,549,000
Cash and short-term investments	90,000	80,000	40,000	10,000
	3,433,000	3,602,000	4,118,000	4,517,000
Current liabilities				
Trade creditors	1,350,000	1,428,000	1,534,000	1,913,000
Bank overdraft	25,000	49,400	549,000	1,008,000
Other			300,000	305,000
	1,375,000	1,477,400	2,383,000	3,226,000
Total assets less current liabilities	4,178,000	4,344,600	4,027,000	3,916,000
Less: loans repayable after more than one year	850,000	744,000	248,000	124,000
Other liabilities	5,000	266,400	319,900	264,400
Net assets	3,323,000	3,334,200	3,459,100	3,527,600
Called up share capital	600,000	600,000	600,000	600,000
Profit and loss account				
Brought forward	2,713,000	2,723,000	2,734,200	2,859,100
Retained for year	10,000	11,200	124,900	68,500
	3,323,000	3,334,200	3,459,100	3,527,600

Customer name and ref	Total amount	Invoices not yet due	Outstanding 1 month	Outstanding 2 months	Outstanding 3 months	Outstanding > 3 months	Action 1 Statement 2 1st reminder 3 2nd reminder 4 Telephone call 5 Warning letter 6 Recovery action implemented					
							1	2	3	4	5	6
MURRAY (C003)	12,000	5,000 (Q796)	7,000 (Q749)				3/10 (Q749)					
Calderwood (C102)	6,000		3,000 (Q511)	3,000 (Q423)			3/9 (Q423)	3/10 (Q423)				
Greenhills (C083)	10,000	2,000 (Q487)			8,000 (Q289)		3/8 (Q289)	3/9 (Q289)	3/10 (Q289)			
Westwood (C098)	1,500					1,500 (Q204)	3/5 (Q204)	3/6 (Q204)	3/7 (Q204)	3/8 (Q204)	3/9 (Q204)	3/10 (Q204)
HAIRMYRES (C034)	5,500				5,500 (Q334)		3/6 (Q334)	3/7 (Q334)	3/8 (Q334)	3/9 (Q334)	3/10 (Q334)	
TOTALS	35,000	7,000	10,000	3,000	13,500	1,500						

Blether Telecom
Extract of Transactions with Debtors in November 20X7

Customer	**Transaction**
Murray	Paid invoice Q749 £7,000. Invoice Q796 remains unpaid. Invoice Q721 £5,000 issued.
Calderwood	Paid invoice Q511 £3,000. Invoice Q423 remains unpaid. Invoice Q611 £6,600 issued.
Greenhills	Paid invoice Q487 £2,000. Invoice Q289 remains unpaid. Invoice Q602 £2,775 issued.
Westwood	Invoice Q204 £1,500 remains unpaid. Invoice Q608 issued £4,000.
Hairmyres	Invoice Q334 £2,750 paid.

Customer profile

Customer	**Profile**
Murray	Medium sized engineering company. Regular customer of 3 years standing. Record of being a good payer.
Calderwood	Independent hotel, 74 employees. Regular customer of 12 months.
Greenhills	Large business services subsidiary, Regular customer, but often purchasing from other suppliers.
Westwood	Small retail organisation. Occasional customer of 12 months.
Hairmyres	Medium sized textile group. Once a regular customer. No use of Blether Telecom's facilities for 4 months.

PRACTICE SIMULATION ANSWER BOOKLET

Task 1

	Actual Nov	Forecast Dec	Forecast Jan	Forecast Feb	Forecast Mar
Revenue					
National (peak)					
National (off-peak)					
International (peak)					
International (off-peak)					
Subtotal					
Direct cost					
National (peak)					
National (off-peak)					
International (peak)					
International (off-peak)					
Subtotal					
Overheads					
Marketing					
Staff costs					
Other overheads					
Premises					
Taxation					
Dividends					
Interest					
Subtotal					

Net cash flow					

Opening cash flow					
Net cash flow					
Closing cash flow					

Note	Actual	Forecast	Forecast	Forecast	Forecast
	Nov	Dec	Jan	Feb	Mar
Call volumes (mins)					
TOTAL CALLS					
National (peak)					
National (off-peak)					
International (peak)					
International (off-peak)					

Task 6

Relevant data

	20X5 £ million	20X6 £ million	20X7 £ million
Working capital (net current assets)			
Total assets (fixed and current)			
Debtors, cash and short-term investments			
Daily operating expenses			
Retained earnings (brought forward plus current year)			
Earnings before interest and taxation			
Interest charges plus annual repayment of loans (excluding bank overdraft)			

Ratios expressed in percentages

	20X5 %	20X6 %	20X7 %
Working capital: total assets			
Retained earnings: total assets			
EBIT: interest charges, plus annual loan repayments			
No credit internal (days)			

Task 7

MEMORANDUM

To:	Millie Will	Date:
From:	Jaymini Patel	
Subject:	MetalBash plc	

Task 9

Blether Telecom Aged Debtors Analysis – November 20X7. Credit Terms: 30 days

Customer name and ref	Total amount	Invoices not yet due	Outstanding 1 month	Outstanding 2 months	Outstanding 3 months	Outstanding > 3 months	Action 1 Statement 2 1st reminder 3 2nd reminder 4 Telephone call 5 Warning letter 6 Recovery action implemented					
							1	2	3	4	5	6
MURRAY (C003)												
Calderwood (C102)												
Greenhills (C083)												
Westwood (C098)												
HAIRMYRES (C034)												
TOTALS												

MOCK SIMULATION 1 QUESTIONS

Data and tasks

Instructions

This simulation is designed to test your ability to operate a cash management and credit control system.

The situation is set out on the following pages.

The tasks for you to perform are detailed on the following pages.

You are allowed fours hours to complete your work.

A high level of accuracy is required. Check your work carefully before handing it in.

Correcting fluid may be used but it should be used in moderation. Any errors should be crossed out neatly and clearly. The use of pencils for your written answers is not acceptable.

You should read the whole simulation before commencing work so as to gain an overall picture of what is required.

The situation

Your name is Henry Naem and you are an accounting technician working as an assistant to the Financial Controller, John Powell, at Fastinfo Ltd. Today's date is the 17 January.

Organisation

Fastinfo Ltd is a company which makes computer components to sell to manufacturers of high technology equipment. It is an established company which plans to develop by setting up a new division to produce a component which it has been developing over the past two years.

Fastinfo Ltd has a 31 December year end.

Personnel

Assistant Accountant	Yourself, Henry Naem
Financial Controller	John Powell
Factory Manager	Mark Bennett
Sales Director	Victoria Bartlett
Credit Control Manager	Brian Herbert

Tasks to be performed

1 Refer to the memo from John Powell (point 1) on page 251, the forecast and actual cash flows for Fastinfo for the final three months of last year on pages 252 and 253, the memo from Mark Bennett on page 254 and the memo from Victoria Bartlett on page 255.

You are required to:

- compare the cash flow forecast and actual cash flow for the final three months of last year in a memo to John Powell, listing any significant differences and suggesting corrective action;
- prepare a cash flow forecast for the first three months of next year for the new division;
- show the effect on the final bank balance of debtors being given an extra month's credit;
- in a note to John Powell comment on the cash surplus or deficit, suggesting three legitimate ways in which it may be improved and also two sources of uncertainty in the forecast.

You should write your answer in the answer booklet where a cash flow format and relevant pages have been reproduced.

2 Refer to the memo from John Powell (point 2) on page 251, the extract from the procedures manual on page 255, the references on pages 256 and 257 and the financial statements extracts for Whittle Ltd on page 258.

- In a memo to John Powell, make a recommendation whether Whittle Ltd should have credit terms extended to it by Fastinfo based on the reference information and ratio analysis of Whittle Ltd.

Your ratio analysis should include the following ratios:

current ratio	(current assets : current liabilities)
acid test ratio	(current assets less stock : current liabilities)
debt ratio	(total short and long term creditors : net fixed assets plus current assets)

You should write your answers in the answer booklet.

3 Refer to the memo from John Powell (point 3) on page 251.

- Using the answer booklet write notes to the new placement student defining a cheque and explaining the difference between a 'stale cheque', a 'post-dated' cheque and a 'crossed' cheque. You should also compare the differences between overdrafts and bank loans.

4 Refer to John Powell's memo on page 251 (point 4), an extract from the aged debtors analysis for November on page 259, an extract from the list of transactions for December on page 260 and the memo from Victoria Bartlett on page 260.

- Using the proforma in the answer booklet, update the extract from the aged debtors analysis listed on page 259 of this booklet.
- List appropriate actions for follow up in a memo to Brian Herbert, together with any recommendations about the writing off of current outstanding debts, using the answer booklet.
- Draft a first reminder letter (one month overdue) using the answer booklet.
- Draft a second reminder letter (more than one month overdue) using the answer booklet.
- Write a memo to Victoria Bartlett explaining the difference between 'with recourse' and 'without recourse' in relation to factoring debts using the answer booklet.

FASTINFO LTD
MEMO

To: Henry Naem
From: John Powell
Date: 14 January
Subject: Work for this week

Henry

I have been unexpectedly called up to Scotland for the week to look at a possible new supplier. As you know there is a lot of urgent work on and I need you to prepare the following for me.

1 I have left a copy of the cash flow forecast and actual cash flow for the final three months of last year on my desk. Please compare the two and write me a memo listing any major differences and suggested corrective action.
There is a strategy meeting with the Managing Director next week and I need to have some cash flow information about the possible new division. I have left cash flow predictions for the first three months of next year from Mark and Victoria on my desk. I am particularly interested in finding out the impact on the bank balance if debtors were given an extra month's credit.
Our overdraft limit is likely to be £60,000 and it is, as you know, company policy to have funding planned before any new ventures are undertaken. When you have calculated the forecast balance, please suggest how the deficit/surplus may best be dealt with and include three suggestions for improving cash flow.
There are always uncertainties in the forecasting; please list two for further consideration.

2 We need to assess the creditworthiness of Whittle Ltd. They have placed a large order and any problems paying would have an impact on our cash flow. I have left two references on your desk (I have not had time to read them) and have obtained extracts from the accounts of Whittle Ltd for the past two years. I need you to go through this information and recommend whether or not we should extend credit to them.

3 A placement student will be starting with us next week and I want to give her the cheques to deal with. Please write out a note explaining what a cheque is and the difference between the various sorts of cheques. Also write a brief explanation of the differences between overdrafts and bank loans.

4 Please update the aged debtors analysis for last month and write a memo to Brian Herbert listing any appropriate actions. We need some standard reminder letters written too. Please prepare drafts for these. Victoria has sent a memo asking for an explanation of factoring. Please also reply to this on my behalf.

CASH FLOW FORECAST FOR THE LAST THREE MONTHS OF LAST YEAR, WHOLE COMPANY

	October £000	November £000	December £000
CASH RECEIVED			
Sales:			
cash	1,300	1,400	1,420
credit	1,200	1,200	1,300
Sale of assets	2	11	5
TOTAL (A)	2,502	2,611	2,725
CASH PAID			
Purchase of:			
land	1,000	–	–
machinery	200	75	75
vehicles	300	200	200
Rent	250	250	250
Wages	30	31	32
Purchases	1,500	1,600	1,800
Selling/administration	25	27	28
TOTAL (B)	3,305	2,183	2,385
B/F cash balance	20	–783	–355
Net cash flow (A-B)	–803	428	340
C/F cash balance	–783	–355	–15

ACTUAL CASH FLOW FOR THE LAST THREE MONTHS OF LAST YEAR, WHOLE COMPANY

	October	November	December
	£000	£000	£000
CASH RECEIVED			
Sales:			
cash	1,200	1,100	1,100
credit	1,100	1,150	1,200
Sale of machine	1	20	10
TOTAL (A)	2,301	2,270	2,310
CASH PAID			
Purchase of:			
land	1,000	–	–
machinery	300	75	75
vehicles	320	210	240
Rent	250	250	250
Wages	38	35	37
Purchases	1,600	1,600	1,800
Selling/administration	28	29	29
TOTAL (B)	3,536	2,199	2,431
B/F cash balance	20	–1,215	–1,144
Net cash flow (A-B)	–1,235	71	–121
C/F cash balance	–1,215	–1,144	–1,265

FASTINFO LTD
MEMO

To: John Powell
From: Mark Bennett
Date: 12 January
Subject: New Division

Further to our conversation I have put together the forecast cash expenditure for the new division next year:

- new equipment will cost a total of £200,000. We need to buy it in January and put down a deposit of £50,000 on 1 January. I have negotiated instalments for the remainder; three equal instalments payable on 1 February, 1 May and 1 September next year. We can get a grant for part of the cost (10%) and this will be received on 1 January also;
- rent for premises will amount to £5,000 per quarter payable in advance, with the first payment being 1 January;
- wages will be £6,000 per month, payable on the last day of the month worked;
- purchases will amount to £10,000 in each of the first two months, then £12,000 in the next two months, increasing by £2,000 every two months for the rest of the year. Purchases will be paid for two months after they have been received.

I look forward to seeing the cash flow forecast and discussing it further.

With regards.

Mark

FASTINFO LTD
MEMO

To: John Powell
From: Victoria Bartlett
Date: 13 January
Subject: Future sales from new division

I have put together some forecast sales for the first three months of next year for the new division. I have been quite conservative so these figures should be achieved with relative ease.

	January	February	March
	£	£	£
Cash sales	12,000	12,500	13,000
Credit sales	12,000	12,500	13,000
Total	24,000	25,000	26,000

Credit sales will be payable by the end of the month after the sale was made. Selling and administration costs will amount to 10% of the sales made in the month and they are payable in cash as incurred.

With regards.

Victoria

FASTINFO LTD
Extract from procedures manual

Extending credit to new customers

The supply of goods/services on credit necessarily involves risk. To minimise that risk the following steps should be taken before extending credit to a new customer:

1 Two references from independent referees should be obtained. Any problems raised by the references should be followed up and further references should be taken if appropriate.

2 The latest set of accounts of a company should be obtained and ratio analysis undertaken. Any problems raised by the analysis should be followed up.

3 Assuming points 1 and 2 are satisfactory, a credit limit should be set by the Credit Control Manager. This should initially be a very conservative limit which is closely monitored. The limit may be reviewed after six months.

FASTINFO LTD
11 Beal Street
Wallington
WL1 9PO
Tel: 0331 8676767

5 January

PRIVATE AND CONFIDENTIAL

Credit Manager
Weston Ltd
Weston Court
Wallington
WL5 8PP

Dear Sir or Madam

We have recently received a request from a customer of ours, Whittle Ltd, giving yourselves as a reference. We would be grateful if you would answer the following questions and return them in the enclosed stamped addressed envelope.

1 For how long has Whittle Ltd been trading with you?

5 years

2 Did you take up references for Whittle Ltd when you began trading with them?

Yes

3 How long a credit period do you normally extend to Whittle Ltd?

Two months

4 Does Whittle Ltd make payments in accordance with credit terms?

Usually

5 Have you ever suspended credit being extended to Whittle Ltd?

Yes

If YES please give date and period of suspension.

Once two years ago for 6 months

6 Please supply any other information which you consider relevant.

Thank you for your help.
Yours faithfully

Brian Herbert

Credit Control Manager

FASTINFO LTD
11 Beal Street
Wallington
WL1 9PO
Tel: 0331 8676767

5 January

PRIVATE AND CONFIDENTIAL

Credit Manager
Greatlygrow Ltd
Long Street
Wallington
WL9 9ZW

Dear Sir or Madam

We have recently received a request from a customer of ours, Whittle Ltd, giving yourselves as a reference. We would be grateful if you would answer the following questions and return them in the enclosed stamped addressed envelope.

1 For how long has Whittle Ltd been trading with you?

1 year

2 Did you take up references for Whittle Ltd when you began trading with them?

2 references

3 How long a credit period do you normally extend to Whittle Ltd?

6 weeks

4 Does Whittle Ltd make payments in accordance with credit terms?

Yes

5 Have you ever suspended credit being extended to Whittle Ltd?

No

If YES please give date and period of suspension.

6 Please supply any other information which you consider relevant.

Thank you for your help.
Yours faithfully

Brian Herbert

Credit Control Manager

EXTRACT FROM THE ACCOUNTS OF WHITTLE LTD: BALANCE SHEET

	This year £000	Last year £000
FIXED ASSETS		
Intangible fixed assets	200	180
Tangible fixed assets	790	670
Investments	900	600
	1,890	1,450
CURRENT ASSETS		
Stocks	200	170
Debtors	800	750
Cash	90	105
	1,090	1,025
CURRENT LIABILITIES		
Trade creditors	900	890
Other	70	68
	970	958
TOTAL ASSETS LESS CURRENT LIABILITIES	2,010	1,517
Less		
Long-term liabilities	500	400
	1,510	1,117
Financed by:		
Called up share capital	1,000	1,000
Profit and loss:		
b/f	117	7
retained	393	110
c/f	510	117
	1,510	1,117
PROFIT AND LOSS ACCOUNT		
Profit after interest and taxation	500	190

EXTRACT FROM AGED DEBTORS ANALYSIS 30 NOVEMBER

Name	Code	Total Owing	<1 month	1–2 months	2–3 months	>3 months
		£	£	£	£	£
Smythe & Co	c0100	6,000	5,000 (inv 8910)	1,000 (inv 3310)		
Happle Ltd	c1190	4,500				4,500 (inv 7914)
Thomas & Sons	c2820	5,000	1,000 (inv 9000)	2,000 (inv 2851)	2,000 (inv 7999)	
Paperclips & Bits	c0991	2,000	200 (inv 2998)	800 (inv 2813)	1,000 (inv 2710)	
TOTAL		17,500	6,200	3,800	3,000	4,500
Percentage		100%	35%	22%	17%	26%

CUSTOMER PROFILES

Smythe & Co

Large manufacturer, established customer for three years, record of being a good payer.

Happle Ltd

Medium sized manufacturer. A regular customer for five years with a history of being a good payer until six months ago. Since then payments have been erratic and there are rumours of liquidity problems. There are no pricing or delivery queries. This debt has been outstanding for five months now.

Thomas & Sons

Large established customer of six years. A regular payer generally one month late.

Paperclips & Bits

Small business, customer for one year, good payer.

COMPANY POLICY ON OUTSTANDING DEBTS

1 When a debt is one month overdue send a first reminder letter.
2 When a debt is two months overdue send a second reminder letter which states that collection will be put into the hands of a third party if payment is not forthcoming.
3 When a debt is three months overdue arrange a meeting with the customer to make a payment agreement. Where no agreement is forthcoming pursue legal action.
4 When a debt is six months overdue make a provision for it in the accounts.
5 If legal action fails write the debt off.

EXTRACT FROM LIST OF TRANSACTIONS FOR DECEMBER

Smythe & Co	Paid invoice 3310. Invoice 8910 remains unpaid. Invoice 1010 £4,000 issued.
Happle Ltd	Invoice 7914 remains unpaid.
Thomas & Sons	Paid invoice 7999. Invoices 2851 and 9000 remain unpaid.
Paperclips & Bits	Paid invoices 2710 and 2813. Invoice 2998 remains unpaid. Invoice 1091 £1,000 issued.

FASTINFO LTD
MEMO

To: John Powell
From: Victoria Bartlett
Date: 13 January
Subject: Factoring debts with and without recourse

John

Further to our recent meeting, I understand the need to improve cash flow but I am a bit hazy on the difference between factoring debts 'with recourse' and 'without recourse'. Could you explain this please.

Regards

Victoria

MOCK SIMULATION 1 ANSWER BOOKLET

Task 1

FASTINFO LTD
MEMO

To:
From:
Date:
Subject:

....

....

....

....

....

....

....

....

....

....

....

....

....

....

....

....

....

....

....

Task 1, continued

CASH FLOW FORMAT
CASH FLOW FORECAST FOR THE FIRST THREE MONTHS OF NEXT YEAR, NEW DIVISION

	January £	February £	March £
CASH RECEIVED Sales: cash			
Sales: credit			
Grant			
Total (A)			
CASH PAID Equipment: deposit			
Equipment: instalment			
Rent			
Wages			
Purchases			
Selling/administration			
Total (B)			
B/F cash balance			
Net cash flow (A–B)			
C/F cash balance			

Task 1, continued

IMPACT ON BANK BALANCE IF DEBTORS PAY ONE MONTH LATER

Task 1, continued

NOTE TO: John Powell
FROM: Henry Naem

Comment on cash surplus or deficit

....

....

....

....

....

....

Legitimate measures Fastinfo can take to improve cash position

....

....

....

....

....

....

....

Sources of uncertainty in cash flow forecast

....

....

....

....

....

....

....

Task 2

FASTINFO LTD
MEMO

To:
From:
Date:
Subject:

Task 3

NOTES FOR PLACEMENT STUDENT

- cheque

....

....

....

- stale cheque

....

....

....

- post-dated cheque

....

....

....

- crossed cheque

....

....

....

- overdraft

....

....

....

- bank loan

....

....

....

Task 4

UPDATED EXTRACT FROM AGED DEBTORS ANALYSIS 31 DECEMBER

Name	Code	Total owing	<1 month	1-2 months	2-3 months	>3 months
		£	£	£	£	£
Smythe & Co	c0100					
Happle Ltd	c1190					
Thomas & Sons	c2820					
Paperclips & Bits	c0991					
TOTAL						
Percentage						

Task 4, continued

FASTINFO LTD
MEMO

To:
From:
Date:
Subject:

....

....

....

....

....

....

....

....

....

....

....

....

....

....

....

....

....

....

....

Task 4, continued

FASTINFO LTD
11 Beal Street
Wallington
WL1 9PO
Tel: 0331 8676767

FASTINFO LTD
11 Beal Street
Wallington
WL1 9PO
Tel: 0331 8676767

Task 4, continued

FASTINFO LTD
MEMO

To:
From:
Date:
Subject:

....

....

....

....

....

....

....

....

....

....

....

....

....

....

....

....

....

....

....

ROUGH WORK

MOCK SIMULATION 2 QUESTIONS

Data and tasks

Instructions

This simulation is designed to test your ability to operate a cash management and credit control system.

The situation is set out on the following pages.

The tasks for you to perform are detailed on the following pages.

You are allowed fours hours to complete your work.

A high level of accuracy is required. Check your work carefully before handing it in.

Correcting fluid may be used but it should be used in moderation. Any errors should be crossed out neatly and clearly. The use of pencils for your written answers is not acceptable.

You should read the whole simulation before commencing work so as to gain an overall picture of what is required.

The situation

Your name is Pat King and you work as an accounting technician at Sleepy Ltd, a company which manufactures and sells timber bed frames to the UK retail trade. The company was established ten years ago and it has consistently increased its turnover and profitability over that period.

Despite the fact that the industry remains very competitive, the company has a stated aim to continue to grow its position in the UK bed market both organically and by acquisition when suitable opportunities arise. As a consequence the company is planning a major expansion of its production facilities in its next financial year. In addition, the company plans to commence the sale of bed frames direct to the public from its factory shop.

Personnel

Accounting Technician	Yourself, Pat King
Financial Controller	Steve Wilks
Production Director	John Lewis
Sales Director	Sue Smith

Tasks to be performed

1 The latest balance sheet of Sleepy Ltd is set out on page 281. Refer to this and to the information provided in the memo from John Lewis on page 282, the memo from Sue Smith on page 282 and the memo from Steve Wilks on page 283.

- Steve Wilks asks you to prepare a cash flow forecast for each of the four months ending 30 April 2005 based on the information provided and using the proforma in the answer booklet. You should use the rough work space provided in the answer booklet to set out your workings for the quantities of wood to be purchased, the number of beds to be produced and the receipts from customers for each of the four months;
- Steve Wilks asks you to calculate the impact on the forecast closing cash balance at 30 April 2005 if the sales price for a bed is only £95 in January, February and March. Use the answer booklet.

2 Steve Wilks asks you to identify those receipts and payments which require careful control and to suggest what action should be taken if receipts fall behind budget. Write a memo to Steve Wilks using the answer booklet.

3 On 31 December 2004 the company placed cash of £150,000 on a four month deposit account earning interest at the rate of 6% per annum. An extract from the Financial Times gilt prices shows that Treasury Stock 9.75% 2008 may be purchased at a price of £112.50. The flat yield is 8.66% and the redemption yield is 6.2%. Steve Wilks asks you to prepare notes to brief the Directors on what is meant by 'gilt-edged securities' and the advantages and disadvantages of investing, at the price shown, in Treasury Stock 9.75 % 2008 as compared with those of the deposit account. Use the answer booklet.

4 The Board of Sleepy Ltd has approved an investment of £1 million for new cutting machinery which is planned to be made in July. Explain in a memo to the Board:

- the advantages and disadvantages of funding the purchase with either a bank overdraft or a bank loan;
- which would be the preferred method of financing.

Use the answer booklet.

5 The company plans to make cash sales from a factory shop with effect from April 2005. No procedures have yet been drafted for the control of cash resulting from these sales. Sue Smith has asked you to set out a draft note of the procedures to be followed for the handling of cash from these sales. You should set this out in the answer booklet.

6 A copy of the request for credit facilities from the Finance Director of Dreams Ltd, a retailer of furniture, is set out on page 284. The company has also supplied its profit and loss account for the year ended 30 June 2004 (page 287). In addition, in accordance with the credit policy of Sleepy Ltd, two trade references have been obtained from Carpets Ltd and Wardrobes Ltd and these are set out on pages 285 and 286. Steve Wilks has asked you to:

- prepare a memo setting out any concerns you have in connection with the request. You should include an analysis of the profit and loss account of Dreams Ltd and refer to the trade references. Use the answer booklet;
- draft a letter, on his behalf, to Mr D Jones in reply to the original request for credit facilities. You should use the answer booklet for this task.

7 The policy for collection of debts is set out on page 287. Extracts from the cash book and sales day book for January are found on page 288 together with an extract from the aged debtors listing at 31 December 2004. Steve Wilks has asked you to:

- update the aged debtors list for the selected accounts at 31 January 2005 stating for each account what credit control action is required. Use the answer booklet;
- draft a note of the matters to be discussed by telephone with Owen Ltd. Use the answer booklet.

SLEEPY LTD - BALANCE SHEET AT 31 DECEMBER 2004

	£	£
Fixed assets:		
Land and buildings		150,000
Plant and machinery	1,800,000	
Less: depreciation	820,000	
		980,000
		1,130,000
Current assets:		
Stock		
Wood	200,000	
Finished goods	120,000	
Debtors	800,000	
Cash on deposit	150,000	
	1,270,000	
Current liabilities:		
Trade creditors	180,000	
Overdraft	520,000	
	700,000	
Net current assets		570,000
		1,700,000
Represented by:		
Share capital		500,000
Retained profits		1,200,000
		1,700,000

DREAMS LTD
17 High Street
Newport
South Wales

Mr S Wilks
Financial Controller
Sleepy Ltd
Tregarn Trading Estate
Cardiff
CF1 3EW

21 December 2004

Dear Mr Wilks

Request for credit facilities

We are a long established company and trade as a retailer of furniture. We are keen to do business with your company. In order to facilitate this we would be grateful if you could confirm that you will be able to provide us with £20,000 of credit on 60 day terms.

I enclose a copy of our latest audited profit and loss account. You may also wish to contact two of our existing suppliers for trade references. I would suggest the following two:

Carpets Ltd
Monnow Way
Bristol
BS7 6TY

Wardrobes Ltd
Pansy Park
Liverpool
L4 1HQ

I look forward to hearing from you shortly.

Yours sincerely

D Jones

David Jones
Finance Director

CARPETS LTD
MONNOW WAY
BRISTOL
BS7 6TY

Pat King
Accounting Technician
Sleepy Ltd
Tregarn Trading Estate
Cardiff
CF1 3EW

28 December 2004

Dear Sir/Madam

In response to your request for credit information on Dreams Ltd our response is as follows:

- We have traded with the company for four years.
- We allow the company £10,000 of credit on 30 day terms.
- We find that on average the company takes 60 days to settle their account with us.
- We are not aware of any other information which you should consider.

Yours faithfully

A Evans

Anne Evans
Credit Controller

WARDROBES LTD
Pansy Park
Liverpool
L4 1HQ

Pat King
Accounting Technician
Sleepy Ltd
Tregarn Trading Estate
Cardiff
CF1 3EW

28 December 2004

Dear Sir/Madam

In response to your request for credit information on Dreams Ltd our response is as follows:

- We have traded with the company for 3 months.
- We allow the company £2,500 of credit on 30 days terms.
- The company settles its account with us in accordance with our credit terms.
- We are not aware of any other information which you should consider.

Yours faithfully

J Corkhill

J Corkhill
Credit Controller

DREAMS LTD

	2004	2003
	£000	£000
Turnover	1,800	1,750
Cost of sales	(1,250)	(1,190)
Gross profit	550	560
Net operating expenses	(500)	(550)
Operating profit	50	10
Interest payable and similar charges	(30)	(20)
Profit/(loss) before taxation	20	(10)
Taxation	–	3
Profit/(loss) after taxation	20	(7)
Dividends	(10)	–
Retained profit/(loss) for the year	10	(7)

DEBT COLLECTION POLICY

- Invoices must be issued on the same day as goods are despatched.
- An aged analysis of trade debtors is to be produced monthly.
- Statements are to be despatched on the first working day of each month.
- A reminder letter must be sent when a debt is 14 days overdue.
- A telephone call to chase payment must be made when a debt is 21 days overdue.
- The customer will be placed on the stop list when the debt is 30 days overdue and a meeting arranged with the customer to discuss the operation of the account.
- A letter threatening legal action will be sent when the debt is 45 days overdue.
- Legal proceedings to be commenced when a debt is 60 days overdue subject to agreement with the Financial Controller.

SLEEPY LTD

AGED DEBTOR ANALYSIS AT 31 DECEMBER 2004 (EXTRACT)

Customer	Total	0–30 Days	31–60 Days	61–90 Days	90+ Days
Adams Ltd	4,120.00	4,120.00			
Hoddle Ltd	1,200.00	800.00	400.00		
Owen Ltd	600.00	600.00			
Ince Ltd	3,500.00			3,500.00	

The agreed credit period for each of these customers is 30 days from the invoice date.

SALES DAY BOOK FOR JANUARY 2005 (EXTRACT)

Customer	Date	Gross	VAT	Beds
Adams Ltd	4 Jan	352.50	52.50	300.00
Hoddle Ltd	6 Jan	587.50	87.50	500.00
Owen Ltd	7 Jan	235.00	35.00	200.00
Owen Ltd	14 Jan	235.00	35.00	200.00
Adams Ltd	28 Jan	587.50	87.50	500.00

CASH BOOK RECEIPTS FOR JANUARY 2005 (EXTRACT)

Receipt	Date	Total	Sales	Sundry
Adams Ltd	7 Jan	3,020.00	3,020.00	
Hoddle Ltd	10 Jan	100.00	100.00	(payment of invoice dated 10.11.04)
Adams Ltd	14 Jan	1,100.00	1,100.00	

MOCK SIMULATION 2 ANSWER BOOKLET

ROUGH WORK

ROUGH WORK

Task 1

SLEEPY LTD

CASH FLOW FORECAST FOR THE FOUR MONTHS ENDING 30 APRIL 2005

	Jan	Feb	Mar	Apr
	£	£	£	£
Receipts				
Trade sales				
Factory sales				
From deposit				
Payments				
Wood suppliers				
Production wages				
Production overheads				
Sales department costs				
Administration costs				
Overdraft interest				
Movement for month				
Bank b/f				
Bank c/f				

Task 1, continued

SENSITIVITY ANALYSIS

Task 2

MEMO

To: Steve Wilks, Financial Controller
From: Pat King, Accounting Technician
Re: Cash flow forecast
Date:

....

....

....

....

....

....

....

....

....

....

....

....

....

....

....

....

....

....

....

....

Task 3

MEMO

Notes on gilt-edged securities

Task 4

MEMO

To: The Board of Directors
From: Pat King, Accounting Technician
Re: Loan and overdraft finance
Date:

Task 5

MEMO

DRAFT PROCEDURES FOR CASH SALES

Task 6

MEMO

To: Steve Wilks, Financial Controller
From: Pat King, Accounting Technician
Re: Request for credit facilities
Date:

....

....

....

....

....

....

....

....

....

....

....

....

....

....

....

....

....

....

....

....

Task 6, continued

SLEEPY LIMITED
Tregarn Trading Estate
Cardiff
CF1 3EW

Task 7

SLEEPY LTD

AGED DEBTOR ANALYSIS AT 31 JANUARY 2005 (EXTRACT)

Customer	Total	0–30	31–60	61–90	90+	Credit Control Action
Adams Ltd						
Hoddle Ltd						
Owen Ltd						
Ince Ltd						

Task 7, continued

Matters to be discussed with the Purchase Ledger Controller of Owen Ltd

....

....

....

....

....

....

....

....

....

....

....

....

....

....

....

....

....

....

....

....

....

....

....

KEY TECHNIQUES ANSWERS

Chapter 1
Cash budgets

▷ ACTIVITY 1

(a) **Tutorial note**: Stock is used up by material usage, and by closing stock. This usage is made up partly from opening stock. The balance must be made up from purchases.

	June	July	August
	£	£	£
Material usage	8,000	9,000	10,000
Closing stock	3,500	6,000	4,000
	11,500	15,000	14,000
Less: Opening stock	5,000	3,500	6,000
Purchases	6,500	11,500	8,000

(b) **Tutorial note**: The main points to watch out for are sales receipts and overheads. Tackle sales receipts by calculating separate figures for cash sales (10% of total sales, received in the month of sale) and credit sales (90% of last month's sales). For overheads, remember that depreciation is not a cash expense and must therefore be stripped out of the overheads cash cost.

Cash budgets, June – August

	June	July	August
	£	£	£
Receipts of cash			
Cash sales	4,500	5,000	6,000
Credit sales	29,500	40,500	45,000
	34,000	45,500	51,000
Cash payments			
Wages	12,000	13,000	14,500
Overheads	6,500	7,000	8,000
Direct materials	6,500	11,500	8,000
Taxation	–	25,000	–
	25,000	56,500	30,500
Surplus/(deficit) for month	9,000	(11,000)	20,500
Opening balance	11,750	20,750	9,750
Closing balance	20,750	9,750	30,250

(c) Cash budgets are an important part of business planning. They highlight future surpluses of cash (enabling managers to make appropriate plans for investing the surplus) and shortfalls of cash (enabling managers to take appropriate action in advance, perhaps by advising their bank of overdraft requirements or raising funds from other sources).

▷ ACTIVITY 2

	Jul £000	Aug £000	Sep £000	Oct £000	Nov £000	Dec £000	Total £000
Receipts:							
Sales	210	200	200	200	200	200	1,210
New issue of share capital	–	–	–	30	–	–	30
Payments:							
Expenses and purchases	160	150	150	150	150	150	910
Expenses and purchases	24	24	24	24	24	24	144
Plant	12	25	13	–	50	–	100
Stock	–	20	–	–	–	–	20
Tax	–	–	–	–	–	30	30
Dividends	–	24	–	–	–	–	24
	196	243	187	174	224	204	1,228
Surplus/(deficiency)	14	(43)	13	56	(24)	(4)	12
Opening balance	40	54	11	24	80	56	40
Closing balance	54	11	24	80	56	52	52

▷ ACTIVITY 3

(a)

	Sept £	Oct £	Nov £	Dec £	Jan £	Feb £
Receipts:						
Cash sales (W1)	18,240	15,200	17,100	16,720	15,960	19,000
Credit sales (W2)	30,000	28,800	24,000	27,000	26,400	25,200
Capital		8,000				
	48,240	52,000	41,100	43,720	42,360	44,200
Payments:						
Purchases (W3)	18,800	19,600	17,600	17,000	19,800	17,200
Wages (W4)	6,800	6,000	6,500	6,400	6,200	7,000
Fixed costs (W5)	6,000	6,000	6,000	6,000	6,000	6,000
Capital	15,000		10,000			4,000
Corporation tax			44,000			
	46,600	31,600	84,100	29,400	32,000	34,200
Surplus/(Deficit)	1,640	20,400	(43,000)	14,320	10,360	10,000
Balance b/f	5,000	6,640	27,040	(15,960)	(1,640)	8,720
Balance c/f	6,640	27,040	(15,960)	(1,640)	8,720	18,720

(b) A spreadsheet is a computer modelling package which comprises rows and columns which intersect to form cells in a matrix. It can be seen that this is the lay-out used in (a) above.

Each cell may be used to store either a label (description), a value, or a formula. The formula may be referenced to the contents of other cells which can automate the calculation of many values in applications such as the cash budget in (a) above.

The spreadsheet may be used simply as an efficient and powerful calculator. However, it is also a powerful presentations device with graphic representations of the data being available. In this regard the user must segregate the output presen-tation and data entry areas of the spreadsheet.

Using part (a) as an example, the row and column headings would be as shown above. The sales values for each month would then be inserted into an input area together with the percentages for cash/credit sales etc. The equivalent of W3 would also be included in this area.

Formulae would then be entered in the input area to calculate intermediate values (e.g. stock used in W3) and in the output area to link with the input area. Some values (e.g. the capital receipt and payments) would be keyed directly into the out-put area since no further calculations are required. Where the same formula is used for a number of time periods, then it would be entered once and copied to the columns of the other periods.

Any of the input variables may then be changed and the effect on the final output will be automatically calculated, this is known as What-If analysis.

Workings

(W1) Since 60% of sales are credit sales, 40% are cash sales, e.g.

	£
September cash sales = £48,000 x 40% =	19,200
5% discount on £19,200	960
	18,240

(W2) August credit sales are paid in September, and so on.
Credit sales = 60% so the September receipt = 60% x £50,000 = £30,000.

(W3)

	July	Aug	Sept	Oct	Nov	Dec
Sales:	44,000	50,000	48,000	40,000	45,000	44,000
Stock used (40% of sales)	17,600	20,000	19,200	16,000	18,000	17,600
Opening stock (50% of 40% of sales)	(8,800)	(10,000)	(9,600)	(8,000)	(9,000)	(8,800)
Closing stock (50% of 40% of Next months sales)	10,000	9,600	8,000	9,000	8,800	8,400
Extra stock					2,000	
PURCHASES	18,800	19,600	17,600	17,000	19,800	17,200
Paid in	Sept	Oct	Nov	Dec	Jan	Feb

(W4) 10% of sales + £2,000
e.g. September: (10% x £48,000) + £2,000 = £6,800

(W5) Fixed costs: £6,000 (£7,500 – £1,500)

Chapter 2
Forecasting and monitoring cash flows

▷ ACTIVITY 4

(a) To calculate the four quarterly moving average trend, the sum of each set of four quarters, moving down the data one quarter at a time, must be calculated. The sum of every two of these values is then calculated to give an eight-period total. These totals are then all divided by eight to arrive at the trend figures. This is shown below.

Year	Qtr	Revenue values (000s)	Sum of 4 quarters	Sum of 8 quarters	Trend
1	1	49			
	2	37			
			211		
	3	58		423	52.875 (423 / 8)
			212		
	4	67		425	53.125 (425 / 8)
			213		
2	1	50		427	53.375
			214		
	2	38		429	53.625
			215		
	3	59		431	53.875
			216		
	4	68		434	54.250
			218		
3	1	51		437	54.625
			219		
	2	40		440	55.000
			221		
	3	60		441	55.125
			220		
	4	70		442	55.250
			222		
4	1	50		445	55.625
			223		
	2	42			
	3	61			

(b) To calculate the seasonal factors another calculation is necessary.

If using the additive model, the components of the time series are shown to be added together i.e.

Data (D) = Trend (T) + Seasonal variation (S)

Hence the seasonal factors can be calculated by subtracting the trend from the actual data.

Year	Qtr	Actual data	Trend	Actual – trend
1	3	58	52.875	5.125
	4	67	53.125	13.875
2	1	50	53.375	–3.375
	2	38	53.625	–15.625
	3	59	53.875	5.125
	4	68	54.250	13.75
3	1	51	54.625	–3.625
	2	40	55.000	–15
	3	60	55.125	4.875
	4	70	55.250	14.75
4	1	50	55.625	–5.625

The deviations (actual – trend) are now collected together to calculate the seasonal variation. For each quarter, in the form of a table, the total and average for each quarter is calculated.

The total of the averages should equal zero. If this doesn't equal zero, the difference is divided between the four quarters, and added to each average figure to give the final seasonal variation value.

Year	Q1	Q2	Q3	Q4	
1	–	–	5.125	13.875	
2	–3.375	–15.625	5.125	13.75	
3	–3.625	–15.00	4.875	14.75	
4	–5.625	–	–	–	
Total	–12.625	–30.625	15.125	42.375	
Number of values	3	2	3	3	
Average	–4.208	–15.313	5.042	14.125	= -0.354
Difference adjustment	0.0885	0.0885	0.0885	0.0885	
Seasonal variation	–4.1195	–15.2245	5.1305	14.2135	
	–4	–15	5	14	

ACTIVITY 5

Memo

To: Ann Drew
From: Assistant accountant

Re: Cash flow report

The cash flow report for January to March shows that actual cash flows have not been as good as expected, and at the end of March there was a cash deficit of £3,300 instead of the budgeted surplus of £8,000.

There appear to be three reasons for this, which should be investigated.

Cash receipts have been lower than budgeted. It seems likely that sales volume is lower than budget, but this should be checked.

Although cash receipts are lower than budgeted, payments for variable cost items (direct materials and direct labour) do not seem to be proportionately lower. It is possible that spending is higher than it should be. This too should be checked.

Only £2,000 of capital expenditure was budgeted but actual capital expenditure was £5,400. The reasons for this additional capital expenditure should be investigated.

The cash deficit is close to the overdraft limit of £5,000. As a matter of urgency, I recommend that we prepare a revised cash forecast, to establish what the future cash position could be. If necessary, we might have to approach the bank to discuss an increase in the overdraft limit.

Measures might also be needed to bring spending on materials and labour under better control, and to defer any further capital expenditures.

Chapter 4
Raising finance

▷ ACTIVITY 6

The following terms could be negotiated.

1 **The term (period) of the loan.** You should try to make sure that the term of the loan is appropriate for its purpose, so that the business will be able to repay the money on time from its expected future income.

2 **The interest rate.** This is likely to be a variable rate. The main point of negotiation should be the margin above base rate or LIBOR that the bank will charge. Negotiating a reduction of just 0.5% in the interest rate would save £2,500 in interest each year on a loan of £500,000.

3 **The repayment schedule.** You should try to make sure that the repayment schedule suits the requirements of the business. The business might want to repay the loan principal in a single payment at the end of the loan term. If so, you should resist any suggestions from the bank for gradual repayment of the principal over the term of the loan. You might also be able to negotiate a frequency of interest payment to suit the business requirements, such as six-monthly interest rather than monthly interest.

4 **Security.** The bank might insist on taking security for the loan. Your business would prefer the loan to be unsecured, but this might be an unrealistic expectation. The nature of the security should be negotiated. You should not agree to give more security than the amount of the loan would justify

5 **Other terms and conditions.** You should check the other terms and conditions proposed by the bank, to make sure that these are acceptable. If they are reasonable, you should probably agree to them. If any seem unreasonable, you should explain why you think they are unacceptable, and negotiate an amendment.

The key objective should be to raise the required amount of money for a suitable term and at a suitable interest rate, without giving excessive security.

▷ ACTIVITY 7

Any three from:

- Flexible means of finance
- Short-term loan finance
- Repayable on demand
- Attractive pricing (usually just over market rates).

Chapter 5
Investing surplus funds

ACTIVITY 8

Task 1
Short-term, highly liquid investments which are readily convertible to cash.

Task 2
Bills of exchange
Certificates of Deposit
Government securities
Local authority short-term loans.

Task 3
On demand.

▷ ACTIVITY 9

Task 1
Interest yield is = (4 / 94.00) x 100% = 4.25%

Task 2
Approximate redemption yield

If an investor buys the stock now at 94.00 and holds it for three years until maturity, he will make a capital gain of 100 – 94 = 6 at redemption. In other words, there will be a capital gain of £6 for every £100 of stock, or for every £94 invested. This gives an average annual gain on redemption of £2 for each £94 invested, which is about 2% per annum. The approximate redemption yield is therefore the interest yield of 4.25% plus 2%, which is about 6.25%.

Chapter 6
Granting of credit

▷ ACTIVITY 10

Any three from:

- Uses a similar benchmark against which all companies are judged.
- Facilitates regular review of the credit-worthiness of customers.
- Highlights potential areas of concern.
- Develops the relationship between the tasks of monitoring credit and establishing credit-worthiness.

▷ ACTIVITY 11

Internal information
(a) Analysis of accounts
(b) Sales staff in regular contact with current or potential customers

External sources
(a) Banks
(b) Credit agencies

▷ ACTIVITY 12

1 The bank reference is sufficient but doesn't appear to be too encouraging ('should be good for your figures'). The first trade reference had offered a £10,000 credit limit for 30 days; the second comes from a customer not a supplier.
There is at present insufficient evidence to grant Crocodile Cuts' request. However, further research should be carried out and possibly a trial period considered where, perhaps offering a lower limit with shorter terms of sale.

2 Two from the following:
- Word of mouth information on the creditworthiness of Crocodile Cuts (from sales staff, trade grapevine, etc). This could be used to gain up-to-date information on Crocodiles Cuts' trading status and activities. Are they reputable and reliable? Are they expanding and perhaps over-stretched?
- Information from credit reference agencies. This could give an external objective opinion on Crocodile Cuts' credit status.
- Historical financial information (such as company reports and accounts, Extel cards, etc). This provides audited data on Crocodile Cuts' financial performance and financial structure, although this could be rather out of date.
- Newspapers and the trade press. Again gives current up-to-date information on Crocodile Cuts and their activities, although may not be completely informed.

3 (a) Legal data
Name and registered address; directors; parent company (if any); county court judgements recorded against it.
(b) Commercial data
Types of business; locations of offices, factories, etc; main features of annual reports; annual sales; abstract of balance sheet.
(c) Credit data
Bankers' opinions; suppliers' opinions; agency credit rating of customer; terms of sale given to it by other customers.

4 Allows access to a credit rating (not publicly available). Gives another opinion of the credit-worthiness of the customer.

Note: Either of the above points is acceptable.

ACTIVITY 13

	Current year	Previous year
Working capital	£90,000	£45,000
Total assets	£477,000	£527,000
Working capital: total assets	0.19	0.09
Debtors, cash and short-term investments	£105,000	£94,000
Daily cash operating expenses (to nearest £100, assuming 365 day year)	£2,400,000/365 = £6,600	£2,700,000/365 = £7,400
No credit interval (in days)	16 days	13 days
Retained earnings	£35,000	£22,000
Total assets	£477,000	£527,000
Retained earnings: total assets	0.07	0.04
Earnings before interest and taxation (EBIT)	£105,000	£53,000
Interest charges	£4,000	£3,000
Loan repayments (20,000 – 30,000)	£10,000	£10,000 (given)
EBIT: interest charges and loan repayments	7.5	4.1

Note: You might be able to se that all four ratios have deteriorated in the current year compared with the previous year. This will give the credit controller a problem. If credit is granted to this customer, the account should be kept under close watch to monitor the customer's payments.

Chapter 7
Managing debtors

ACTIVITY 14

Debtor collection period = (52,000 / (2,500 x 365)) x 365 days

= 20.8 days

ACTIVITY 15

The cost of offering the discount is:

(£1.50 / £98.50) x (365 days / (60 – 14) days) x 100% = 12.1 %

▷ ACTIVITY 16

Task 1

EKAT Aged Debtors Analysis – 31 May 20X7. Credit terms: 30 days

Customer name and ref	Total amount	Invoices not yet due	Outstanding 1 month	Outstanding 2 months	Outstanding 3 months	Outstanding > 3 months	Action 1 Statement 2 1st reminder 3 2nd reminder 4 Telephone call 5 Warning letter 6 Recovery action implemented					
							1	2	3	4	5	6
Gartcosh	£10,000	£5,000 K521		£5,000 K496			03-Apr K496	03-May K496				
Strathaven	£6,600	£6,600 K511										
Coatbridge	£5,775	£2,775 K502			£3,000 K411		03-Mar K411	03-Apr K411	03-May K411			
New Mains	£14,000	£4,000 K508		£2,000 K487		£8,000 K289	03-Jan K289 03-Apr K487	03-Feb K289 03-May K487	03-Mar K289	03-Apr K289	03-May K289	
Castlemilk	£11,000			£11,000 K472			03-Apr K472	03-May K472				
Rutherglen	£1,000			£1,000 K481			03-Apr K481	03-May K481				
Cambuslang	£1,500					£1,500 K204	03-Dec K204	03-Jan K204	03-Feb K204	03-Mar K204	03-Apr K204	05-May K204
Easterhouse	£16,000	£3,000 K510		£13,000 K392			03-Apr K392	03-May K392				
Airdrie	£2,750					£2,750 K234	03-Feb K234	03-Mar K234	03-Apr K234	03-May K234		
Stewartfield	£5,000	£5,000 K513										
TOTALS	£73,625	£26,375		£32,000	£3,000	£12,250						

Task 2

Gartcosh
A good customer that appears to take over 60 days to make payment. Consider ways of encouraging prompt payment, e.g. settlement discounts.

Coatbridge
A large customer seemingly abusing their credit terms at the expense of a small supplier (EKAT). Consider ways of improving relationship and obtaining prompt payment, e.g. provision of settlement discount.

New Mains
A particular problem seems to exist with invoice K289, and invoice K487 is outstanding for two months. Establish whether a query exists with the invoice regarding quality or service. If there are no problems, consider ways of enforcing payment, using the legal process or a debt collection agency.

Cambuslang
A small customer with one outstanding invoice (K204). Establish whether this is in dispute. If not enforce payment using the legal process or a debt collection agency. Be prepared to write-off the debt.

Airdrie
Establish why K234 has been part-paid. Investigate why action has not been taken to recover this earlier. Negotiate with Airdrie for full payment.

Task 3

$$(2.5 / (100 - 2.5) \times (365 / (60 - 7))) = 17.66\%$$

Task 4

Two of the following:

- To reduce the cost of the administrative effort in collecting the debt
- To reduce the risk of default
- To reduce the cost of funding if it is likely that such a customer will make late payment
- To improve its cash flow

Or other reasonable answers.

Chapter 8
Collection of debts

▷ ACTIVITY 17

Any **three** from:

- Well known and respected locally
- Financially sound
- Operates a trust account with its bank that is regularly audited and will pay the client promptly
- It is licensed under the Consumer Credit Act 1974
- Level of charges
- Information about track record of success in collecting debt

▷ ACTIVITY 18

	£	£
Annual cost of using the factor:		
Fee: 2% x [(£125,000 x 12/3) – £30,000]		(9,400)
Loss of profits		(15,000)
		(24,400)
Annual benefits of using the factor:		
Administration savings	20,000	
Reduction in bad debts: 3% x [(£125,000 x 12/3) – £30,000]	14,100	
		34,100
Net savings		9,700

The net annual saving from using the factor is £9,700 (although this solution ignores interest costs).

▷ ACTIVITY 19

		Costs of factoring	Savings
		£	£
Sales ledger administration	2% × £200,000×12	48,000	
Administration cost savings			30,000
Credit protection insurance	1.5%×£200,000×12	36,000	
Reduction in bad debt losses	2.5% £200,000×12		60,000
Cost of factor finance	7.75%×80%×£200,000 × 2 months	24,800	
Overdraft interest saved	8%× 80%×£200,000 ×2 months		25,600
Total		108,800	115,600
Net benefit from factoring	(115,600 – 108,800)		6,800

PRACTICE SIMULATION ANSWERS

Task 1

	Actual Nov	Forecast Dec	Forecast Jan	Forecast Feb	Forecast Mar
Revenue					
National (peak)	57,393	57,761	59,090	61,055	62,851
National (off-peak)	644	649	672	685	705
International (peak)	31,080	31,161	33,574	32,533	33,490
International (off-peak)	1,129	1,142	1,246	1,272	1,309
Sub total	90,246	90,713	94,582	95,545	98,355
Direct costs					
National (peak)	37,304	38,163	39,431	40,591	42,137
National (off-peak)	433	448	457	470	488
International (peak)	19,884	21,424	20,759	21,370	22,184
International (off-peak)	732	799	815	839	871
Sub total	58,353	60,834	61,462	63,270	65,680
Overheads					
Marketing	5,000	5,000	5,000	5,000	27,000
Staff costs	13,350	13,350	13,350	13,350	13,817
Other overheads	5,800	5,800	5,800	5,800	5,800
Premises	9,350	9,350	9,350	9,350	9,350
Taxation		8,500			
Dividends					8,000
Interest				24,750	
Sub total	33,500	42,000	33,500	58,250	63,967
Net cash flow	–1,607	–12,121	–380	–25,975	–31,292
Opening cash flow	51,784	50,177	38,056	37,676	11,701
Net cash flow	–1,607	–12,121	–380	–25,975	–31,292
Closing cash flow	50,177	38,056	37,676	11,701	–19,591

Note: Call volumes (mins)

Total calls	1,598,765	1,630,740	1,678,703	1,742,654	1,774,629
National (peak)	1,231,049	1,271,977	1,309,388	1,359,270	1,384,211
National (off-peak)	31,982	32,615	33,574	34,853	35,493
International (peak)	319,754	309,841	318,954	331,104	337,179
International (off-peak)	15,980	16,307	16,787	17,427	17,746

Task 2

The cash surplus in the four months to February 20X8 should be invested in an interest-bearing bank deposit account. This should provide easy access to the money and be placed with an institution with an excellent credit rating. Therefore, the emphasis is on safety and liquidity.

The deficit in March 20X8 should be funded by a short-term credit facility (e.g. an overdraft) as it appears to be a short-term requirement.

To improve the cash position, Blether Telecom could:

- consider improving working capital management, which creates a cash requirement, particularly in a fast growing business like Blether Telecom. It could also consider reducing the credit period granted to businesses although this will have an impact on sales
- consider reducing the rate of growth of the business, perhaps by reducing expenditure on marketing
- cancel or postpone the dividend payment.

Task 3

Examples might include:

- other capital expenditure (operations manager)
- capital receipts from sale of capital equipment (operations manager)
- share options/rights issues, raising new capital (finance director)
- extraordinary dividend (finance director).

Task 4

EMAIL

To: Douglas Gulland Date:
From: Jaymini Patel
Subject: Cash forecast

With respect to the cash flow forecast I produced, I suggest:

- November to February – invest cash surplus in safe and liquid investment (e.g. bank deposit account)
- March - short-term credit line (e.g. overdraft).

  It is important to recognise the short-term funding requirement early (i.e. at the time of making the forecast) and make arrangements to negotiate a short-term line of credit, in accordance with the organisation's credit procedures, on the best possible terms.

Task 5

Introduction

To date, Blether Telecom has been operating using a mix of short- and long-term funding. However, in the next 18 months as the growth in our business slows, we will be forecasting a cash surplus. Therefore, a crucial issue will be how this is managed.

Key elements of an investment management policy

The most important considerations when investing cash are:

- safety
- liquidity
- profitability.

Safety refers to the likelihood that the value of the investment will fall. The **liquidity** of an investment can be thought of as how easily it can be sold and/or converted into cash. The **profitability** of an investment is the overall return on the investment.

Clearly the most important factor is safety, with the returns on an investment relatively insignificant compared to the actual amount of the investment. Clearly liquidity is very important, if Blether Telecom needs to invest its cash for working capital purposes (i.e. pay creditors) or capital purposes (i.e. make an acquisition or purchase capital equipment).

Cash investments

Cash investments are usually deposits in a bank or building society. The essence of cash-based investment is that the security of the capital sum is certain, or as certain as anything can be. Bank deposit accounts go by the name of deposit accounts, option deposits and so forth. Building society deposits are typically termed term shares, escalator bonds, notice shares, instant access accounts.

Marketable securities

Marketable fixed interest securities are types of investment. Their prices are affected by their coupon rate (i.e. the interest rate), the length of time to maturity, and the risk associated with the payment of interest and the eventual repayment of capital. Here, UK Government securities are considered (relatively) risk free, but others are not.

Examples of marketable securities

UK Government securities

Also known as gilts, they form the largest part of the 'fixed interest' market. Gilts are usually classified by their maturity (e.g. shorts – up to 5 years, longs – 15 years, etc). A limited number of variable rate, index-linked and convertible gilts are also available.

Commercial paper

The term used for certificates issued by a company promising to pay an amount to the person bearing the note on a specified date. Commercial paper is an unsecured borrowing issued for a short period of time, usually no more than one year (and often less).

Debentures

Similar to commercial paper, being debt stock issued by a company. However, debentures are usually secured on a particular asset and the loan is for the long term (i.e. usually five or ten years).

Certificates of deposit

Certificates of deposit are issued by institutions and are negotiable instruments certifying that a sum has been deposited with the issuer (a bank or building society) to be repaid on a certain date. The term can vary from seven days to up to five years.

Bills of exchange

Bills of exchange are similar to cheques. Examples of bills of exchange include: term bills (short term with a maturity from two weeks to six months), trade bills (drawn by one non-bank company on another company) and bankers' acceptances (drawn by a bank).

Summary: an outline policy for Blether Telecom

When considering how to invest cash, due consideration should be given to the following (in descending order): the safety of the investment, its liquidity and the return on the investment.

- To manage risk, limits should be in place to ensure cash is invested in a spread of marketable securities, leaving no over-exposure to a particular market or instrument.
- Credit ratings should be employed, so for example, Blether Telecom should invest in securities rated AA (long term) or A+ (short term).
- Overnight cash surpluses should be invested in a cash deposit account, with surpluses expected of, say, over a month invested in a marketable security (of assessed credit quality) to gain a better return.
- All investments should be reviewed by senior management every month.

Task 6

Relevant data

	20X5	20X6	20X7
	£ million	£ million	£ million
Working capital (net current assets)	2,124.600	1,735.000	1,291.000
Total assets (fixed and current)	5,822.000	6,410.000	7,142.000
Debtors, cash and short-term investments	2,738.000	3,210.000	3,559.000
Daily operating expenses	86.332	90.438	102.422
Retained earnings (brought forward plus current year)	2,734.200	2,859.100	2,927.600
Earnings before interest and taxation	284.000	285.500	205.500
Interest charges plus annual repayment of loans (excluding bank overdraft)	169.472 (W)	555.775	203.240

Ratios expressed in percentages

	20X5	20X6	20X7
	%	%	%
Working capital : total assets	36.49	27.07	18.08
Retained earnings : total assets	46.96	44.60	40.99
EBIT : interest charges plus annual loan repayments	167.58	51.37	101.11
No credit interval (days)	31.71	35.49	34.75

Workings

Interest charge and annual repayment (20X5)

		£000	£000
Interest			63,472
Loan repayment	20X4	850,000	
	20X5	744,000	
			106,000
			169,472

Interest charge and annual repayment (20X6)

		£000	£000
Interest			59,775
Loan repayment	20X5	744,000	
	20X6	248,000	
			496,000
			555,775

Interest charge and annual repayment (20X7)

		£000	£000
Interest			79,240
Loan repayment	20X6	248,000	
	20X7	124,000	
			124,000
			203,240

Task 7

MEMORANDUM

To: Millie Will | Date:
From: Jaymini Patel
Subject: MetalBash plc

Purpose of the ratios

The working capital : total assets ratio identifies the business's investment in working capital as a proportion of total assets. A high ratio indicates excessive investment in working capital, whilst a very low ratio could suggest a lack of liquidity caused by overtrading.

The no credit ratio shows the number of days an organisation could survive, by paying its regular, day-to-day expenses from cash and short-term investments. It indicates liquidity and the safety margin which a business has.

The retained earnings : total assets ratio shows the retained earnings as a proportion of total assets. Usually this figure would be quite high as an organisation with substantial fixed assets will need significant capital to maintain them, use them effectively and replace them.

The earnings before interest and taxation : interest charge plus annual repayment of loans ratio indicates a company's ability to meet its obligations to lenders. Typically, earnings need to be significantly higher than these obligations (perhaps by a factor of two or three) to ensure that the organisation can survive a temporary fall in earnings.

Trends in ratios

Working capital has fallen over the period, both in absolute terms (pounds) and relative terms (percentages). This is mainly due to a growth in current liabilities, most noticeably the bank overdraft.

The no credit interval period rose between 20X5 and 20X6, and deteriorated slightly in 20X7.

The fall in retained earnings as a proportion of total assets over the past two years, despite the increase in retained earnings in pounds, suggests the dividend policy is too generous for a company with rapidly growing assets.

Earnings did not cover interest charges and loan repayments in 20X6 and only just in 20X7. This may explain the company replacing long-term credit with short-term debt. However, this ratio improved dramatically in 20X7 indicating this position may soon (favourably) reverse.

Conclusion

On the evidence supplied by the historic accounts, MetalBash is not a good credit risk. Blether Telecom should not grant credit to MetalBash. Trading with MetalBash should only be conducted if MetalBash can provide some additional form of guarantee, perhaps from their bank, and should be for a reduced credit period.

Task 8

It is important to:

- convey that Blether Telecom are not prepared to trade on the proposed terms at present, but that they are willing to trade on credit if a suitable guarantee is provided
- that the situation can be reviewed in the future
- that this is communicated in a firm yet polite manner, regardless of MetalBash's reaction.

Task 9

Blether Telecom Aged Debtor Analysis – November 20X7. Credit Terms: 30 Days

Customer name and ref	Total amount	Invoices not yet due	Outstanding 1 month	Outstanding 2 months	Outstanding 3 months	Outstanding > 3 months	Action 1 Statement 2 1st reminder 3 2nd reminder 4 Telephone call 5 Warning letter 6 Recovery action implemented					
							1	2	3	4	5	6
MURRAY (C003)	10,000	5,000 (Q721)	5,000 (Q796)				3/10 (Q749)					
Calderwood (C102)	9,600	6,600 (Q611)			3,000 (Q423)		3/9 (Q423) 3/10 (Q511)	3/10 (Q423)				
Greenhills (C083)	10,775	2,775 (Q602)				8,000 (Q289)	3/8 (Q289)	3/9 (Q289)	3/10 (Q289)			
Westwood (C098)	5,500	4,000 (Q608)				1,500 (Q204)	3/5 (Q204)	3/6 (Q204)	3/7 (Q204)	3/8 (Q204)	3/9 (Q204)	
HAIRMYRES (C034)	2,750					2,750 (Q334)	3/6 (Q334)	3/7 (Q334)	3/8 (Q334)	3/9 (Q334)	3/10 (Q334)	3/10 (Q204)
TOTALS	38,625	18,375	5,000	0	3,000	12,250						

Murray (C003)

Murray is a regular payer and has one outstanding debt. The required action is to send Murray its regular statement. No further action.

Calderwood (C102)

Calderwood has one invoice now outstanding for three months. Although the required action indicates a second reminder, perhaps a telephone call would also be useful given the indication that Calderwood is an irregular payer.

Greenhills (C063)

This customer has one invoice outstanding over 3+ months. As Greenhills has been a regular customer this suggests there is a problem with the invoice, possibly relating to a quality or service issue. A visit to the customer is recommended before legal action is taken. Consider treating as a bad debt.

Westwood (C098)

Westwood has an invoice long overdue. However, Blether Telecom is still trading with the customer, indicating a problem with its credit function. No further credit should be allowed to Westwood. Blether Telecom should attempt to contact Westwood to ascertain the problem. If a satisfactory answer cannot be found, recovery action should be instigated. Consider treating as a bad debt.

Hairmyres (C034)

Hairmyres has now paid half of its long overdue account. Before proceeding to take court action to recover the remaining amount due Blether Telecom should establish whether a dispute exists with the customer, and their credit status.

Task 10

Notes

Three weeks after we have served the debtor (John Chancer) with a statutory demand, we can petition the court for a bankruptcy order.

For a bankruptcy order to succeed:

- the debt must be in excess of £750
- the debt must be unsecured
- the debtor must be domiciled in England and Wales.

However, if the statutory demand has been complied with or there is a reasonable prospect of Chancer paying the debt, the petition will be dismissed.

The consequences of a petition are:

- if Chancer pays money to creditors or disposes of property, these transactions are void
- any other legal proceedings relating to the debtor's property or debts are suspended
- an interim receiver is appointed, to protect the estate (by selling goods that may diminish in value).

The consequences of a bankruptcy order are:

- the official receiver takes control of Chancer's property
- a statement of Chancer's assets and liabilities is drawn up (a statement of affairs)
- the receiver summons a meeting of creditors, within 12 weeks of the bankruptcy order
- the creditors appoint a trustee in bankruptcy
- Chancer's assets are realised and a distribution of these assets made to the creditors.

Different types of creditor are paid in a certain order. These different claims are ranked in order:

(1) fees paid by an apprentice or articled clerk in training

(2) preferential creditors such as HM Revenue and Customs for PAYE and VAT; subcontractors in the building industry; national insurance contributions; pension scheme contributions; employees' wages for four months up to £800

(3) ordinary creditors.

The consequence is that if Blether Telecom does successfully petition for Chancer to be made bankrupt, it may be placed towards the back of the queue when the receiver distributes what is left of Chancer's assets. That the debt has been outstanding for such a period and that Blether Telecom are considering such severe action indicates that they should treat this as a bad debt for accounting purposes.

MOCK SIMULATION 1 ANSWERS

Task 1

FASTINFO LTD
MEMO

To: John Powell
From: Henry Naem
Date: 17 January
Subject: Cash flow - October to December

As requested I have compared the cash flow forecasts for the last three months of last year to the actual cash flows for the same three months.

The major difference between forecast and actual figures is in the sales figures. Both cash sales and credit sales are significantly below the forecast figures, with cash sales in particular being well below the budgeted figures in each month.

There have been some minor increases in revenue expenditure over the forecast figures however the major difference in expenditure has been in capital expenditure. Although the purchase of the additional land was at the budgeted figure the purchases of machinery and vehicles are both higher than was anticipated.

The combination of significantly less cash flow from sales (£970,000 less than forecast) and higher cash outflow on capital expenditure (£170,000 more than forecast) has led to a dramatically different cash balance than forecast. The forecast showed our overdraft due to decrease from £783,000 in October to just £15,000 in December. However the reality is that the overdraft has remained at around £1.2 million for the three months with a final overdraft figure at the end of December of £1,265,000.

I suggest that initially the procedure for forecasting sales, cash sales in particular, is considered. If the forecasts were overly optimistic then in future they should be more realistic. Alternatively there may be operational problems which may have caused the drop in sales from the forecast figures, in which case additional marketing may be required in order to boost sales at the start of this coming year.

The reasons for the overspend on fixed assets should also be investigated as they appear to be continuing expenditure possibly on lease payments that are more expensive than was forecast.

The overdraft balance of £1.2 million is too high and very expensive. Much of this has been caused by £2,220,000 of capital expenditure during the three-month period. This long term expenditure would be more appropriately funded by longer term finance than an overdraft and therefore the bank might be approached with the aim of replacing all or much of the overdraft with a term loan to match the life expectancy of the fixed assets.
I hope this has been useful.

Task 1, continued

CASH FLOW FORMAT

CASH FLOW FORECAST FOR THE FIRST THREE MONTHS OF NEXT YEAR, NEW DIVISION

	January £	February £	March £
CASH RECEIVED			
Sales: cash	12,000	12,500	13,000
Sales: credit	–	12,000	12,500
Grant	20,000		
Total (A)	32,000	24,500	25,500
CASH PAID			
Equipment: deposit	50,000		
Equipment: instalment		50,000	
Rent	5,000		
Wages	6,000	6,000	6,000
Purchases			10,000
Selling/administration	2,400	2,500	2,600
Total (B)	63,400	58,500	18,600
B/F cash balance	0	–31,400	–65,400
Net cash flow (A-B)	–31,400	–34,000	6,900
C/F cash balance	–31,400	–65,400	–58,500

IMPACT ON BANK BALANCE IF DEBTORS PAY ONE MONTH LATER

Amended cash received

	January £	February £	March £
CASH RECEIVED			
Sales: cash	12,000	12,500	13,000
Sales: credit	–	–	12,000
Grant	20,000		
Total (A)	32,000	12,500	25,000
CASH PAID	63,400	58,500	18,600
B/F cash balance	0	–31,400	–77,400
Net cash flow	–31,400	–46,000	6,400
C/F cash balance	–31,400	–77,400	–71,000

Task 1, continued

NOTE TO: John Powell
FROM: Henry Naem

Comment on cash surplus or deficit

Under the original forecast assumption of one month's credit to customers the overdraft limit is exceeded by £5,400 in February and is close to the limit in March. However if an additional month of credit is extended to customers the overdraft limit is exceeded by £17,400 in February and £11,000 in March. This is not likely to endear us to the bank in such early stages of the division's life.

Legitimate measures Fastinfo can take to improve cash position

Take out a medium-term loan to finance the capital expenditure rather than financing it by the overdraft.

Lease the new equipment rather than purchase outright.

Make all sales for cash rather than allowing credit for half of the sales.

Negotiate a longer credit period from suppliers (although as this is two months already any extension is unlikely).

Factoring of the debts from the credit sales.

Invoice discounting for the credit sales.

(**Note** only three measures were required.)

Sources of uncertainty in cash flow forecast

Sales forecasts.

Period of credit to customers.

Purchases forecasts (dependent upon actual sales and stock levels).

Amount of overdraft allowed by the bank.

(**Note** only two uncertainties were required.)

Task 2

FASTINFO LTD
MEMO

To: John Powell
From: Henry Naem
Date: 17 January
Subject: Whittle Ltd – credit assessment

We have received two trade references for Whittle Ltd. The reference from Greatlygrow Ltd is positive stating that Whittle is allowed six weeks of credit and always pays in accordance with the stated credit terms. However Greatlygrow Ltd has only been trading with Whittle Ltd for one year.

The other reference from Weston Ltd indicates that in the five years of trading with Whittle Ltd there was a suspension of credit to Whittle Ltd two years ago for a period of six months.

I have analysed the financial statements of Whittle Ltd for the last two years and calculated the following ratios:

		This year	Last year
Current ratio	(current assets : current liabilities)	1.1 : 1	1.1 : 1
Acid test ratio	(current assets less stock : current liabilities)	0.9 : 1	0.9 : 1
Debt ratio	(total short and long term creditors : net fixed assets plus current assets)	49%	55%
Return on owners equity	(profit after tax and interest : share capital plus reserves)	33%	17%

Whittle Ltd appears to be increasingly profitable and to be marginally reducing its level of debt compared to equity. However both the current ratio and acid test ratio are fairly low although they have remained constant over the two year period.

I recommend that initially we contact the Credit Manager of Weston Ltd in order to find more detail about the suspension of credit to Whittle Ltd. If that is satisfactorily resolved then a period of credit of, say, one month with a fairly low credit limit should be set and the movement on Whittle Ltd's account should be closely monitored by Brian Herbert, and the credit limit then reviewed after six months.

Task 3

NOTES FOR PLACEMENT STUDENT

- **Cheque**

  A cheque is a written instruction to a bank authorising and requiring the bank to pay a stated amount to a third party. A cheque has three parties to it. The drawer who is the person writing the cheque. The payee being the person to whom the cheque is payable and the drawee, the bank on whom the cheque is drawn.

- **Stale cheque**

  A cheque must be dated. If a cheque is presented to a bank for payment more than six months after the date of the cheque then that cheque is viewed to be stale and the bank would not pay on it and would return it to the drawer.

- **Post-dated cheque**

  A cheque should be dated with the date on which it was drawn. If a later date is put on the cheque then it is known as a post-dated cheque and it should not be paid by the bank until that date.

- **Crossed cheque**

  A crossed cheque is one on which there are two vertical lines on the face of it. This simple general crossing means that the paying bank must only pay the cheque into another bank account. Most pre-printed cheques also have the words 'account payee' written between the two lines instructing the paying bank (the drawee) only to pay the cheque into the account of the payee.

- **Overdraft**

  An overdraft is a facility granted by the bank whereby if payments out of a current account exceed the payments in, the bank finances the deficit by means of this overdraft. The overdraft facility on the current account if granted by the bank does not have to be used but it is a short term form of temporary lending which is available if required. Technically an overdraft is repayable on demand.

- **Bank loan**

  In contrast to an overdraft a bank loan is a longer term method of financing where the customer borrows a fixed amount from the bank which will be paid back with interest over an agreed period of time or at the end of an agreed period.

Task 4

UPDATED EXTRACT FROM AGED DEBTORS ANALYSIS 31 DECEMBER

Name	Code	Total Owing £	<1 month £	1–2 months £	2–3 months £	>3 months £
Smythe & Co	c0100	9,000	4,000 (inv 1010)	5,000 (inv 8910)		
Happle Ltd	c1190	4,500				4,500 (inv 7914)
Thomas & Sons	c2820	3,000		1,000 (inv 9000)	2,000 (inv 2851)	
Paperclips & Bits	c0991	1,200	1,000 (inv 1091)	200 (inv 2998)		
TOTAL		17,700	5,000	6,200	2,000	4,500
Percentage		100%	28%	35%	11%	26%

FASTINFO LTD
MEMO

To: Brian Herbert
From: Henry Naem
Date: 17 January
Subject: Aged debtor analysis

I have updated the aged debtor analysis to 31 December.
According to our company policy on outstanding debts the following actions should be taken:

Smythe & Co – As invoice 8910 for £5,000 is now more than one month overdue a first reminder could be sent. However this is a long-established customer who is generally a good payer and appears to pay off invoices which are between one and two months old, therefore you may not consider this action necessary.

Happle Ltd – Invoice 7914 for £4,500 has now been overdue for six months therefore legal action should be taking place to recover the debt. The position of the legal action should be checked but in any case a provision should now be made in the accounts against the recoverability of this debt.

Thomas & Sons – In line with past payment practice this customer has invoices outstanding which are over two months old. As this is a long-established customer who generally pays one month late no action is recommended if we are happy with this payment practice.

Paperclips & Bits – According to our company policy a first reminder letter should be sent regarding invoice 2998 for £200 which is now more than one month overdue.

Task 4, continued

FASTINFO LTD
11 Beal Street
Wallington
WL1 9PO
Tel: 0331 8676767

Accounts Payable Department

Account No:

Dear Sir

Further to our invoices detailed below, I do not appear to have received payment. I trust that this is an oversight and that you will arrange for immediate payment to be made. If you are withholding payment for any reason, please contact me urgently and I will be pleased to assist you.

Invoice number	Terms	Due date	Amount

If you have already made the payment please advise me and accept my apology for having troubled you.

Yours faithfully

Brian Herbert

Credit Control Manager

Task 4, continued

FASTINFO LTD
11 Beal Street
Wallington
WL1 9PO
Tel: 0331 8676767

Accounts Payable Department

Account No:

Dear Sir

Further to our invoices detailed below and reminder letter dated ……………..I do not appear to have received payment. I trust that this is an oversight and that you will arrange for immediate payment to be made. If you are withholding payment for any reason, please contact me urgently and I will be pleased to assist you.

Invoice number	Terms	Due date	Amount

I regret that unless payment is received within the next seven days I will have no alternative but to put the collection of the amounts due into the hands of a third party.

If you have already made the payment please advise me and accept my apology for having troubled you.

Yours faithfully

Brian Herbert

Credit Control Manager

FASTINFO LTD
MEMO

To: Victoria Bartlett
From: Henry Naem
Date: 17 January
Subject: Debt factoring

A debt factoring arrangement is one where the factor takes over the debts of the company and gives the company a cash advance. The factor will then collect the debts of the company. A 'with recourse' factoring arrangement is one whereby the factor can recover any debts that are not paid by customers from the company. The company effectively still bears the risk of bad debts.

A 'without recourse' arrangement is one whereby the factor bears any bad debts and has no recourse to the company for reimbursement for any debtors that do not pay.

I hope this addresses your concerns. If you have any further questions, please let me know.

Henry

MOCK SIMULATION 2 ANSWERS

WORKINGS

Working 1 – trade sales

	Jan	Feb	Mar	Apr
Number of beds	5,000	5,400	5,800	6,200
Sales revenue	£500,000	£540,000	£580,000	£651,000
Receipts from sales				
Dec sales	£500,000	£300,000		
Jan sales		£200,000	£300,000	
Feb sales			£216,000	£324,000
Mar sales				£232,000
Trade sales receipts	£500,000	£500,000	£516,000	£556,000

Working 2 – cash on deposit

	£
Deposit	150,000
Interest (150,000 x 6% x 4/12)	3,000
	153,000

Working 3 – payments to wood suppliers
Production budget

	Jan	Feb	Mar	Apr
Number of beds being sold – trade	5,000	5,400	5,800	6,200
factory shop				100
	5,000	5,400	5,800	6,300
Opening stock of beds	(2,000)	(2,200)	(2,400)	(2,600)
Closing stock of beds	2,200	2,400	2,600	2,800
Sales	5,000	5,400	5,800	6,300
Production	5,200	5,600	6,000	6,500

Wood purchases budget

	Jan	Feb	Mar	Apr
Opening stock	(40,000)	(40,000)	(40,000)	(30,000)
Closing stock	40,000	40,000	30,000	20,000
Wood required for production	52,000	56,000	60,000	65,000
Purchases (metres)	52,000	56,000	50,000	55,000

Wood supplier payments (one month in arrears @ £5 per metre)

	£	£	£	£
December creditors	180,000			
January purchases		260,000		
February purchases			280,000	
March purchases				250,000
	180,000	260,000	280,000	250,000

Working 4 – production wages

	Jan	Feb	Mar	Apr
Production quantity	5,200	5,600	6,000	6,500
Hours worked	10,400	11,200	12,000	13,000
Wages cost @ £5 per hour	£52,000	£56,000	£60,000	
@ £5.25 per hour				£68,250

Task 1

SLEEPY LTD
CASH FLOW FORECAST FOR THE FOUR MONTHS ENDING 30 APRIL 2005

	Jan	Feb	Mar	Apr
	£	£	£	£
Receipts				
Trade sales (W1)	500,000	500,000	516,000	556,000
Factory sales				12,000
From deposit (W2)				153,000
	500,000	500,000	516,000	721,000
Payments				
Wood suppliers (W3)	180,000	260,000	280,000	250,000
Production wages (W4)	52,000	56,000	60,000	68,250
Production overheads (105,000 – 15,000)	90,000	90,000	90,000	90,000
Sales department costs (20,000 – 1,500)	18,500	18,500	18,500	18,500
Administration costs	25,000	25,000	25,000	25,000
Overdraft interest	5,200	3,907	3,441	3,050
	370,700	453,407	476,941	454,800
Movement for the month	129,300	46,593	39,059	266,200
Bank b/f	–520,000	–390,700	–344,107	–305,048
Bank c/f	–390,700	–344,107	–305,048	–38,848

Task 1, continued

SENSITIVITY ANALYSIS

	Jan	Feb	Mar	Apr
Number of beds	5,000	5,400	5,800	6,200
Sales revenue @ £95	£475,000	£513,000	£551,000	
@ £95 x 1.05				£618,450
Receipts from sales				
Dec sales	£500,000	£300,000		
Jan sales		£190,000	£285,000	
Feb sales			£205,200	£307,800
Mar sales				£220,400
Trade sales receipts	£500,000	£490,000	£490,200	£528,200

Revised cash flow forecast

	Jan £	Feb £	Mar £	Apr £
Receipts				
Trade sales (from above)	500,000	490,000	490,200	528,200
Factory sales				12,000
From deposit (W2)				153,000
	500,000	490,000	490,200	693,200
Payments				
Wood suppliers (W3)	180,000	260,000	280,000	250,000
Production wages (W4)	52,000	56,000	60,000	68,250
Production overheads (105,000 – 15,000)	90,000	90,000	90,000	90,000
Sales department costs (20,000 – 1,500)	18,500	18,500	18,500	18,500
Administration costs	25,000	25,000	25,000	25,000
Overdraft interest	5,200	3,907	3,541	3,409
	370,700	453,407	477,041	455,159
Movement for the month	129,300	36,593	13,159	238,041
Bank b/f	–520,000	–390,700	–354,107	–340,948
Bank c/f	–390,700	–354,107	–340,948	–102,907

Task 2

MEMO

To: Steve Wilks, Financial Controller
From: Pat King, Accounting Technician
Re: Cash flow forecast
Date: January 2005

Most of the figures in the cash flow forecast for the four months to 30 April 2005 will require careful control and monitoring.

Clearly the major income of the company is from trade sales. The quantity of trade sales must be monitored as not only will lower sales mean less income but without an alteration in the production schedule this will also lead to increased stocks of completed beds. The payment pattern of trade debtors should also be monitored as if this varies significantly from the assumed pattern of 40% after 1 month and 60% after two months then this will affect the income. I have also noted that no allowance has been made for possible bad debts. If a debtor does not pay then again this will reduce the income level.

The purchase of wood is the major expense of the business and the quantity purchased should accord with the production schedule otherwise there could be an unacceptable increase in stocks or possible shortage. If the production schedule changes due to altered sales figures then the purchase schedule must also be altered in accord. The price of wood has been assumed to remain at £5; the buying department should therefore ensure that this is the price that is paid for each metre of wood and no more.

There should be control of the number of hours worked. If the employees are inefficient then this will mean that more than two hours per bed are worked and this will increase the overall wages bill especially if overtime hours are worked.

Production overheads, sales department costs and administration costs are all treated as fixed costs. Any variances from the budgeted amounts should be monitored and investigated.

Task 3

MEMO

Notes on gilt-edged securities

Gilt-edged securities or gilts are marketable British Government Securities. They are fixed interest securities and can have a short life, less than a year, ranging through to a life of 20 years or more. There are indeed some undated stocks such as Consolidated Stock 1½% which have been in issue for decades.

Gilts are marketable, their market price will change throughout their lives. The return on the gilt can be expressed in one of two ways. The interest yield or flat yield is the return on the gilt if it is held for a year based upon the current price. In the case of the Treasury Stock 9 ¾% at a price of £112.50 the flat yield is:

$$(9.75 / 112.5) \times 100 = 8.66\%$$

However the flat yield takes no account of the fact that the stock is redeemable. The gross redemption yield, in the case of this Treasury Stock, is 6.2%, which takes into account both the interest payable until redemption and the redemption value.

Both the flat yield and the redemption yield are higher interest rates than the 6% earned on the deposit account which might indicate that the Treasury Stock would be a better investment. However this does not take into account risk and the timing of the interest payments.

The cash on deposit is virtually completely risk free as the initial amount invested of £150,000 will be repaid on 30 April together with the interest accrued. Although Government stocks are relatively risk free, as the Government will not become insolvent and not repay the stock, there is an element of risk in investing in them for a short period of time as the price that they could be sold for on 30 April is not guaranteed. If £150,000 of Treasury Stock were purchased at a price of £112.50 there is no guarantee that on the date of sale the interest earned and selling price would necessarily achieve as high a return as the quoted yields as market forces or economic conditions might have suppressed the price. Therefore the potentially higher return on the Treasury Stock must be weighted against the slightly higher risk.

The investment of £150,000 is only for a four-month period. The interest on Treasury Stock is normally only paid every six months. Suppose that the interest on the Treasury Stock were payable on 8 June and 8 December. For administrative purposes the Government declares gilts ex interest some time before the due date of payment. Let's suppose that the stock went ex interest on 20 November 2004 and again on 20 May 2005. When we purchased it on 31 December we would be expecting to receive the 8 June interest but as we sell before this date anyone owning the gilts up to 20 May 2005 would get the interest. The price at which we would buy and sell the gilts should reflect the interest position but again there is some risk.

Task 4

MEMO

To: The Board of Directors
From: Pat King, Accounting Technician
Re: Loan and overdraft finance
Date: January 2005

A bank overdraft is effectively a short-term source of finance. An overdraft facility is made available by the bank in order to fund short-term shortfalls of income compared to outgoings. A bank overdraft attracts a relatively high rate of interest and therefore would be a very costly form of finance for a £1,000,000 investment.

Companies should aim to match their sources of finance to the purposes for which they were raised. A bank overdraft is a short-term source of finance suitable for funding short term working capital changes. However the purchase of machinery is a medium- to long-term investment and as such would be more appropriately funded by a medium to long-term source of finance such as a bank loan.

The bank loan could be negotiated to be paid off over the approximate life of the machinery with repayments covering both interest and capital. Alternatively the interest could be paid off periodically but the repayment of the capital would all happen at the end of the loan term. Bank loan finance will tend to be at a lower interest rate than a bank overdraft.

For the purchase of fixed assets a bank loan will generally be the preferred method of financing rather than a bank overdraft.

Task 5

MEMO

DRAFT PROCEDURES FOR CASH SALES

- The cash must always be kept in a locked till.
- The key must be kept by the person responsible for accepting the cash from customers.
- If cheques are to be accepted they must be covered by a valid cheque guarantee card - if the price is to be £120 per bed then this guarantee limit must be £150 or £200.
- If credit cards are to be accepted authorisation must be sought for payments which exceed the floor limit.
- At the end of each day the cash, cheque and credit card vouchers in the till must be reconciled to the till records by someone other than the person responsible for making the sales.
- If the cash is to be banked that day it must be securely transported to the bank using different routes and at different times (ideally two people should take the cash to the bank).
- The paying-in slip should be made out by someone other than the person paying the money into the bank and should be reconciled to the till records for the day.
- If the cash is not to be banked until the following day as the shop does not shut until the bank is closed then either the cash must be kept in a locked safe on the premises or it should be lodged in the bank's overnight safe.
- All cash should be banked as soon as is possible.

Task 6

MEMO

To: Steve Wilks, Financial Controller
From: Pat King, Accounting Technician
Re: Request for credit facilities – Dreams Ltd
Date: January 2005

In the context of the request from Dreams Ltd for £20,000 of credit on 60 day terms I have considered the profit and loss accounts of the company for the last two years and the two trade references which we have received.

The following ratios have been calculated for each of the two years:

	2004	2003
Gross profit margin	30.5%	32%
Operating profits margin	2.8%	0.6%
Interest cover	1.7 times	0.5 times

Although the company has a reasonable, although declining gross profit margin, its operating profit margin is very small. In 2003 the operating profit was not enough to cover the interest payments due and even though this improved in 2004 the interest cover is still very low. This raises some concerns about the long term existence of the company.

We have not been provided with a balance sheet and this would have been useful for assessing the short and longer term liquidity of the business. From the profit and loss account we can see that the interest cost has increased by 50% from 2003 to 2004 which would indicate an increase in gearing.

I have also considered the trade references that we have received. Carpets Ltd inform us that they allow credit of £10,000 on 30-day terms but that Dreams takes an average of 60 days to settle their account. They have been trading with Dreams Ltd for four years.

Wardrobes Ltd allow credit of just £2,500 on 30 day terms and state that Dreams Ltd have settled their account within that time. However they have only been trading with Dreams Ltd for three months so there is very little evidence for this to be based upon.

My concerns are that only one of the trade references can reasonably be relied upon and that it would appear that even with offering of 30 days of credit we would not be paid until 60 days after the invoice. Neither company allows credit to Dreams Ltd of anything like the £20,000 they are requesting from us.

I have further concerns about Dreams Ltd itself. Its profit and loss account and implied gearing position do not look healthy from the amount of information that we have been provided with.

Task 6, continued

SLEEPY LIMITED
Tregarn Trading Estate
Cardiff
CF1 3EW

Mr D Jones
Finance Director
Dreams Ltd
17 High Street
Newport
South Wales

January 2005

Dear Mr Jones

Re: Request for credit facilities

Thank you for your enquiry regarding the provision of credit facilities by us of £20,000 of credit on 60-day terms. We have examined your profit and loss account and taken up your trade references.

We have some concerns about your level of profitability and would like the opportunity to examine your balance sheets for 2003 and 2004. As one of your trade references has only been trading with you for three months we would request details of a further supplier that we could contact for a trade reference.

At this stage I am not able to confirm whether we can provide you with a credit facility but will reconsider the situation when we receive your balance sheets and additional trade reference.

Thank you for your interest in our company.
Yours sincerely

Steve Wilks
Financial Controller

Task 7

SLEEPY LTD
AGED DEBTOR ANALYSIS AT 31 JANUARY 2005 (EXTRACT)

Customer	Total	0–30	31–60	61–90	90+	Credit Control Action
Adams Ltd	940.00	940.00				No action required
Hoddle Ltd	1,687.50	587.50	800.00	300.00		Send reminder letter/maketelephone call for £800. Place on stop list and arrange meeting for £300.
Owen Ltd	1,070.00	470.00	600.00			Send reminder letter/ make telephone call for £600.
Ince Ltd	3,500.00				3,500.00	Check on progress of legal proceedings.

Matters to be discussed with the Purchase Ledger Controller of Owen Ltd

- Make sure you know the name of the purchase ledger controller
- £600 is 21 days or more overdue (check invoice number/s outstanding)
- Ask for any reasons for, or disputes that have caused non-payment
- If no problems, then ensure controller agrees amount and terms of payment
- If told cheque is in the post – ask for cheque number, date it was posted, address to which it was sent – may need to request cheque to be stopped and new cheque issued
- If told cheque is drawn up but waiting to be signed by cheque signatory ask to speak to cheque signatory
- If told payment is made on monthly computer run ask for a manual cheque to be drawn up.

GLOSSARY

Term	Description
Accruals concept	Transactions are reflected in the profit and loss account in the period in which they occurred rather than in the period when the cash was received or paid.
Administrative order	Where an amount of less than £5,000 is owed this can be paid into the court on a regular basis and the court then pays the creditors.
Aged debtors analysis	Analysis of each debtor balance showing how long each invoice has been outstanding.
Attachment of earnings order	The business is paid directly from the debtor's employer out of the individual's pay packet.
Bad debt	A debt that will never be recovered.
Bank of England	The UK's central bank.
Bank overdraft	A facility offered by the bank as an addition to funds in a bank account which is technically payable on demand.
Bank reference	Reference from a potential customer's bank concerning their financial position.
Bill of exchange	An order in writing addressed by one person to another requiring the addressee to pay a certain amount to another party.
Cash flow	The total of net cash receipts and payments for a period.
Cash/settlement discount	Discount for payment of invoices within a certain timescale.
Certificate of deposit	Document issued by a bank certifying that a deposit has been made with that bank which is repayable to the bearer on surrender of the certificate at maturity.
Certificate of deposit	Issued by a bank or building society which certifies that a certain sum has been deposited with it to be repaid on a specific date.
CHAPS	Clearing House Automated Payments System which is an electronic clearing system for large value same-day sterling payments.
Charging order	A court order which puts a charge on the debtor's property so that the debt can be paid out of the proceeds of sale if necessary.
Cheque crossing	Instruction on the face of a cheque to the bank as to how the cheque should be paid.
Collection agency	An agency appointed to collect the debts of a business.
Collection letter	A letter sent to an overdue customer asking for payment.
Commercial paper	Sale by companies of promissory notes.
Consideration	The provision of a promise or action by both parties to a contract.
Convertible loan stock	Debentures that are convertible, on the choice of the holder, into ordinary shares of the company.

Term	Description
Credit insurance	Insurance against non-payment of debts arranged through a broker.
Credit terms	The terms of payment for credit customers.
Debentures	Long term loan stock finance raised by a company.
Debt factoring	Sale of all debts to a factor for a proportion of cash upfront.
Debt factoring	A service provided whereby the debts of a business are collected by a factor and the factor provides cash in advance.
Final reminder	A further letter to an overdue customer possibly threatening legal action.
Finance lease	Use of an asset for most of its useful economic life in return for regular lease payments.
Financial intermediaries	Financial institutions which bring together savers and borrowers.
Garnishee order	An order whereby a third party from whom the debtor is owned money pays the business directly the amount due.
General provision	A percentage of total debtors that is provided against on the basis of past experience.
Gilts	Government securities.
Hire purchase	Purchase of an asset by instalments rather than by cash.
Interest yield	The yield on a fixed interest security if it is held for one year.
Invoice discounting	Only limited debts are assigned to a factor.
Invoice discounting	A service where the invoices of a company are purchased by supplying cash in advance but the business continues to collect the debts and repays the invoice discounter.
Money markets	Markets buying and selling different forms of money or marketable securities.
Offer and acceptance	The essential elements of an agreement in contract law.
Operating cycle	Debtors payments period plus stock turnover period less creditors payment period.
Overtrading	When a company expands too quickly and over-stretches its working capital due to inadequate financing.
Primary banks	The commercial, retail or clearing banks.
Profit	The profit made in a period applying the accruals concept.
Ratio analysis	Consideration of a potential customer's recent financial statements in order to determine their reliability as a credit customer.

Term	Description
Redemption yield	The yield to the redemption date on a fixed interest security, which will include both interest received and capital growth.
Retail deposits	Current account deposits held by individuals or organisations in connection with their payments and receipts.
Revenue payments/receipts	Payments or receipts incurred in the normal trading activities of the business.
Seasonal variations	Similar patterns in the time series during corresponding time periods.
Secondary banks	Merchant banks, other British banks and foreign banks in the UK.
Sensitivity analysis	Calculations to show the sensitivity of the individual estimates to change and the resulting change in cash balance.
Specific provision	A provision against a particular debt which it is thought is doubtful will be received.
Stale cheque	A cheque dated more than six months ago.
Sterling Commercial Paper	Short-term promissory notes with a fixed maturity .
Surplus of funds	An anticipated excess of funds.
Time series	A set of values for some variable over a period of time.
Time series analysis	Analysis of a time series into a trend and seasonal variations.
Trade reference	Reference from another supplier that a potential customer regularly uses.
Trend	The general direction in which the time series is moving.
Wholesale deposits	Large interest-bearing accounts with negotiated interest rates.
With recourse factoring	A service where the business has to repay the factor for any monies advanced on a debt that is bad.
Without recourse factoring	A service where the factor bears the risk of any bad debts.
Working capital	Stocks, debtors and creditors.

INDEX